A Fighting Union

SARHWU banner showing support for the ANC and the SACP.

A Fighting Union

An oral history of the
South African Railway and Harbour Workers Union, 1936-1998

Margaret Kiloh with Archie Sibeko

RAVAN PRESS

First published in 2000 by

Ravan Press
P O Box 145
Randburg
2125

Typesetting and design: Flight Graphics
Cover illustration: SARHWU
Cover design: David Selfe

The publishers would like to thank the following who gave permission for copyright material to be included in this book:

William Matlala, Xolo Tshabalala, The Star newspaper, Transnet Heritage library, Mayibuye Centre, SARHWU, M. Kiloh.

Printed by Clyson Printers, Maitland, Cape Town

Contents

Dedication

This book is dedicated to the members of SARHWU, both past and present. It is their story.

Acknowledgements

We would like to give special thanks to Transnet, SACTU and the Open University (UK) for financial help with this project.

Thanks are also due to our spouses, Joyce Leeson and George Kiloh, and to our families for their patience and support; to John James for reading and commenting on the manuscript and to the officers and members of SARHWU and SATAWU, without whom it could not have happened.

Interviews and Written Contributions

The authors and publisher would like to express their thanks to the following for their valuable contributions to this book.

Evan Abrahamse
Ray Alexander
Otto M. Balfour
Meshak Baloyi
Mtobeli Bangiso
Johan Beaurain
Lizwi Lennox Buso
Davilene Davids
Charles Sabelo Dywili
David Muraga Dzenhe
Eliphus Zomgezile Fosi
Johnson Msonuba Gamede
Christopher Educator Gcinikhaya Gobinca
Xolani Gogwana
Sanku Gwala
Magezi Amos Honwani
Thobile Christopher Jekwa
Bonakele Jonas
Elizabeth Kekana
Sekitla Justice Langa
Mzaman Silas Mabunde
Ezrom Mabyana
Mluleki Macdonald Madolo
Thembekile Majalisa
Jonas "Trompie" Nkhansiweleni Makhavhu
Robert Mfana Mashego
Albert Mashoai
Stephen Matlou
Nomanesi Signoria Maxhakana
Boyce Melitafa
Nomayeza Veronica Mesatywa
Gilbert Wilson Miya
Francis Moabi
Vanguard Mbuyiseli Mkosana
Ntaote David Moeti
Johnson Mokhesi
Kedibone Mokonyane
Monica Morobane
Isaac Morudu
Tshidiso Moshao

Arthur Mosikare
Nombukiso (Bukie) Motloung
Thobile Wiggett Mseleni
Eric Mtshali
Nomvuyo Mtyekisane
Simon Mulomoni
Vuyani Elivs Mzayifani
Billy Nair
Justice Pumezo Ncanywa
Nelson Ndinisa
Ratshivhanda Samson Ndou
Rita Alita Ndzanga
Eric Vuyisile Ngcingwana
Johannes Ngcobo
Wonder Ndwebisa
Neil Newman
Sisa Njikelana
Bongani Nogaga
Sello Ntai
Charles Ntlangula
Mzwandile Nimrod Nyamakazi
Methews Thembinikosi Oliphant
Thapelo James Phera
Johnny Potgieter
Kgatledi Jeremiah Raphela
Mike Roussos
Martin Sebakwane
George Sihlayi
Mandla P. Nzama
Derrick Simoko
Bafana Sithole
Duncan Speelman
Elliot Mshiyeni Sogoni
Nadeema Syms
Bonnie Thekisho
Sello Tshwaribe
Ben Turok
Vic van Vuuren
Barnabas Mziwandile Wondo
Joseph S. Xasi

Foreword

This is the story of the South African Railway and Harbour Workers Union. We have called the book A Fighting Union because SARHWU not only had to fight against bosses for workers' rights but also had to confront the racist regime directly. It has always been in the front line of the struggles of the people of South Africa.

SARHWU is one of the oldest of the trade unions that still exist in South Africa. It was formed in 1936 when most of the black railway and harbour workers were migrants, 'red-blanketed men' from the rural areas who had come to work in town for a limited time and then intended to return home to plough. They had little if any education.

Why, then, did people like them become involved in working-class struggles, and learn to organise a union?

Of course it was because of their experience. They were deprived of human dignity, herded into primitive and overcrowded compounds, badly fed and paid very low wages. In this they were like most South African workers, but what was special about the railway and harbour workers was that their boss was the racist regime. Their managers were directly accountable to cabinet ministers, and their industry was the guinea-pig for apartheid labour policies. All South Africa's discriminatory labour laws were first tried and then perfected on the railways.

Black workers could only be labourers, forced to do hard, unskilled manual work with no job security. By contrast, white workers were bought off by job reservation, security, pension funds and sick pay. The least able and least educated white man could always get a job on the railways, where he would be a foreman in charge of black workers.

In addition, the full power of the state machine was available to the railway and harbour authorities and was readily used against black workers. Spies, informers, railway police, other police and, if necessary, the army were used to 'control unrest' and in particular to break strikes in this key state sector, the transport industry.

Small wonder, then, that people who were exploited and harassed like this could not take it lying down. They fought back, and in fighting back they found ready allies in the political movements, some of which had valuable organising skills. Many members and leaders of SARHWU became members and leaders of the South African Communist Party and the African National Congress.

Archie Sibeko (Zola Zembe), Honorary Life President of SARHWU (SATAWU).

These links had many organisational benefits for the union. They also broadened members' outlooks and created links in the townships with other unions. However, a price was paid later when political organisations were banned. Many of the union's leaders were also banned, arrested, murdered or forced underground or into exile.

This history of SARHWU then is also part and parcel of the history of South Africa's struggle for freedom and democracy.

As we have seen, SARHWU had to be a militant union because it was fighting the state every time it took up a trade union issue. The employer would never talk. In response to a grievance its answer was always to sack and arrest the workers' spokesmen and to make brutal attacks on the workers themselves. The workers could respond only by action, and this meant strikes and meeting violence with violence.

Militancy contributed to the struggle against apartheid, but meant that the union entered the post-apartheid era with no experience of negotiations, let alone compromise. (The same applied, of course, to the employer, which created a labour relations office only in the late 1980s.)

Even today negotiations can be problematic for unions. Elected officers are sent to negotiate without much room to manoeuvre. They are expected to win full acceptance of all the union's demands and to agree nothing without reference back. This version of democracy has cost the union dear, not only financially but also in terms of loss of experienced leaders, and in other ways too, as the events of 1991 dramatically showed. It also cost me dear personally. Almost certainly the stresses of trying to rescue the union from disaster in 1991 led directly to the minor stroke that forced me to retire from politics.

SARHWU has a proud history in the struggle for democracy and a better life for working people. There are many new challenges to be faced now in carrying forward that struggle in the new South Africa.

There are new skills to be learned, for example in collective bargaining, but there are broader educational needs too, if the union is to function effectively.

Most workers in the industry still have little education and are uncomfortable in talking in English or reading in any language. This means that communications have to be by word of mouth, translated by officers or shop stewards to the membership and back again. As a result, policies can sound different from what was decided at a conference by the time the message reaches the workplace, and sound different in different workplaces. Union democracy and worker participation in progressive change demand that this is tackled, and the union needs to push hard for the employer to provide good basic adult education for all employees. The union has a major need to develop trade union education.

SARHWU's well-known militancy needs to be deployed today in support of the industry itself, as well as defending workers' interests within the industry. Much of the rest of the world is discovering the importance of transport by rail and sea as an alternative to the unending growth of private cars and trucks. More and better railways in South Africa would create jobs in the industry, reduce road accidents and pollution and make it easier for the millions without cars to get around. SARHWU would find many allies with 'green' interests and sustainable development agendas in a campaign to promote public transport.

This story has seemed to be about working men, with the women remaining invisible, but as Chapter Seven reminds us, South Africa is now committed to equal opportunities regardless of gender as well as regardless of race. SARHWU has made a start on this, for example by requiring that every regional delegation to national conferences must include at least one woman. However, there are still no women among the senior office holders and as the testimony of the women themselves shows there is still a long way to go to put this right.

Why are we writing this book now?

This seemed to be the right time to write SARHWU's story, for two reasons.

The first one is obvious. The year 1998 saw the end of the name SARHWU. After prolonged negotiations, mergers took place with two rival unions, BLATU, the Black (Transnet Allied) Trade Union (formerly the Black Staff Association), and TATU, the Transnet Allied Trade Union, and a new transport union, the South African Transport and Allied Workers Union, SATAWU, was born.

That is not the end of the story. There are two more steps to be taken. As we write, arrangements for a merger with the Transport and General Workers' Union are well under way, and then the final step to the objective of 'One industry, one union' will be to find a way to merge with the historically white unions.

Our own people and our own comrades need to know what SARHWU is and where it came from.

The other reason is even more pressing. Time and again the apartheid regime destroyed our offices and all the records and papers in them. This meant that our main resources were the memories of those who played parts in the story. These are a rapidly diminishing band.

We travelled up and down the country recording the history of their union as they had lived it, and a rich resource this turned out to be. There are gaps, of course. Many have passed on, some killed in the struggle, and not all the living people we wanted to see could be traced; but we learned a lot.

We think you will find, then, that this book is not a 'dry as dust' history book but a moving story told by the participants, of how one group of working people lived and survived in the harsh struggle against the daily experience of apartheid.

It has been a great experience for me to meet old comrades and be reminded, or even hear for the first time, about parts of SARHWU's eventful past.

One particular thing has stuck with me. When we interviewed Ray Alexander she produced a photograph taken at the founding conference of SARHWU in 1936. In it were Ray herself, so influential in the union and with me personally, and Johnny Mtini. Johnny was a hero of mine, and as chairman of SARHWU the Western Cape he was the one who persuaded me to work full time for the union in 1954. Since that time I have always been involved in this powerful union, proud to be carrying on the work started by these great predecessors of ours.

This personal link reminds me of a slogan we had in the movement, that the flag of the freedom struggle must never be allowed to fall down. When one person can no longer carry it others must be ready to pick it up and carry it on until we reach our destination. Johnny and Ray passed it on to those leading the transport workers today. I know that these leaders will always remember that the workers' organisation is not owned by them. It is like the flag of the struggle. When they took office they accepted the duty of caring for it and then passing it on, stronger than ever, to those who will follow them.

Archie Sibeko
June 1999

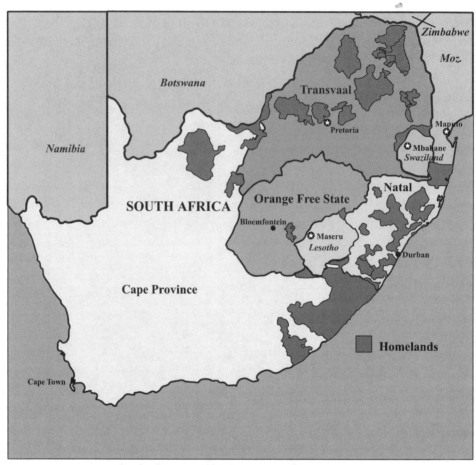

South Africa pre-1994: Provinces and major towns.

Introduction
Historical Background

Government directly employed railway workers and none of the industrial laws covered the railways. Further, almost all the African workers were casuals, taken on each morning for that day only and even within that day liable to be sacked by the foreman at any time. All this was on top of the general situation that no black union could negotiate on behalf of members. So in the case of the railwaymen, even more than most workers, the task was to organise and educate them for the long trade union and political struggles ahead. [1]

This book tells the story of the South African Railway and Harbour Workers Union, how it was formed, the part it played in the struggle against apartheid and the challenges it faces today as it adopts a new name and a new role in South African society.

SARHWU was founded in March 1936. It is one of the oldest black trade unions in South Africa and has survived to continue, after merging with other transport unions, as the South African Transport and Allied Workers Union. Throughout its history it was actively involved in the economic and political struggle of black workers and was closely identified with the African National Congress, the South African Communist Party, the South African Congress of Trade Unions and its successor, the Congress of South African Trade Unions. Its story is, therefore, both unique of itself and at the same time part of the wider picture of social and political change in South Africa.

Every story must have a beginning, but sometimes it is difficult to know quite when to begin. If we were just looking for a date then it would be simple – we would say that SARHWU began on 26 March 1936, and leave it at that. But real life is not simple. Real life doesn't begin and end at fixed points and our story is no different. It has its roots buried deep in past events and, like a tree, although it has a single trunk, it branches out in various directions. For this reason we must look further back if we want to identify the political and economic conditions which led to the setting up of the union and to understand the influences which affected its growth.

---

1.   A. Sibeko, 1996, p. 36.

The major historical influences on the development of African trade unions such as SARHWU were the growth of wage labour, the nature and level of industrialisation and the labour policies pursued by the various governments in power.

The Origins of Wage Labour

The development of wage labour in South Africa began with the settlement of Europeans from 1652 onwards, but it was not until the discovery of gold in the Transvaal in 1886 that the process of industrialisation and urbanisation began in earnest. Before then, South Africa was still an agricultural society and although white settlers seized land and established colonial administrations they were resisted. Independent chiefdoms kept considerable power over land and labour and even after the final defeat in 1879 of the strongest of these, the Zulu Kingdom, the settlers often found it wiser to bargain with chiefs for the supply of labour rather than resort to force.

As long as Africans retained control of enough land it was possible for chiefs to control the supply of labour. In some places and in periods of labour shortage, individuals could obtain quite high wages, sometimes by withdrawing their labour and returning to their villages as a bargaining point. Many managed to avoid wage labour altogether either by operating entirely within a subsistence economy, by earning income selling their own produce or by farming as share-croppers on land surplus to the needs of white farmers.[2] Others used the system on their own terms, entering the wage economy to avoid traditional obligations or to earn cash for specific purposes (such as buying cattle for bride price) and leaving it again when their needs were satisfied.[3]

This situation changed with the development of the mining industry in the Rand (named after the ridge of high ground in the Transvaal which has produced more gold than anywhere else in the world). The mines needed two kinds of labour. The first of these was skilled labour. The rural Afrikaners (the descendants of Dutch farmers) were not equipped to provide this and high wages were used to attract skilled immigrants from England and other European countries. The second kind was unskilled labour. Because of the depth and low ore content of the seams there was a need for a large supply of cheap manual labour in order for gold to be mined profitably. For this the mining companies looked to the black population, and when voluntary labour was slow to appear, a variety of methods were used to 'encourage' recruits. Special recruiting corporations were

2.   See Durban LACOM, 1986, Chapter 1.
3.   See L. Callinicos, 1987, for stories and accounts of the experiences of early migrant labourers.

set up which paid local chiefs to supply fixed amounts of labour to the mines on a regular basis. Hut, poll and labour taxes were imposed which increased the need for Africans to enter the wage economy, and measures were brought in to restrict the ability of Africans to make a living from their own land or by renting or squatting on land taken over by white farmers. At the same time legislation was used to introduce pass, contract and compound systems to regulate the influx of black labour and to curb the rights of migrants in 'white' areas.

From the beginning of wage labour, Africans were tied by contracts to work for a fixed wage. Contracts were backed by legislation such as the 1850 Masters and Servants Ordinance which imposed criminal sanctions for 'desertion'. In 1896 the Boer parliament of the Transvaal (the Volksraad) supplemented this legislation by bringing in two 'pass' laws which restricted the right of Africans to remain on the Rand to those employed by a 'master' and required all Africans to carry a metal badge (later a signed pass). Those entering a 'labour district' to look for work also needed a special pass, and if they failed to find work within three days they were forced to leave the area. Blacks caught without a pass were fined, put in jail and then returned to their home villages. Wages were kept low and recorded on each pass. The pass laws created a system of circulatory migrant labour that was regulated by the government in line with the demand for a low-paid workforce from the mining companies and other employers.

As mining developed, new towns grew up to provide the necessary economic infrastructure. These provided alternative employment to the farms and mines and Africans found jobs as labourers, domestic servants and in a host of other occupations. By 1899 the largest of these towns, the capital of the Rand, Johannesburg, had a population of 100 000 of whom only half were white. There were also about 250 000 migrant mine workers housed in compounds outside the town. These workers were isolated from others, guarded by special mine police and subjected to strict controls.[4] Single-sex compounds or hostels were also built to house municipal workers. Later regulations required any employer of 50 or more black workers to provide similar compound-type accommodation. Domestic workers frequently lived at their place of work, where they were constantly on call, but others had to house themselves as best they could. Official policy was to confine Africans to separate black townships ('locations'), outside the boundaries of the white town, but as the towns grew these soon became overcrowded and blacks often spilled over to share slum housing areas with low-paid workers of other races.

Following the Act of Union in 1910 the migrant labour system was consolidated by the Land Act, 1913, which largely dispossessed Africans of their land.

---

4. See L. Callinicos, 1987, pp. 39-40.

Most land was allocated to whites with only 7,5% (later increased to 13%) being kept as 'Native Reserves', which were used as a pool from which labour could be drawn depending on the needs of the white economy. These were recognised, even by whites, as 'inadequate to the support of the race, even if they were not, as they are, almost fatally depreciated by overstocking and exhaustion'.[5] During 1912-14 a series of droughts, diseases and locusts struck the rural areas hard. Families could no longer provide for their needs from the infertile and over-crowded land to which they were confined and many thousands were forced to work for local farmers or migrate to find work in the mines or the towns.

In the agricultural sector sharecroppers were no longer allowed to share the crops they produced and were forced to become labour tenants who worked for their landlord in return for living on the land, or to work as contracted wage labourers. Work was seasonal, conditions were extremely harsh and accommo-dation rudimentary. Many drifted to the towns in search of a better life, but in the mine compounds and slum yards conditions were little better. Workers were paid only a single man's wage which was not enough to maintain family life. To a large extent, women, children and the elderly were left to support themselves from the land, and the 'breadwinners' would return only at infrequent intervals. Those women who did migrate to the towns had to maintain themselves by working, often as domestic servants, or by making a difficult living in the informal economy.[6]

Industrialisation and Labour Policy

In the period leading up to the 1914-18 war the South African economy was based almost entirely on mining and agriculture. There were small repair shops and factories producing those mining supplies that could be made easily and cheaply locally. Other small factories producing light consumer goods such as boots, blankets, candles and soap had also developed to a limited extent. On the whole, however, South Africa remained a supplier of raw materials to Europe and an importer of finished products. Most of the profits from mining were not reinvested in the local economy and were exported to Europe.

During the course of the war this situation changed. Britain was unable to deliver manufactured goods to South Africa and as a result South African secondary industries were given a boost. The economy underwent a period of industrial boom that continued after the war so that in 1919 -20, 4 300 factories with a workforce of 30 000 whites and 74 000 others (Indians, Africans and

---

5.   G. Gordon Brown, 1937, p. 242.
6.   D. Hindson, 1983, p. 309.

coloureds) were recorded. The total employed in all manufacturing establishments reached more than 180 000 by the end of 1920.[7] By this time, however, the expanding post-war British and American economies were beginning to bring increasing competition to these industries from imported goods. At the same time the price of gold on the world market (on which the South African economy relied) fell by a quarter. A number of mines closed, and inflation and unemployment grew.

The Rand Revolt

Mine owners attempted to protect their profits by reducing the wages of white workers and replacing them in a number of semi-skilled jobs by black workers doing the same job at a lower rate of pay. (White workers' wages were ten times higher than those of black workers.) The white workers resisted and in 1922 there was a violent strike, which became known as the Rand Revolt. Twenty-five thousand white miners went on strike for eight weeks and were joined by other white workers, many of whom were unemployed, behind a banner reading 'Workers of the World Fight and Unite for a White South Africa'. Strikers were organised into 'commandos' that attacked African and other employees continuing to work. The Smuts government responded with full military force, 153 people were killed in clashes between strikers and troops, 5 000 strikers were arrested and were imprisoned or fined, and four men were sentenced and hanged for their role in the strike.

Although the miners were defeated, the revolt highlighted for the government the danger of unrest in the industrial workforce and the scale of the 'poor white' problem, which was caused by the drift from the land of poor, unskilled and disaffected Afrikaners. A commission appointed by the government in 1921 proposed large-scale land settlement as a solution but in many rural areas the white population continued to decline. Another commission, appointed in 1928, reported that out of a white population of over 1 800 000, 22% were 'pauperised' and 34% were below 'normal' living standards, unable to clothe, feed, house and educate their children.[8] Unskilled whites were unable to obtain work in the towns 'at anything like a white South African living wage' because the ratio of skilled to unskilled wages was kept down to around 7:1 by the availability of cheap black labour. Unskilled whites did, however, possess voting power and could exact from the government still further measures of relief and assistance as the

7. H.J. Simons and R.E. Simons, 1969, p. 220.
8. Report of the Carnegie Commission 1930-32, quoted in G. Gordon Brown, 1937, p. 226.

price of their support.[9] In the election of 1924 they used this to bring down the South African Party government, which had been in power since the Act of Union, and replace it with a new one more favourable to their interests.

The Pact government

The new government, led by the Nationalist General Herzog, was the result of an alliance between the National Party and the Labour Party and was therefore known as the Pact government. Its policies represented the different emphases of the two parties. The National Party aimed to foster the interests of the Afrikaner bourgeoisie, who were strongly represented in the leadership of the party, and to encourage the growth of a strong national capitalist class that could be counted on to provide future political support. This was supported by the Labour Party with the condition that there should also be policies to protect its supporters among the white working class against de-skilling and to provide them with employment.

The National Party objectives were achieved by measures to encourage the development of manufacturing industry, thus favouring the interests of local (Afrikaner), rather than foreign (British), capitalism. A Tariff Act was passed to tax imported goods and protect home industries. Manufacturing industry began to grow again and the value of goods produced rose from £322 (R644) million in 1925 to £460 (R920) million in 1929. By 1931 manufacturing industry was producing nearly a sixth of the country's wealth.[10]

The labour requirements of manufacturing industry were different from those of either agriculture, with its seasonal pattern, or mining, where there was a racially divided workforce consisting of a small number of highly-paid white craft workers and supervisors and a large unskilled migrant labour force. Machine-based mass production needed a readily available supply of cheap semi-skilled labour and this provided an opportunity for black workers. Between 1918 and 1920 the number of Africans in non-mine employment grew from just over 67 000 to more than 92 000, the majority of the increase being in manufacturing as against the service occupations which had previously predominated (although these still represented a large percentage).[11] Initially employers hired both black and white workers on equal terms but the Pact government introduced what it called a 'Civilised Labour' policy. The aim of this was to protect white

---

9.   G. Gordon Brown, 1937, p. 225.
10. L. Callinicos, 1987, p. 119; H. Houghton, 1969, p. 135; other sources give different figures and care has to be exercised about what is being counted but all sources show a definite increase.
11. P. Bonner, 1982, p. 272.

workers (supporters of the Labour Party side of the pact) against competition from cheaper black labour while at the same time promoting the interests of local capitalists (supporters of the National Party side).

The 'Civilised Labour' policy

When the Pact government came into power in 1924 the position of white workers had already been strengthened by the Apprenticeship Act of 1922 and the Natives (Urban Areas) Act, 1923, which had been passed by the previous government led by General Jan Smuts. The first of these was intended to give employment to unskilled Afrikaners by opening skilled trades to 'poor white' youths and effectively excluding other races. The second extended the existing pass laws by barring Africans from urban areas except for the purposes of employment, and further restricting their right to own land in towns.

The Pact government added to this approach by using new legislative and administrative policies designed to provide employment for 'poor white' Afrikaners and protect their conditions of employment. All government departments were instructed to replace 'uncivilised' (i.e. black) labour with 'civilised' (i.e. white) workers. Between 1925 and 1926 this produced jobs for 1 400 whites at the expense of blacks.[12] Nevertheless, it was felt necessary to increase this number by extending the colour bar into the private sector, in particular the mines.

The Mines and Works Act of 1911 had reserved skilled jobs in the mines for whites only. This had been declared unlawful by the courts, however, and mine owners had continued to employ blacks in these categories in order to save labour costs (a practice which had been a major factor in provoking the Rand Revolt of 1922). The Mines and Works Act of 1926, known as the 'Colour Bar Act', revived the 1911 Act and prohibited the employment of any other than whites in skilled occupations for which a certificate of competence was required.

Elsewhere in private industry, government influence was less direct. The employment of white labour was encouraged by means of tax relief and wage legislation. The Wages Act of 1925 set up a Wage Board, which fixed minimum wages for workers not covered by industrial councils. To some extent this allowed black workers to raise the level of their wages but in the main the system worked in favour of white workers by fixing the wages in semi-skilled occupations at a 'civilised' level and so prevented black workers from undercutting white wages. Such government policies were successful in protecting white

---

12. J. Lewis, 1981, p. 34; quoted in L. Callinicos, 1987, p. 128.

xxiii

workers against the worst effects of the depression that was soon to hit the economy.

The Depression

At the beginning of the 1930s the South African economy was hit by a combination of drought, the effects of the world trade depression and Britain's abandonment of the gold standard. Capital was drained from the economy and by 1932 over £12,5 (R25) million had been sent out of South Africa for investment. The price of agricultural exports fell and cheap imports of manufactured goods (the result of Britain's devaluation) led to a drop in the gross output of manufacturing plants from £112 (R224) million in 1930 to £91 (R182) million in 1932.[13] Mines and factories closed and thousands of workers were laid off until the depression was ended by the decision of the government to abandon the gold standard and thus restore the value of its exports.

Although rural 'poor whites' suffered too, the brunt of the hardship caused by the drought and depression was borne by Africans as jobs and wages were cut and the government again extended the protection of whites. In 1932 a government commission reported that in many cases it was impossible for black families to live off either what could be produced on the land or the level of wages paid in towns.[14] No definitive unemployment statistics exist, but it is estimated that in 1932, 14 000 Africans were looking for jobs in Johannesburg alone. During the depression the number of blacks working in factories fell by 18% and in mines by 10%.[15]

The government response was to extend existing legislation so as to increase state control and to introduce measures to cushion the effect of the depression on white workers. The Riotous Assemblies Act was amended in 1930 to give the government power to banish, ban or prohibit individuals, meetings or books without trial. The 1924 Urban Areas Act was also amended to tighten pass laws to prevent black job seekers, driven from the land by the drought, from entering the towns. Simultaneously, subsidised relief projects were set up to employ unemployed whites and coloureds. In September 1933, the Department of Labour employed around 30 000 whites on subsidised relief works and 8 500 in municipalities. A further 12 500 were employed on other subsidised projects not classified as relief works, and local councils were subsidised so that they could

---

13. H.J. Simons and R.E. Simons, 1969, p. 462.
14. *Report of the Native Economic Commission* (1932).
15. H.J. Simons and R.E. Simons, 1969, p. 454.

increase their proportion of 'civilised' labour to at least one-fifth of their unskilled labour force.[16]

The experience of the effects of the downturn in world trade gave a fresh impetus to the alliance between government, white workers, mining and manufacturing industry to protect their interests in the face of external and internal threats. The National Party and the South African Party came together to form a new party, the United Party, which came to power in 1933. The new government protected manufacturing and farming through a system of tariffs and export bonuses and backed up the 'civilised labour' policy with social welfare benefits such as help in education, health care and housing for poor whites. Legislation controlled the supply of black labour by increasing the number of Africans who were allowed to work but at the same time strictly controlling the places where they were allowed to work and their terms and conditions of employment.

Economic growth

South Africa was led out of the depression by the recovery of the gold mining industry. In 1933 there was a dramatic rise in the price of gold and an Excess Profit Tax was levied on the mines. This produced funds to help local industry and enabled the development of state-run industries such as the South African Railways, the Electricity Supply Commission and the Iron and Steel Corporation of South Africa. The mining companies also invested directly in established industries or set up their own concerns. Foreign investment increased, and between 1933 and 1939 production almost doubled. Employment also increased. In December 1933 it was estimated that there were a total of 389 000 'natives' employed in South Africa, 273 507 from within the Union and the remainder from neighbouring territories. There were 261 312 workers employed in the mines and 128 540 in other occupations. By the end of the decade manufacturing industry employed 236 000 workers; fewer than half of them were white. Manufacturing represented some 18% of national income, compared with 11% in 1920 – still less than mining's 23%, but poised to overtake it.[17]

The country's new prosperity accelerated the drift of Africans to towns. Most Africans still lived in rural areas, but by 1936 there were over 500 000 Africans (mainly men) living on the Witwatersrand, around 200 000 in Johannesburg alone. Many of these were under-employed or unemployed and a large number were in domestic service or in unskilled casual jobs. A legal minimum wage was

16. As above, pp. 454-55; G. Gordon Brown, 1937, pp. 226-27.
17. G. Gordon Brown, 1937, p. 236; Union Statistics for Fifty Years, 1960. Table S-3; H. Houghton, 1969, p. 125.

set for male European workers of some £3 10s – £6 10s a week (R7,13). The median wage for Africans was around 19s per week (less than R2) and over 300 000 men lived in single-sex compounds or hostels where deductions for accommodation and food reduced their wages still further.[18]

Trade Unions and the Organisation of African Workers

With the industrial development of South Africa came the development of organisations to protect the interests of workers. Craft unions, which predominated in the mines, the state-run railways and in heavy industry, such as the metal industry, were the first to develop. These were followed by a variety of industrial unions (mainly white but often with 'parallel' black counterparts), which developed in the growing manufacturing sector at the end of World War I. Finally came separate African trade unions, the first of which was the Industrial and Commercial Workers' Union, founded in 1919, and also the growth of exclusive Christian Nationalist unions.

Craft unions

At first trade unionism in South Africa was dominated by labour relations in the country's major industry, mining. As we noted in the last section, there were two kinds of workers on the early Rand. Skilled workers, often immigrants from England and other European countries, were a minority of the workforce; they were experienced in industry and could earn high wages. In contrast, there was a mass of unskilled workers, mainly Afrikaner and black newcomers to the towns and to wage labour. Competition for employment kept their wages low and the conditions in which they worked and lived were often very bad.

The end of the nineteenth century and the early years of the twentieth century was a time of struggle during which mining companies attempted to keep wages down and replace expensive skilled labour by cheaper unskilled workers. The skilled workers, many of whom brought with them from Europe a knowledge and experience of trade unionism, responded by forming protectionist craft unions, both in the mines and in the industries which serviced the mines. A number of British craft unions (such as the Amalgamated Engineering Union) opened branches in South Africa. These were followed by local unions, such as the South African Typographical Union and the Transvaal Miners' Association.

---

18. B. Hirson, 1990, pp. 22-24.

These were mostly white but not exclusively so, especially in the Cape, where coloured members were accepted.

Craft unions were threatened by the ability of capital to restructure the industrial process to de-skill workers. They responded with a confrontational class-consciousness and adopted a militant strike policy when jobs were threatened. Major confrontations occurred in 1897, 1902, 1907, 1913 and 1914 and the mining unions in particular remained a threat to employers until the Rand Revolt of 1922 and their subsequent alliance with the state.

Industrial unions

Changing economic and social circumstances and the growth of manufacturing industry at the end of the 1914-18 war brought a different dimension to trade union organisation. From the mid-1920s a new proletariat was developing in South Africa as both whites and blacks left the land to work in the fast growing industrial sector. Large numbers of semi-skilled workers entered the new factories and new trade unions, organised on the basis of industry rather than occupation or craft, developed to protect their interests.

The new industrial workforce was less well paid and more varied than that represented by the craft unions. The division of labour in the early years of the new manufacturing industries was not on racial lines, and the new unions could see the advantage of organising both black and white workers so that their wage rates were not undercut. Some of the new industrial unions, such as the Garment Workers Union and the Furniture Workers Union, formed and held joint meetings with parallel African unions in the same industry and some, such as the Johannesburg Boot and Shoe Workers' Union, accepted coloured and African members as well as whites. The new unions tended to be more open and more progressive than the essentially conservative craft unions. On the other hand, the leaders of the industrial trade unions were often more radical than the membership, and non-racial worker solidarity was undermined by government policy that discriminated against blacks in favour of white workers.

The Industrial Conciliation Act

Following the Rand Revolt the policy of government was to control industrial unrest by channelling disputes through recognised industrial relations machinery. The Industrial Conciliation (IC) Act was introduced by the Smuts government in 1924. Under this Act employees could form trade unions which would be approved, recognised and registered. Joint boards or industrial councils were set up on which these registered trade unions were represented. All disputes were to be mediated by these councils and then taken through a process of conciliation before strikes were permissible.

Africans were not covered by the Act, however. All government and municipal employees, all contract workers, all farm workers, all domestic workers and all workers 'regulated by any Native Pass Laws and Regulations' were specifically excluded from the definition of an employee covered by the Act. These workers were covered by the Wage Board set up by the Wage Act of 1925 to set minimum wages but this excluded agricultural, domestic and mineworkers. The result of the legislation was to divide black workers from their white counterparts by excluding blacks from membership of registered unions and to leave them with no legal means of negotiation.

In contrast to white workers, the majority of black workers were illiterate migrants and had no tradition of organisation. There was, however, a history of resistance to poor conditions and treatment which showed itself both in individual acts of 'indiscipline' or desertion, and in spontaneous, usually short-lived, mass action. The first recorded African collective action took place in November 1895 when 200 African dock workers in Durban demanded an increase in pay, and in 1913, soon after a major strike by white miners, 9 000 African mineworkers struck against low wages and poor conditions. There were further strikes in the mining industry in 1918, 1919 and 1920, when a strike of over 70 000 black mineworkers spread over 12 days in all. Troops were used to force workers underground to work and three strikers were killed and 40 injured.

Development of separate African unions was hindered by a combination of factors. The African labour force consisted of different ethnic groups. Some were migrants who returned periodically to the reserves; others had left farm employment to become more or less permanent town dwellers. Once in towns they formed a variety of different associations, including clan associations, church groups, youth clubs, trade and tenants associations as well as loose work-based organisations which took up demands for improved wages and conditions. Trade union organisation cut across these other forms of association but did not replace them. Workers' loyalties were divided and new forms of combination, such as trade unions, did not always come first. The indifference (or hostility) of white trade unionists, government oppression and the financial and organisational problems faced by those who attempted to set up unions were also formidable obstacles to African trade unionism. These difficulties are illustrated by the history of the Industrial and Commercial Workers' Union (ICU), the first nationally based African trade union to be established in South Africa.

The Industrial and Commercial Workers Union and early African unions

The ICU was set up in January 1919 with a base among coloured and African dockworkers in Cape Town and soon became a broad general union with branches throughout South Africa covering some 100 000 workers at its peak in 1927.[19] Under the leadership of its Secretary, Clements Kadalie, the union was initially successful, winning a wage increase of nearly 100% after a strike by about 2 000 Cape Town dockworkers in December 1919. But this victory was won in the teeth of scabbing by white workers and violence by the state.

A protest march by the Industrial Commercial Workers Union. The ICU was a general black workers' organisation which peaked in the late 1920s. It became the Council for Non-European Trade Unions, which differed from the ICU in that it organised urban workers into industrial unions. In a time of economic growth, many of these unions won real wage increases for their members.

In the decade that followed, the ICU grew rapidly. By the mid-1920s it had branches in Port Elizabeth, East London, Central and Eastern Cape, Orange Free State, the Transvaal and Natal. Nevertheless, it failed to repeat its early success. As pointed out above, under the 1924 Industrial Conciliation Act Africans were excluded from registered unions because by definition they were not employees. They could form their own segregated unions but as these bodies had no legal

---

19. Membership figures for African unions at this time must be treated with some caution. Membership fluctuated and in the absence of reliable records of paid-up members all figures must be treated as estimates.

standing and were not recognised by employers it was virtually impossible for the ICU to negotiate any improvement in the wages and conditions of its members. For a trade union to attract support it is necessary for it to be able to deliver economic rewards to its members. In the face of superior force, however, such success is rare and in these circumstances support for a union has a tendency to wither away. This, in a nutshell, was the fate of the ICU.

In addition to constant police harassment and the built-in discrimination of government legislation, the union also suffered from a lack of resources, financial corruption, internal conflicts and inherent weaknesses in its structure. The ICU was a general union, organising workers in a variety of different industries. Although the membership was large it was primarily rurally based and the ICU had more of the features of a social movement than of a trade union. Its members were scattered in small workplaces and farms rather than concentrated in the industrial sector and its communications were poor. There were also differences between Kadalie and a group of ICU organisers who were members of the Communist Party of South Africa who advocated that the union should be reorganised from a general union into disciplined industrial unions. However, that was not the only bone of contention. Kadalie was also criticised for the lack of democratic controls over the union's funds and elections, for the failure to pursue more militant policies and for using members' dues to embark on a number of business ventures.

In an attempt to win the backing of foreign labour movements, such as the British Trade Union Congress, Kadalie tried to steer the union away from strikes and militant action. He purged members of the Communist Party from the ranks of the ICU in 1926, and in 1927 applied for affiliation to the South African Trade Union Council. (The application was rejected by the leadership of the SATUC.) Rivalry developed between Kadalie and AWG Champion, the leader of the union in Natal, and in 1928, following an internal crisis concerning the misuse of funds, the national structure began to disintegrate into a number of different sections, the largest being Natal, with about 30 000 members. By the early 1930s the ICU as a national structure had virtually collapsed.

Following the disintegration of the ICU there were a number of attempts by former organisers, many of them communists expelled by Kadalie, to start African industrial unions. In the late 1920s the Native Laundry Workers, Native Bakers, Native Clothing Workers and Municipal Workers Unions were formed by communists TW Thibedi and Bennie Weinbren in the towns on the Rand. In 1929 these were joined by unions in the dairy, meat, food and drink, soap and chemical, canvas and other industries, but the depression of the early 1930s and the growth of African unemployment weakened them to the extent that only the Clothing Workers Union and the Laundry Workers Union survived.

The 'Christian Nationalist' trade unions

Afrikaner nationalists first achieved political power through the Pact government in 1924 but the economy, civil service, army and police force were still dominated by English speakers. In order to penetrate these fields the nationalists had formed the semi-secret Broederbond society in 1918, and it was through this organisation that they promoted the formation of racist Christian Nationalist trade unions in those industries which had the most Afrikaner workers. Alternative Afrikaner unions were formed which infiltrated the membership of the National Union of Railway and Harbour Servants (NURAHS), the white Mineworkers Union (MWU), the Iron and Steel Trades Association (ISTA) and the building, clothing and leather industries. The policy was most successful in the railways, where workers relied on the government for their jobs, and in the mines, where most white workers were supervisors and held racist beliefs. Afrikaner nationalists were less successful in the industrial unions where, although members also held racist beliefs, they recognised that their interests as workers linked them to some extent to other workers, both black and white, who were not necessarily Afrikaner.

Trade union federations

With a few exceptions, early trade unions were organised on a provincial rather than a national basis and even the federations through which they co-operated with one another showed the same tendency. From the early 1900s Trades and Labour Councils were formed in most major cities and these came together at provincial level in Industrial Federations. In 1914 these amalgamated to form the South African Industrial Federation (SAIF) to which unions from all provinces were invited to affiliate.

The SAIF supported a policy of support for white labour, believing that employers used black labour to drive wages down. Most unions throughout the country affiliated, but the Cape Federation of Labour Unions (CFLU), which represented a large number of coloured workers, refused to do so. Under its secretary, Archie Crawford, the SAIF grew to be a large and powerful organisation, taking control of negotiations with employers and government on behalf of its affiliates. It was active in the Rand Revolt of 1922, but after this splits developed in its ranks. In 1923 membership, which had once been over 60 000, had fallen to only 2 000. In 1925 the federation collapsed and was replaced by the South African Trade Union Council (SATUC).

The SATUC represented a mixture of the strands present in the South African trade union movement. It was formed as a result of a special congress called by the Minister of Labour, Colonel Cresswell, who wanted to be able to negotiate with a single trade union body. Its members were all registered under the IC Act and all were white. Many of its members were conservative craft unions (although some of these refused to join). At the same time, however, there was a progressive strand represented by the new industrial unions. The secretary of SATUC, Bill Andrews, was a member of the South African Communist Party, and by 1928 even the right-wing unions had recognised that black workers should also be organised in trade unions, though most felt that these should not be in the same unions as white workers.

In 1930 SATUC merged with the Cape Federation of Labour Unions to form the South African Trades and Labour Council (SATLC). Like SATUC, the SATLC incorporated both conservative craft unions, white industrial unions, white unions with parallel black organisations and the relatively progressive non-racial registered trade unions.[20] The minority of progressive trade unionists within the Council campaigned for the inclusion of Africans as 'employees' under the IC Act and for the abolition of racial labour laws, and officially the SATLC supported the formation of non-racial unions. In practice, however, the Council did little to help the development of African unions and it was deeply split on racial questions. Many union leaders held racist views, and the issue was further complicated by the growth of Afrikaner nationalism in the trade union movement.

African unions were forced to form their own federation. In 1928, 150 delegates representing different African industrial unions came together to form the Federation of Non-European Trade Unions (FNETU). At this time the federation claimed a total of some 10 000 - 15 000 members. It followed a policy of dealing with economic issues rather than the broad political demands pursued by the ICU and there was some limited success. Gains for workers were obtained through the Wage Board and through the use of strikes to force employers to negotiate, but with the depression of 1930-33 many black workers lost both their jobs and their hard won gains.

At the same time the FNETU was severely affected by splits within the Communist Party of South Africa (CPSA), with which it was closely associated. The adoption by the CPSA of the 'Black Republic' policy which emphasised

---

20.   In 1937 there were seven craft unions accounting for 7 871 members and 25 industrial unions representing 8 809. By 1947 this had risen to 70 855 and 60 033 respectively.

support for black nationalism, brought about a rift with those members who believed that the party should be building an alliance between black and white workers. A number of trade unionists, including Bill Andrews, Bennie Weinbren, Gana Makabeni of the African Clothing Workers Union and TW Thibedi of the Native Laundry Workers, were expelled from the party and the FNETU rapidly collapsed.

It was not until the mid-to late 1930s that the period of industrial expansion which followed the end of the depression led to renewed efforts to organise African workers. The revision of the IC Act in 1937 extended the operation of industrial councils by laying down that African workers should be represented by an official from the Department of Labour and that wage agreements would be ratified only if they fixed rates for black employees as well as for whites. The Wage Board had already fixed minimum wages for the baking, laundering, furniture and clothing industries and it became clear that African unions could exploit the upturn in the economy and increase wages by putting their case to the Board and the industrial councils.

With the assistance of the white liberal South African Institute of Race Relations and the Trotskyite, Max Gordon, the Laundry Workers Union was revived and a number of new African unions were formed. A Joint Committee of African Trade Unions was formed in 1939 and by 1940 its membership was reported to be 21 unions with a combined membership of 25 000 (30% of the African workforce). Like others before it, however, the Joint Committee was short lived. In 1940 Gordon was interned and the Committee promptly split following disagreements about white domination of the organisation. A small group of affiliates joined with the former communist, Gana Makabeni then secretary of the African Clothing Workers Union and of a grouping of unions called the Co-ordinating Committee of African Trade Unions, and in 1941 the Council of Non-European Trade Unions (CNETU) was formed.

The role of the Communist Party

The Communist Party of South Africa was formed in 1921.[21] Its initial membership was small, consisting mainly of immigrant Europeans. Its influence on the South African trade union movement was, however, disproportionate to its size. Communists were involved in most of the progressive industrial unions and, as noted above, one of the founders of the party, Bill Andrews, became secretary of the South African Trade Union Council when it was formed in 1925. In particular, its activists were

---

21. The party was preceded by the International Socialist League, which split off from the Labour Party in 1915. It was renamed the South African Communist Party (SACP) in 1953.

almost the only members of the recognised trade unions who showed any commitment to the organisation of black workers. At the same time, however, factionalism and changes in political line made the party less effective than it could have been. The party was closely associated with the Communist International (Comintern), the Soviet-backed organisation to promote international communism, and changes in Comintern policy led to disagreements within the South African party, which, in turn, had repercussions for the trade union movement as a whole.

Until the Rand Revolt of 1922 the party supported the view that the African worker was insufficiently proletarianised and that working class gains could be achieved only through the power of the white trade unions. However, a number of trade unionists within the party argued that the lesson of the failure of the Rand Revolt to bring about political change was that the state would use race as a means of dividing the working class. They saw the organisation of black workers as vital to the overthrow of the ruling class and argued that it was therefore necessary to shift from a position which saw the white working class as the sole instrument of revolution in South Africa.[22]

Further disillusioned by the accommodation between the National Party and the Labour Party and the adoption of the 'civilised labour' policy, the CPSA began actively recruiting black members. Political education classes were organised with the aim of bringing more Africans into the party and attracted a number of able recruits including Albert Nzula, who became the first black general secretary of the CPSA, Johannes Nkosi, Gana Makabeni and Moses Kotane. It was these activists who, together with a number of other black communists expelled by Kadalie, worked to build up the remnants of ICU branches to form African unions in a variety of industries.

Between 1928 and 1934, however, the party split over the policy of support for national liberation and formation of a 'Black Republic' in South Africa which was adopted by the sixth congress of the Comintern. Those who opposed the policy saw it as support for middle-class bourgeois nationalist movements and an abandonment of class-based organisations such as trade unions. During this period there was another exclusivist 'ultra-left' twist in Comintern policy which resulted in many purges. *This* policy was later changed in line with changes at Comintern level. Many of the leaders of the new industrial unions and black recruits such as TW Thibedi and Gana Makabeni were expelled. The party was disastrously weakened; membership fell from 4 000 to 851 and it was not until the end of the 1930s, when the leadership moved from Johannesburg to Cape

---

22. See H.J. Simons and R.E. Simons, 1969, for a full account of these debates.

Town, that changes in policy, in particular the adoption of the more inclusive United Front policy, brought about a recovery.

Summary

The first forty years of the twentieth century saw a rapid expansion in African wage labour, first on the land, then in the mines and in service occupations and finally in the manufacturing sector. The system of contract labour controlled and regulated African employment, slowing down the process of proletarianisation. Most Africans continued to be rural dwellers but many also had links with town-based and work-based social associations that grew in importance. Government policies discriminated against black labour, and wages and conditions of work were poor. White trade unions failed to support African workers and a number of African trade unions were founded but these were unrecognised and weak and tended to be short lived. The Communist Party played an important role in the progressive trade union movement and in the founding of African unions, but developments were hindered by sectarianism.

1

The Beginnings of SARHWU

Introduction

The South African Railways and Harbours Administration (SARH) occupied a unique position as an employer. The railways provided the main line of communication between the industrial interior and the coast. Before the Act of Union the railways of the different provinces were worked independently.

On 31 May 1910 all these provincial railways, amounting to 7 000 miles (over 11 000 kilometres) of line, were amalgamated into the South African Railways and Harbours and became the property of the Union of South Africa. By 31 December 1916 the grand total of miles of railway within the Union and the Protectorate of South West Africa had grown to over 11 000 miles (nearly 18 000 kilometres).

The SARH was a major employer of labour both in the docks, where it employed harbour-side workers (on-board stevedores being employed by the private shipping companies) and on the railways and later, when air travel developed, it extended its influence to cover the national airline, South African Airways (SAA). It employed workers in a variety of different occupations and from its beginning it employed a large number of whites – not only in craft occupations but also in the special category of 'skilled labourer'.

Government policy was to use state employment of this kind to combat the threat of the growth of an unstable class of discontented unemployed 'poor whites' but it was obstructed in this by the closed shop operated by the militant craft unions and by the lack of education and skills among white recruits.

1

De-skilling and 'Civilised Labour'

Thousands of unskilled, barely literate 'poor whites' were recruited into the railway service, which over the following two decades provided them with the training and education which enabled them to progress through an elaborate system of promotion and upgrading.[1]

Native and coloured workers who do the hardest, most dangerous work are not given the chance of becoming skilled workers. They are often employed on semi-skilled work, for instance assisting the white artisans with repairs on furnaces at the height of 100-150 feet, helping them to splice wire (which weakens the eyesight), and to shift heavy machinery where the cranes cannot do it – but they cannot become skilled workers because this would mean higher status, higher wages.[2]

The power of the craft unions was broken using a combination of legislation and the reorganisation of work previously performed by skilled workers. As a first step the 1912 Railways and Harbours Services Act made striking by railway employees punishable by fine or imprisonment. This was followed by the 1914 Riotous Assemblies and Criminal Law Amendment Act that prohibited strikes in essential services and made picketing illegal.

At the same time the SARH adopted a policy of de-skilling (the substitution of skilled labour by semi-skilled). New moulding machines were introduced to do the job previously performed in the railway workshops by craftsmen moulders. The Moulders Union refused to operate the new machinery so the work was given to semi-skilled operatives instead, at lower wages. Throughout the railway service a new class of employee was created which was dependent for its employment not on scarce skills or union strength but on government policy.

This fact was clearly shown when there was a change in government policy during the depression that hit South Africa at the beginning of the 1920s. The government introduced several economy measures. The number of white railway labourers was cut, their privileges were withdrawn and they were placed on a casual basis. The result was an electoral backlash in 1924 that replaced the Smuts administration with one that promised to put the interests of white workers first.

The 'civilised labour' policy adopted by the new Pact government has been described as 'a massive operation in social engineering, designed to repair and maintain the racially hierarchical division of labour'.[3] In the words of a government report, the intention was to raise the poor whites above the level of the

1.   J. Lewis, 1984, p. 75.
2.   *Negro Worker* 6(8), October 1936: 7-12.
3.   J. Lewis, 1984, p. 75.

blacks since 'The European minority, occupying the position of the dominant race, cannot allow a considerable number of its members to sink into [poverty] and to fall below the level of the non-European workers'.[4]

As part of this policy the SARH recruited thousands of unskilled poor whites and introduced schemes of education and training to fit them for semi-skilled and supervisory grades.

> The principle was adopted at this time that labourers ... could obtain almost any position in the Service. Except in cases requiring technical training, all promotions were to be made through and from the labourer's ranks ...The administration was establishing a thorough-going system of rehabilitation designed to secure the incorporation of poor whites and ensure their political support.[5]

South African Railways and Harbours employees, blacksmith's shop, Colenso.

A system of 'learnership' was developed and a probationer scheme was introduced in 1927. In that year 1 331 junior labourers were promoted to the probation grade and in 1928 a further 1 767 were added. The category of European labourer continued until 1938 by which time the upgrading of white workers and a growing labour shortage had reached such an extent that it was proving difficult to recruit whites as labourers.

---

4. Quoted in R.H. Davies, 1979, p. 80.
5. Quoted by J. Lewis, 1984, pp. 75-76.

The main beneficiaries of these changes were Afrikaners and the main losers were blacks and coloureds. By 1929 the Railway Administration announced that it had found employment and often housing for approximately 25 000 workless men 'who were regarded as "poor whites", without any prospect or hope'.[6] The number of black employees is reported by Jon Lewis, in his study, *Industriali-sation and Trade Union Organisation in South Africa,* to have fallen by almost 6 000 from 47 157 in 1924 to 41 533 in 1929, while the number of whites increased from 39 024 (including 4 760 labourers) to 58 562 (16 248 of whom were classed as labourers).[7]

This racial distribution of employment was reinforced by the effects of the depression that hit South Africa at the beginning of the 1930s. Government employment schemes raised the number of whites from nearly 29% of the total workforce in 1929 to nearly 39% in 1934. The number of employees of SARH who were Afrikaners increased from 42% of white railway workers in 1926 to 57% in 1939 – when it has been calculated that every eleventh adult male Afrikaner was a railway worker![8]

The rise of Afrikaner trade unionism

The SARH was an especially powerful employer as a result of the large size of its workforce and its special relationship with the government. The railways and harbours were considered to be an essential service and the SARH did not have to conform to the Industrial Conciliation Act. Workers were represented by a variety of different sectional unions and staff associations representing different grades. The National Union of Railway and Harbour Servants (NURAHS) which had been formed in 1915 was nominally non-racial, although white dominated. The craft unions and those representing higher grades were exclusively white.

The position of workers was weak and made weaker by the divisions between different unions and between races, created by company policy. The large number of poor whites recruited between 1924 and 1929 'could be in no doubt that they owed their jobs and their economic salvation to the government's "civilised labour" policy'[9] and formed a compliant workforce. Between 1928 and 1934 further de-skilling took place with the introduction of even simpler moulding machines. At the same time the administration introduced a piecework system and an hierarchical organisational structure which increased the super-vision of work. The craft unions protested but the new workers benefited from

---

6. As above, p. 76.
7. As above, p. 75.
8. As above, p. 69; O'Meara, 1983, p. 90.
9. J. Lewis, 1984 , p. 77.

the reorganisation. The position of skilled workers and their unions was undermined, clearing the way for what Lewis calls 'the eventual triumph of state-oriented and racially exclusive company unionism'.[10] Before that happened, however, there was a growth of a new kind of 'Christian Nationalist' trade unionism.

Support for Afrikaner nationalism and Afrikaner 'cultural' associations, such as the Broederbond, was particularly strong among white railway employees. The aim of the nationalists was to unite all Afrikaners in order to take over political and economic power. In order to separate Afrikaners from other workers and ensure that their primary loyalty was to the nationalist movement they decided to form separate trade union organisations.

English-speaking whites had traditionally dominated the higher grades in the railway organisation but their position was coming under challenge from the Afrikaners who formed the majority of the lower grades. In 1934 HJ Klopper, a railway official active in the Broederbond and other Afrikaner cultural organisations, formed the union 'Die Spoorbond'. At first the Spoorbond represented salaried staff and its main aim was to fight perceived discrimination against Afrikaner office workers on the railway but this policy soon became broadened to include the replacement of all black workers by Afrikaners. The Spoorbond supported the advancement of Afrikaners within the railways in order to separate them from any class alliance with English-speaking whites or black employees. In the words of JBM Hertzog, the leader of the National Party, Afrikaner trade unions would 'weld the Afrikaner worker and the Afrikaner nation into a mighty unity'. In line with this the Spoorbond rejected strikes, calling instead for loyal service and adopting the motto *Verower deur Diens* (Conquer through Service). Benefits for members were achieved through political, not industrial, pressure and a membership of some 16 000 was soon built up, overshadowing NURAHS, which had failed to organise effectively among the influx of unskilled workers taken on to the railway payroll at the beginning of the 1930s.

The success of the Spoorbond has been attributed to three main factors. As well as being a Nationalist organisation it successfully represented the economic interests of white workers by campaigning against substitution by cheap black labour. It was a successful alliance of salaried staff and manual labour that could present a united front to the employer, and its use of negotiation rather than conflict and its pro-state policy won it the protection of powerful friends.[11] As a result of its success, however, it was felt by SARH to be too powerful. In 1941 the union was weakened when employees were divided into new categories for

10. As above, p. 75.
11. See O'Meara, 1983.

5

the purposes of negotiation and it lost its right to negotiate for all categories of staff. Some of this ground was made up again at the end of the war but it never again achieved the predominance which it enjoyed during its early years.

Working conditions of black railway and harbour workers

The wives and children of waterside workers are never sure of seeing them again as they leave them in the morning. Accidents are frequently taking place. Broken fingers, broken backs and injuries here and there are the order of the day ... There is a tendency on the part of the Company Authorities and Administration to pay very little attention to the danger threatening the workers. Casual men do not receive any sick pay whatsoever. Injured on duty pay is 60% of the worker's pay but this is only granted provided the injured worker is incapacitated for not less than seven days ... If the worker stays at home he does not receive any pay. After returning to work he has to go through weeks of begging until he gets his sick pay which only amounts to a few shillings.

The life of a worker is cheap in the eyes of the Railway and Harbour Authorities. When a worker was crushed to death by a heavy bucket of sand they thought that £29 [R58] was sufficient to compensate the widowed mother, despite the fact that the son who was her main support was killed through the negligence of the Government and the crane driver. [12]

The majority of black employees of the SARH were migrants, working on contracts and housed in company labour compounds. Pay was low and conditions were harsh and there was a tradition of resistance among black railway and harbour workers going back to World War I and even earlier. Strikes by African harbour workers in Durban are recorded in 1895 and 1903; in May 1917 a successful strike of railway workers on the Rand for an additional 3d (2,5 cents) a day triggered off a wave of other strikes, and it was a successful strike by Cape Town dock and harbour workers in 1919 that led to the formation of the ICU (described in the Introduction). [13]

The initial Cape Town strike – against the export of scarce foodstuffs – was organised by a strike committee of black and white workers consisting of Cape Town dockworkers and representatives of NURAHS. The strike was built on by Clements Kadalie, the Secretary of the ICU, who issued a demand for an increase in wages from 4s to 8s 6d (40c to 85c) a day but this was only partially successful.

---

12. *Negro Worker* 6(8), October 1936: pp. 7-12.
13. H.G. Ringrose, 1951, pp. 7-8, 14.

A number of private companies offered an increase to 8s (80c) a day but the SARH refused to recognise the ICU or to give any increase. Police and troops were called in, Africans were ejected from the dock labour compound and prosecutions for breach of contract brought under the Master and Servant Act which still governed industrial relations and made desertion a criminal offence.

The 'civilised labour' policy meant that blacks were excluded even from labouring jobs and that whites were rapidly promoted to supervisory and artisan positions which were closed to other races. Co-operation between management and white labour meant that white workers were protected against the worst effects of the depression of 1929/30. Railway wages fell between 5% and 20% in 1929 but it was black SARH employees who were particularly badly affected.[14] Before September 1931 casual harbour workers in Cape Town (some 28 000 of the non-European workers employed by the Railway and Harbour Administration) were paid 4s 6d (45c) for an eight-hour day and pro rata for less than eight hours. In 1931 the administration saved itself some £160 000 (R320 000) by cutting the wages of all 'non-European workers' by 6d (5c), and in 1932 it made a further cut of 3d in the wages of Africans and 4d in the wages of coloured workers. At the same time it fixed the working week at 60 (later 56) hours.[15]

Small-scale strikes against these cuts, and the increase in hours which accompanied them, occurred in Durban, Port Elizabeth, Dundee and Newcastle. In 1932 in Durban, 1 000 black port workers went on strike. Work in the port was halted and only 300 day-labourers continued working; in Port Elizabeth 240 workers struck. On both occasions the workers were defeated by the management's tactics of replacing Africans first by white or coloured workers and then by fresh labour brought in from the reserves.[16] Again, in 1937, casual SARH workers at Durban docks struck for an increase in the daily rate of pay but after a two-week lockout were forced to return to work for the same wages.

A contemporary publication describes the wages and working conditions of black and coloured Railway and Harbour employees in Cape Town as extremely harsh:

> A single native [African] railway worker starts with 3/6d a day and the single coloured workers with 4/- a day. After eleven years of hard, dangerous work, they rise for a single native worker to 4/6d a day and for a single coloured worker to 5/- a day. Married native workers start with 4/- and married coloured workers receive 5/4d a day, after eleven years service!

14. B. Hirson, 1990, p. 20.
15. SARHWU, 1937.
16. A.T. Nzula, 1979, p. 151.

> The native and non-European workers are not only sweated on very
> low wages, but also suffer under miserable conditions of work. For
> example, while white labourers get raincoats and rainboots, the native
> and non-European workers do not, although many are employed in the
> engine rooms, standing the whole day in water, whilst others are
> employed on cleaning tubes of boilers but do not get dust masks thus
> breathing in the dust.[17]

The livelihood of the black workers was also extremely insecure. About 28 000
of the 45 000 employees of the Railway and Harbours Administration nationally
were casual day labourers. In Cape Town those from the Eastern Cape and further
afield were housed in labour compounds. Others travelled in daily from the
surrounding rural areas and, having no means to pay their fare, were compelled
to walk distances every morning to the Cape Town docks in search of work. At
the docks the workers lived in a former prison. Speaking in 1936 Z Musopha, a
worker in the Alfred Dock, described the housing of African dock workers as
'slum conditions':

> The old breakwater jail is the avowed residence of the Natives, where
> they stay in halls or what were previously cells ranging from eight men
> upwards according to the capacity … Bunks are arranged on raised
> supports side by side on floor space on which men sleep.[18]

At the docks workers were as often as not faced with the iniquitous system of
'standing by'. Sometimes men who had not worked for a whole week were
requested to stand by for a ship which was expected. More than once these men
had to wait in vain and to return home with nothing for the hours they had waited.
Even those with more long-term employment had little security. There were no
benefits for death in service and although there was a 'Gratuity Fund' for workers
dismissed after fifteen years it was the practice of the government to dispense
with a worker's services before this time to avoid payment.

The continual speeding up of work and cutting back on staff resulted in an
increase in accidents for which there was little or no compensation. A typical
case was that of Andries Armoed, aged 30, crushed to death by a load of timber.
Returning a verdict of accidental death, the magistrate commented on the fact
that the trolley which should have been in the charge of six men had, in fact been
operated by only three.[19] In the event of death it was common for £7 to be paid
to the dependants in full compensation, and in one case an African labourer who

---

17. *Negro Worker* 6(8), October 1936: pp. 7-12.
18. *Negro Worker* 6(8), October 1936: p. 13.
19. Interview: Ray Alexander, Cape Town, October 1997. *Cape Argus*, 7 November 1936.

lost an eye while on duty received sick pay only on return from hospital and was then discharged, although he had been with the administration for eight years.

The formation of SARHWU

On the first of April 1936, in the same hall that the ICU and the Cape Town Stevedoring Union were built, on the corner of Buitengracht and Dock Road, we convened a meeting and we formed the Railway and Harbour Workers Union. The crowd was so big. There was a stoep *(verandah)* and I had to speak outside on the stoep so that the people could hear me – because the hall was so full – upstairs, on the steps, the people were everywhere.[20]

It was against this background that the South African Railway and Harbour Workers Union was formed in Cape Town in 1936. The depression was finally over and Cape Town, which as one of South Africa's most important ports had played a major role in the recovery of the economy, was booming. Cape Town Harbour had built up a world reputation for the quick discharge of cargo and in that year a total of 1 938 015 tonnes of cargo was loaded and unloaded on its

Delegates to the founding conference of SARHWU, Cape Town, 1936. (Ray Alexander, back row 6th from the left; Johnny Mtini is last on the right, back row.)

20. Interview: Ray Alexander (Simons), Cape Town, November 1997. (The report of the formation of the union in *Negro Worker* gives 26 March 1936 as the date of the meeting.)

wharves. During the first quarter of 1936-37 South African Railway earnings increased by £494 212 (R988 424), Harbours by £47 443 (R94 886) and Airways by £6 294 (R12 588).[21] White employees on the docks and railways had by that time recovered the wage cuts which they had suffered during the lean years. Nevertheless, African wages had still not been restored to pre-depression rates.[22]

The formation of SARHWU was a direct result of the unique combination of political, geographical and economic circumstances of this time. As has been noted in the Introduction, blacks were barred by the IC Act from joining most of the white-dominated craft and industrial unions, and both Kadalie's Industrial and Commercial Union and later attempts to form separate African trade unions and federations in the Rand had met with little success.

In the Western Cape, however, circumstances were more favourable. From the earliest days of industrialisation a large proportion of the workers were coloured rather than African and were not therefore excluded from joining registered trade unions. Most unions were non-racial (although they and the Cape Federation of Labour Unions were dominated by white leaders) and they in turn influenced the adoption of a non-racial policy by the South African Trades and Labour Council (SATLC) when it was formed in 1930. Following the split in the CPSA over the 'Black Republic' thesis of the Comintern, the central office of the party moved from Johannesburg to Cape Town. According to Ben Turok, who was a member of the CPSA (by then renamed the SACP) in the 1950s:

> The Communist Party in Cape Town was a little bit different to the party in the rest of the country, including the ANC. Cape Town was different largely because of the *Guardian* which was the mouthpiece of the left. Somehow the CP tradition had been more deeply rooted here than in the rest of the country, something perhaps to do with the fact that the HQ of the party was here for a good many years. Moses Kotane had his HQ in Cape Town when he was general secretary. Also Cape Town in a way was more working class than the rest of the country. Because of its coloured population and its long industrial history it had a more classical proletarian culture than other parts of the country. Therefore the party was more identified with working-class issues than in the rest of the country and even the ANC here was more linked to the party.[23]

Activists such as Ray Alexander, Bill Andrews, Johnny Gomas, Eli Weinberg and James Shuba, had been influential in the setting up of black trade unions in the garment, leather, rope, milling and chemical industries following the decline

---

21. G. Gordon Brown, 1937, p. 149.
22. SARHWU, 1937.
23. Interview: Ben Turok, Cape Town, October 1997.

of the ICU. It was Ray Alexander, in particular, who was responsible for fostering the organisation of SARHWU in 1936.

Ray's story

Ray Alexander was born in Latvia. She was a committed communist and had joined the underground Communist Party in her home country when she was still only fourteen. To escape the persecution of Jews and communists she emigrated to South Africa in 1929 when she was 16. On her arrival she immediately joined the Communist Party of South Africa and in 1935, aged 21, she took on the task of challenging the Spoorbond and helping to form a union for black railway and harbour workers. Her own account of how this happened illustrates both the important role played by this dedicated group of trade unionists and also the enthusiastic response of black workers to the idea of forming a trade union:

> In December 1935 NURAHS, the National Union of Railway and Harbour Servants, a union that was established in 1910 and had workers of all races, was infiltrated by the Broederbond. They formed a union called Spoorbond. These workers came to the NURAHS conference, which they also belonged to, and they took over the membership and passed a resolution that the union should only consist of whites so the coloureds and the Africans and the Indians were pushed out.
>
> I was the secretary of the Commercial Workers Union and I was elected to go to an anti-fascist conference in Johannesburg – an Anti-Fascist League Conference – in 1935 [The League against Fascism and War]. Johnny Gomas was going to the ANC and All-African Convention conference in Bloemfontein. The conference was to start on the 16th December so it must have been the 14th December when the new General Secretary of the Cape Town Stevedoring Workers Union, Henry October, got to hear what happened at the NURAHS conference and told us. We were sitting there at the station, Jimmy Emmerich, Donald Molteno, I, Johnny Gomas and others; we were going to the two conferences so we were a big crowd and there was no apartheid business, we were all sitting together and discussing it.
>
> Just then the bedding men came to make the beds so right away we had a meeting with them and started to talk to them about it. We told them that they were out of a union and we said to them, 'We'll help you to organise another union. Don't be without a union.' Then, I'm telling you, at every station we stopped at on the way to Johannesburg – Beaufort West, Kimberley and everywhere – the bedding men introduced us to other non-European – non-white – workers and told

11

them what they had heard from us and that we were organising and I right away started to write down the names and addresses of the workers.

In Johannesburg the bedding men said they'd take us to the railway laundry (the Railway and Harbours Administration had a laundry in Braamfontein) and they took us to the laundry and introduced us and whispered that we would organise a union and that they must give us more names of other workers. Gomas did work in Bloemfontein, the same work as I did in Johannesburg, and on the way back from the conference we did this again at all the different stations.

Ray was dismissed from her employment for attending the conference in Johannesburg and began to work full-time for a number of unions from offices at 57 Plein Street, Cape Town. From there she began to organise the Cape Town railway workers. With Johnny Gomas she visited the Salt River railway works, the stations and the harbour, recruiting workers. They were greeted enthusiastically and on 26 March SARHWU was launched at an inaugural meeting that was filled to capacity and attended by delegates from all provinces. Willy Driver, a coloured harbour worker, was elected as the union's first Secretary.

In the same month as the meeting in Cape Town Ray travelled to Johannesburg on Communist Party business and took the opportunity of spreading the word about the formation of the union among both blacks and whites.

We spoke to the Secretary of NURAHS, who was a bitter and broken man because of what happened to him [the destruction of the union by the Spoorbond] and asked him to give us the names of white workers who were in opposition to Spoorbond and he gave us names. One was a man by the name of Bill Merrington, a white man. He had started another breakaway union, the Railway and Harbour Employees Union, but we worked close together and became friends. Bill Merrington and Henry October and I had a meeting. We each contributed 2/6d and bought the paper, stencil and ink and I typed and duplicated a leaflet about the forming of the union and calling a meeting. While I was in Johannesburg I took with me copies of the leaflets and copies of the constitution and we had a meeting with lots of workers from the laundry and others, I think in the Trades Hall. I told them that the union was established and we started to build the union.[24]

---

24. Interview: Ray Alexander (Simons), Cape Town, November 1997.

The first national conference

The response of black workers was so enthusiastic that it was reported that by July the new union already had a membership of over 1 300.[25] On 3 and 4 August twenty-six accredited delegates, including representatives from Durban and Braamfontein and from other dock unions, met for their first national conference in Cape Town. Officers and an Executive Committee were elected, largely from among the coloured workers who not only tended to have more literacy skills than their African counterparts but also formed the majority of employees in the harbour area where the union had the most members.

The main focus of the conference was on the low wages and appalling conditions of African and coloured railway and harbour workers and on their unequal treatment in comparison with white workers. From the beginning SARHWU followed a policy of campaigning for improvements in working conditions at the same time as raising the political awareness of its members. Following a debate, the conference decided to affiliate to the South African Trades and Labour Council and to the International Trade Union Committee of Negro Workers, and in the discussion of the Secretary's report to the conference FC Welcome of the Cape Town Stevedoring Union identified the causes of the workers' problems as being political and therefore requiring a political response:

> The way the Government treats the native workers is ridiculous. Smuts and Hertzog joined hands with one aim, and that is to oppress us more and more and therefore we must learn to join hands. Today, brothers, we are only starting. Last month we met in Bloemfontein and we established the All African Convention into a permanent organisation. Now we meet here, and we must see that all our brothers employed at the Railway and Harbour Administration should join the Union. We must also educate the white workers that they are our brothers and that we all have to join hands to free ourselves from the terrible exploitation.[26]

After discussion the conference adopted a list of demands to be presented to the Minister of Railways including a minimum wage of 1s per hour for all 'non-European and native' workers, a 48-hour week, annual leave of one week on full pay, an end to the replacement of 'non-European and native' workers by whites, adequate pensions and compensation for injury and measures to improve safety.

---

25. *Negro Worker* 6(8), October 1936: p. 7.
26. As above, p. 13.

It was agreed that the Conference would meet again in April 1937 in Port Elizabeth. Africans had no right to rent premises in the towns, which were considered to be white areas. The union therefore established itself in the same offices at 57 Plein Street as the Cape Town Stevedoring Workers Union and the Garment Workers Union, which were rented in the name of white Communist Party supporters.

In August 1936 and again in September 1937 memoranda were sent to the Railway Administration, supported by the Trades and Labour Council, asking for improvements in the various issues raised by the conference. On the second occasion the Railway Administration set up a departmental sub-committee to investigate the grievances but, as was to be generally the case over the next fifty years, the workers were not allowed to make representations or give evidence. On both occasions after long delays the management stated that, 'It was not practicable to consider further concessions.' [27]

'We Want to Live'

Ray Alexander describes below how, in response, a pamphlet was prepared and distributed under the auspices of the union:

> The conditions of the workers were horrible so we went out on a campaign. I wrote a little book called *We Want to Live*, setting out the conditions and how the union was established. I got the information by having interviews with workers and I typed it up myself but English wasn't my mother tongue. Jack Simons [later to be her husband] had just come from England with a letter from Harry Pollitt [the leader of the Communist Party of Great Britain] so he corrected the English and we brought it out and published it. The union was growing from strength to strength and we started to persevere and pressurise to get improved conditions and higher wages. [28]

We Want to Live, published in 1937, provided further graphic details of the conditions of railway and harbour workers, pointing out that although revenue had increased by 26,5% and the harbours and railways operations together showed a surplus of £6 671 182 (R13 342 364), the wages paid by the administration were much less than those fixed under the various Wage Determinations and Agreements which existed for corresponding classes of work. In the Cape Peninsula, where railway workers earned 3s 6d to 4s per day, the Cape Town

---

27. Interview: Ray Alexander, Cape Town, October 1997.
28. Interview: Ray Alexander, Cape Town, November 1997

City Council paid its labourers 6s 8d per day and the Cape Town Tramway Company paid its shed employees a princely 10s (R1). In Bloemfontein a minimum wage of 3s 6d a day was fixed for workers in a number of occupations but the Railway Administration was exempt from the terms of the award and paid less than this general rate, and in a number of other parts of the country workers in certain categories earned only between 2s and 3s a day. In 1937 the 28 000 casual labourers earned on average under £32 (R64) a year – lower than the average wage paid to black workers in 1920, 17 years earlier.

In addition to being paid low wages workers worked long hours. The 'bedding boys' on the trains, who were among the first workers that the conference delegates had recruited, could be called on at any time to attend to passengers. Catering staff began work at 5.30 a.m. They had no definite hours of duty and (unlike the whites employed in the dining cars) they were not guaranteed time off between trips. The laundry workers in Braamfontein (the second group to be recruited) worked in excessive heat from 7 a.m. to 3.30 p.m. on weekdays with two 15-minute breaks and 7 a.m. to 12.30 p.m. on Saturdays with one 15-minute break. African workers received no paid leave apart from three public holidays per year (Good Friday, Christmas Day and Union Day), a concession granted only in 1936 subject to the condition that they must be at work on the weekday immediately before and after the public holiday, no matter what their length of service. [29]

We Want to Live included an application form for membership of the South African Railway and Harbour Workers Union, and called upon all black railway and harbour workers to form one big union so that they would be a force to be reckoned with and able to compel the Railway and Harbour Administration to treat them 'as human beings, not as animals'. Addressing white railwaymen, other workers and the public in general, it appealed for support in the struggle against poverty and disease.

Early problems

Support for the union continued to grow, both in Cape Town (where it attracted both coloureds, who formed the majority of the labour force at the harbour, and Africans, who were concentrated in the railway works at Salt River) and in other provinces. But low wages and the casual nature of employment hampered the organisation of members. There was no such thing as 'stop orders' (also known as 'check off', a method of collecting subscriptions at source where money is

---

29. SARHWU, 1937.

deducted directly from wages by the employer). The union relied on organisers collecting subs by hand every pay day. This had some important political and organisational advantages. It brought organisers and workers together and provided the opportunity for discussion of issues and the expression of grievances. On the other hand it meant that income was irregular and there was no financial stability. The result was financial difficulties – a problem which was to be a recurrent theme throughout the union's history.

At the same time the union experienced problems with its Secretary, placing an added burden on Ray Alexander's shoulders:

> David Wells was the Chairman – he was a coloured man, very well respected by the people, an honest man. The Treasurer was Comrade Cotton. Willy Driver [the Secretary] unfortunately took to drink. He had made wonderful progress. I taught him to take minutes and to draft letters and he was really doing well but I think that somebody in the Railway and Harbour Administration had sent somebody to take him for drinks because all of a sudden he would disappear from the office and come late in the afternoon – drunk. This was a terrible time for me. I was persevering and it was agreed that he would never leave the office without me seeing with who and where he was going to. It lasted for a long time. Afterwards the union dismissed him and Comrade Cotton took over as Secretary. That was about two years later, at the end of 1938.[30]

At this time Ray Alexander was surviving on about £3 (R6) a month paid to her by the Garment Workers Union plus whatever the other unions she helped could afford, but there was very little to spare and she often relied on the charity of others. Unfortunately, however, members of the CPSA did not always find themselves welcomed, even by other trade unionists.

> In 1939, April, we were having an annual conference in Bloemfontein and I was asked to come there as their secretary. Normally nobody had money so Comrade Bill Andrews gave me the address of a white railway worker who was in the AEU [Amalgamated Engineering Union] and said that he would put me up. So from the train in Bloemfontein I looked up the address and I went to the place. I showed him the note from Bill Andrews but he said there was a problem with his wife because she was an Afrikaner and if she got to know what my politics are she wouldn't have me. So I said, 'Don't tell her!' but she didn't like the idea of a young woman coming to stay at their place. They made up a bed for me

---

30. Interview: Ray Alexander, Cape Town, November 1997.

in the passage on a settee and in the morning she told me to go. All she gave me was a plate of porridge and for supper I think she gave me some soup and a slice of bread!

We had to go to the location for the conference and at about 12 o'clock the Special Branch came in and arrested me because, being a white woman, I had to get permission to go into the location – they must have got the tip-off about who I was. I was removed without any money. I think I just had a shilling on me. The government, the police, told me that I must leave Bloemfontein before that night as a punishment. The comrades came to the station to say goodbye to me and told me about the conference and said they were very sorry. I said to Comrade David Wells, 'Comrade, I've only one shilling on me. I've not another penny for a bed or for food.' I think he gave me five shillings, something like that, but I didn't buy a bed. I slept on a bunk and I used the five shillings to buy food! [31]

Clearly the first three years of SARHWU's life were not easy ones and it might well have died like so many unions before it, but in 1939 war broke out and the situation in South Africa changed.

Wartime: 1939-1945

The 1939-45 war influenced the fortunes of the trade union movement as a whole and of SARHWU to a considerable extent. In 1933 the total number of 'natives' recorded in employment was 273 507.[32] By the beginning of the war in 1939 the number had increased by some 243 000 and the number of African employees of the Railways and Harbours Board nationally had almost doubled to some 47 000.[33] The outbreak of war necessitated a restructuring of the economy of the country, leading to a rapid increase in manufacturing and a further influx of Africans into towns. During the first three years of the war almost as many blacks were recruited into employment as in the previous ten years, and by the time it ended there had been almost a two-thirds increase in the industrial labour force drawn from the black population.[34] Between 1943-44 the volume of output of manufacturing industry increased by 127% and industrial employment increased by 96%. The non-white labour force increased particularly quickly.[35]

---

31. A full report of the conference can be found in the CPSA newspaper, The *Guardian*, 1939.
32. G. Gordon Brown 1937, p. 238.
33. *Union Statistics for Fifty Years, 1900-1960*, quoted in B. Hirson, 1990, p. 22.
34. Board of Trade and Industries Report No. 282, p. 46.
35. B. Bunting, 1964, p. 115.

Because the government needed the co-operation of workers in the war effort, it became more conciliatory for a while. In 1939 and 1942 substantial wage increases were agreed by the Labour Department as Wage Determinations. The average wage increased and a compulsory cost of living allowance was paid to all workers. This policy of 'conciliation' backfired, however, because it encouraged black demands that the government was not prepared to meet. Despite the increase in wages, the standard of living of African workers fell. The price of basic foodstuffs increased by around 58% on the Rand and in Pretoria. This was made worse by profiteering by those merchants supplying African shops (which added a further 15% to costs) meaning that workers found it difficult to maintain even a minimum standard of living.[36]

As a result workers frequently simply downed tools and walked off the job. Between 1942 and 1945 there were strikes in the laundry, steel, coal, milling, power, distributive and municipal sectors. Some 5 000 struck work in 35 strikes in 1941, rising to 12 800 in 58 strikes in 1942. In response to the threat of interruptions to wartime production the Smuts government returned to a policy of repression. Troops fired on African strikers in Pretoria in 1942, killing 16, and in the same year the government introduced War Measures Acts 9 and 145. These allowed for intervention by the Minister of Labour in any dispute designated as harmful to the war effort and for a ban on strikes and lockouts. Strikes by Africans were punishable by a £500 (R1 000) fine or three years' imprisonment. Later regulations prohibited gatherings of more than twenty persons on mine company and government property, making picketing and union meetings at workplaces almost impossible to organise. Despite this wave of repression, 1943 -1945 saw very little reduction in the number of strikes by Africans or in the numbers involved (7 400 in 1943, 12 000 in 1944 and 14 700 in 1945).[37]

The extent to which strikes were organised rather than simply spontaneous outbursts of discontent varied. Many were short-lived 'wildcat' protests but others were taken up by, if not originally organised by, trade unions. Officially there was a truce between the government and the trade unions, with even the CPSA supporting the war effort against Nazi Germany following Hitler's attack on the Soviet Union.[38] The Labour Department supported some kind of recognition and control of African trade unions and when, in November 1941, the Council of Non-European Trade Unions (CNETU) was formed the Minister of Labour, Walter Madeley, opened its first conference and indicated that recognition was a possibility.

---

36. *Race Relations News* 6(1), quoted in B. Hirson, 1990, p. 26.
37. H.J. Simons and R.E. Simons, 1969, pp. 556-57; B. Hirson, 1990, p. 87.
38. See I. Edwards, 1986, pp. 66-70.

SARHWU was one of the unions which were able to use the negotiating advantage provided by the war effort and by the increased reliance on black labour to win increased wages. Writing in 1951, an observer noted that SARHWU 'has achieved a degree of success which is outstanding among purely Native trade unions'.[39] Its interests spread into different parts of the country and in 1944 a conference of representatives in Johannesburg met the Minister of Transport who said that the SARH would recognise the union whether it was registered or not, provided that it could show that it was representative. An agreement was subsequently made that the SARH would collect subscriptions by stop order and forward the money to the Head Office of SARHWU but there is no record that this was ever implemented.

In fact there was ambivalence on both sides. At the same time as the CPSA was busy collaborating with the government it did not neglect the organisation of workers at grassroots level, building up cells in factories and hostels. In Durban African workers were especially militant, partly as a result of the influence of Indian workers who had a much longer history of trade unionism and were recognised in terms of the Industrial Conciliation Act.[40] In 1941 dock-workers went on strike under the leadership of a migrant worker, Zulu Pungula. The strike was spontaneous but not unorganised. The CPSA was successful in developing a close relationship with Pungula but the strike was defeated by government repression. As a result trade union organisation was forced under-ground. As Billy Nair, a veteran member of the CPSA in Durban recalls,

> [In Durban] the Railway Workers Union and the Dock Workers were joined together in one single union. This has a history because in the thirties and forties the workers themselves organised secretly. This is largely because one of their leaders exposed himself by actually becoming a spokesman, a famous Zulu Pungula. When it was found out that he was the ringleader in organising the workers he was actually deported, never to come back to Durban again.
>
> The workers learnt a bitter lesson from this and decided to organise secretly so their leaders were never exposed again. But annually, especially during the peak period, when the ships used to dock in the Durban harbour in their hundreds, the workers used to strike at the right moment, in order to push their demands. The workers were met with hostility on the part of the authorities. Police, sometimes the army, were called and even the security [force] of the Stevedoring Company was also let loose,

---

39. H.G. Ringrose, 1951, p. 56.
40. I. Edwards, 1986, p. 71.

to bash their heads and pressure them to get back to work and so on. Force was one of the themes that ran through the reaction to workers' struggles for improvements.[41]

Because of the compound system it was especially easy for the Durban authorities to identify and target striking workers and to deport not just the 'ringleaders' but also whole work groups, or gangs, back to their rural area. But official harassment also took place in other parts of the country against other workers, especially those in the public sector.

By the end of 1945 the number of workers incorporated in the CNETU was reported as being around 158 000 organised in 119 unions.[42] But as the following report at the time suggests, many of these were weak:

> Even the best organised of these independent Native Trade Unions lead a very precarious existence. In the first place, they usually experience great difficulty in getting in subscriptions ... The money must be collected separately from each individual member and, due to the low average standard of education of Natives employed in industry, the number of members competent to act as shop stewards or collection agents is small. Again, the low wage received by most Native employees limits their ability to pay, so that the general rule is that small amounts must be collected at frequent intervals.[43]

Further difficulties were met in finding suitable office accommodation at a reasonable rent, as many landlords refused to let to Africans. On one level the war had seemed to provide an opportunity for black trade unions to gain recognition but the policy of moderation pursued by the CNETU and the CPSA (as part of the prioritisation of the drive to defeat fascism) failed to produce any concrete results. Black unions had been unable to take advantage of the situation to advance the interests of their members and in the succeeding years their position weakened once again.

This was partly because black workers were still insufficiently proletarianised and organised to constitute a critical mass. Although the number of black workers had tripled between 1934 and 1946, the workforce was only a quarter of a million out of an economically active black population of five million (i.e. 5%) and urbanised blacks were still only 23% of the total black population. Many urban Africans were scattered among small employers or working in the informal sector; casual work and high labour turnover were the norm and most

41.   Interview: Billy Nair, Cape Town, October 1997.
42.   R. Fine, 1991, i.e. 40% of all Africans employed in commerce and private industry. Such figures are difficult to substantiate, however.
43.   H.G. Ringrose, 1951, pp. 56-57.

establishments employed only five to ten workers. Trade unions throughout the world have found it difficult to organise labour in these conditions. To a large extent the growth of black trade unions was dependent on the state's willingness to make concessions. When this was withdrawn trade unions were forced back on to strikes and political opposition as the only means of obtaining economic gains.

Summary

SARHWU had its origins in Cape Town in 1936. The spurs to the formation of the union were the 'civilised labour' policy pursued by the SARH and the dissolution of the non-racial NURAHS and its replacement by the Afrikaner nationalist Spoorbond. The new union was helped by the Cape Town Stevedoring Workers Union but spread to include workers in Johannesburg as well as in the ports of Cape Town and Durban. It was greatly assisted by Ray Alexander and other members of the CPSA and allied itself with the political stance of the progressive unions in the Trades and Labour Council against the government's labour policy. Evidence from the union's first conference and from the pamphlet *We Want to Live,* produced for the union, tells us much about the harsh conditions experienced by black and coloured railway and harbour workers and about the response of the SARH administration to efforts to improve them.

Although most Africans still came from a rural background, increasing numbers were entering the workforce through the migrant labour system and finding themselves trapped in a spiral of low wages, poor housing and racial discrimination. The majority of the white working class was allied with the ruling regime that bought its support by protecting white jobs and wages at the expense of black workers. The trade union movement was to a large extent divided along racial lines and black trade unions were not recognised, making the task of improving the conditions of the workers an uphill struggle. After considerable debate, the Communist Party had decided that black workers were an essential force in bringing about revolutionary change in South Africa. Activists like Bill Andrews and Ray Alexander took the lead in encouraging and supporting the foundation and development of black trade unions. In Cape Town, Ray used her skills and her contacts to set up an office base, and she provided education and training in how to run an effective trade union. She also made sure that workers' leaders understood the links between workers' experiences and capitalism and racism.

2

Under Attack

Introduction

In the last chapter we saw how the story of SARHWU had its beginnings in the political and economic turmoil of 1930s South Africa. During the course of the Second World War there had appeared to be the prospect of an accommodation between the government and the trade union movement. However, the crushing of the 1946 African mineworkers strike showed that the state was still prepared to use violence to support employers and that black trade unions were not yet sufficiently developed to resist.

The introduction of apartheid by the National Party government in 1948 put an end to any possibility that African trade unions might be incorporated into the industrial relations system. Legislation was used to regulate and control black labour and to suppress any attempt at opposition. Trade unions were not recognised and were prevented from making economic gains for their members through negotiation. Strikes were put down with the full force of the state and union leaders arrested.

The South African Railways were a stronghold of the National Party, and railway and harbour workers suffered some of the worst forms of working conditions and discrimination. As SARHWU grew in the 1940s and 50s it retained its links with the Communist Party, becoming also a firm ally of the revitalised African National Congress against the National Party apartheid government and a founder member of SACTU (South African Congress of Trade Unions) when it was formed in 1955. As a result it suffered the fate of all opposition to the state.

Black trade union leaders were harassed, banned, imprisoned, killed and driven into exile, but a number of them survived to revive SARHWU once more at the beginning of the 1980s and to bear witness today to the events of that period. Among these are Archie Sibeko, who became Honorary Life President of SARHWU in 1992, and Rita Ndzanga, Billy Nair, Curnick Ndlovu, Samson Ndou, Sam Pholotho, and Ben Turok, all of whom became Provincial or National Members of Parliament in the first non-racial election of 1994.

Trade union activity, 1945-1948

During the war opposition to government policy had been muted. The left supported the anti-fascist war effort and even Communist Party members were welcomed on public platforms. At the same time the government had placated the trade unions in order to prevent strikes and disruption of the war economy. Under the leadership of Gana Makabeni the Council of Non-European Trade Unions (CNETU) had opposed strike action whilst making attempts to work with progressives on the Trades and Labour Council (TLC) to campaign for government recognition of African unions. However, co-operation with the government was at odds with the approach of more militant members (including L Molapo, the Transvaal secretary of SARHWU, who was arrested for picketing on behalf of striking mill workers in September 1944). The end of the war saw a further expansion in the black urban labour force, which brought with it a worsening of the misery experienced by those forced to live in overcrowded slum conditions on poverty wages. Organised opposition to government policy came mainly from an overlapping coalition of Communist Party, ANC and progressive trade union leaders.

Until the outbreak of war the ANC was primarily a middle-class organisation which sought to bring about change by moderate means such as petitioning Parliament. These methods proved to be ineffectual and in 1943 a group of young supporters, including Nelson Mandela, Oliver Tambo, Walter Sisulu and Anton Lembede, formed the ANC Youth League and began to advocate more radical demands. In the CNETU too, support for more radical policies gained strength and in 1945 Makabeni was replaced by JB Marks, the leader of the mineworkers union and a prominent member of the CPSA.

It was recognised that the typical small-scale wildcat strike, which had characterised the war years, was ineffective and that working conditions would only improve if enough key workers could be organised. The obvious target was the mines which occupied a central place in the South African economy, but, like

23

the dockworkers, African miners were housed in separate labour compounds where police guarded them.

The African mineworkers strike

The mines were notorious for their brutal treatment of the migrant African workforce and until 1941 it had proved impossible to form a trade union. After visiting the founder of the Industrial and Commercial Workers Union, Clements Kadalie, Govan Mbeki, then a student at Fort Hare, decided to visit a mine compound to assess the situation.

> Amongst other things Kadalie says to me, 'The mineworkers can't be organised.' I said, 'Why?' He says they can't be organised because the police would not allow it. So I went to the mines – I had relatives who were working on the mines as clerks. I went there during the December holiday because I wanted to get direct how it is that the mines can't be organised. I spent days there, Croesus Mines, Crown Mines and other mines. You had to produce a pass to enter the compound, to come into the mine property, to say nothing of spending a night there. But because my relatives were clerks there they slipped me in. At every step around the compound there were police. Then I came away with a view different from Kadalie. I said to my friends, to my colleagues, my comrades then, 'Let us organise the mineworkers way back where they come from. Let us go and organise them in the Transkei, organise them in the Ciskei or whatever but not here because we can't get at them here.'[1]

Mbeki's analysis was not accepted at the time but in 1941 the African Mineworkers Union (AMWU) was formed, following a conference organised by the CNETU, the CPSA and the ANC. Under the leadership of JB Marks the union built up its organisation through secret meetings, both in the mine compounds and in the townships and rural reserves.

Unrest in the mines in 1942-43 led to the setting up of the Lansdown Commission to investigate the wages and conditions of African mineworkers. The union gave evidence about low wages, long hours, poor food and compound accommodation and the contract labour system but its demands for a 10s per shift minimum payment and improvements in conditions went unanswered. Cuts in rations and severe food shortages led to demonstrations and spontaneous stoppages. The union leadership was cautious about the danger of striking and

---

1.   Interview: Govan Mbeki, Cape Town, October 1997.

tried to find ways of negotiating a settlement, but in August 1946 it was forced to take action when a meeting of over 1 000 delegates voted for a strike.

On 12 August 70 000 - 100 000 African miners went out on strike but the action was short lived and unsuccessful. Once the workers were on strike the full might of the state was turned on them and the violence began. Smuts ordered the police to fire on the striking black mineworkers, as he had done when faced by the white miners in 1922. Thirteen Africans were shot dead and many others were injured in violent clashes on the Reef. An attempt was made by the CNETU to call a sympathy strike in support of the miners. Unfortunately, however, there was a lack of practical planning. The strike failed and the organisation of the AMWU was severely damaged. Many strikers were arrested under the Riotous Assemblies Act and the Native Labour Regulation Act and members of the central executive of the Communist Party, including JB Marks, Moses Kotane and Jack Simons, were charged with sedition (although they won the case after a lengthy trial). [2]

The defeat of the miners had a major impact. Having already failed to take advantage of the improvement in workers' bargaining power during the war, unionism had now suffered another major setback. The strike also played an important part in determining the direction of the labour policies of both the National Party and the United Party, and has been credited with responsibility for the Nationalists' election victory in 1948.

The two parties had a choice between following a policy of confrontation and repression of black trade unions or one of buying off the trade union leadership and controlling the nature of their organisations by bringing them into the industrial relations system ('incorporation'). On the government side the United Party, which traditionally represented the interests of urban capital, was alarmed by the danger of African unions falling under the influence of communist 'agitators' if they continued to be unrecognised. Its main aim was to avoid the threat of further disruption in key areas of the economy. Thus it introduced measures to control the pace and direction of African trade union development rather than to stem it entirely.

In 1947 a new Industrial Conciliation (Natives) Bill was tabled which recognised the status of Africans as employees under the law and proposed a qualified recognition of African trade unions. But the restrictions imposed made it clear that the main aim was to control rather than to encourage the development of black unions. Africans would be recognised as employees, but only in order that the state could regulate their organisations. Trade unionism was to be made a

---

2. In 1944 AMWU membership was reported to be over 25 000. By 1950 the paid up membership had fallen to just 700 out of a potential 308 377. See R. Fine, 1991, pp. 11, 29-33.

25

criminal offence for Africans in mining, farming, the railways, government and domestic service. Despite the protests of the Trades and Labour Council it was proposed that all trade unions must be racially segregated and the internal organisation of African unions was to be controlled through a process of registration that prevented members of other racial or national groups from holding office.

Severe though it was, this measure was still unacceptable to the rurally-based National Party, which insisted that Africans had no rights in towns and that African labour should remain migratory. Smuts's policies aroused the hostility of Afrikaner poor whites, who saw the miners' strike as proof that blacks were in competition for their jobs, and these fears were capitalised upon by the National Party.

The victory of the National Party

In the run-up to the general elections of 1948 the National Party addressed itself in particular to the white working class, promising to guarantee a proper wage, introduce sickness, accident and unemployment insurance and provide protection against 'communist-supported' encroachment by African workers. In 1947 it published a new policy of apartheid (separate development) aimed at 'preserving and safeguarding the White race' by treating Africans in urban areas as 'migratory citizens not entitled to political or social rights equal to those of the Whites.' This meant that 'natives must stay in their own territories and should come to the city only temporarily as workers.' [3]

The result of the 1948 general elections was a victory for the National-Afrikaner Party coalition by five seats (although on a minority of votes). The Smuts Bill was abandoned and the new government set up its own Industrial Legislation Commission of Enquiry. When the Commission made its report, its proposals were similar to those of the Smuts Bill in that they recommended qualified recognition of African trade unions, but this approach was rejected. Instead, the new government set about the process of enshrining its apartheid ideology in legislation and ensuring that all opposition was effectively crushed.

The Introduction of Apartheid

In order to understand the struggle of SARHWU during this time it is necessary to understand the nature of the policy of apartheid introduced by the National

---

3.   National Party pamphlet, quoted in B. Bunting, 1964, p. 114; J.G. Strijdom, Nasionale Jeugbond meeting, Bloemfontein, 14 July 1947, quoted in B. Bunting, 1964, p. 118.

Party following its electoral victory in 1948. Over the next fifteen years and beyond the new regime set about introducing a raft of legislation directly aimed at implementing the policy of apartheid and restricting the rights of non-whites in all fields.

Apartheid legislation can be divided into that intended to control the residence, movement and employment of different racial groups (giving supremacy to whites) and that directly aimed against political opponents of the regime who fought against this process. The consequences for Africans in general and for workers and their trade unions in particular were devastating, entailing years of struggle for social and political rights and economic gains.

The Pass Laws and the Control of Labour

Foremost among the new laws in their day-to-day impact on Africans were the 'pass laws'. These were based on the segregation of land and control of the right of the 75% of the population who were black to live and work outside those areas which had been designated (some 7,5% under the 1913 Land Act, extended to 12% in 1936). Although Africans were already severely restricted by previous legislation, the National Party brought in even more severe new laws.

- *The 1949 Native Laws Amendment Act* created special labour bureaux for Africans, designed to restrict the flow of workers to the towns so that an abundant supply of labour would always be available for the mines and farms.
- *The 1950 Population Registration Act* established a racial register of the population that classified people in three main groups – European, coloured and African. Ultimately everyone would have to carry an identity card on which his or her race would be indelibly stamped.
- *The 1950 Group Areas Act* provided for the establishment of racial ghettos in urban areas in which ownership and occupation of land were restricted to a specified population group.
- *The 1952 Natives (Abolition of Passes and Co-ordination of Documents) Act,* despite its name, did not abolish the carrying of passes but made the pass laws even harsher. Passes were consolidated into a single document to be known as a reference book and issued to all Africans over the age of sixteen. The document was pasted in front of the identity card issued under the Population Registration Act. The book had pages relating to labour bureaux and influx control, signatures of employers, poll tax receipts, taxes, etc. As the books were issued fingerprints were taken and recorded in a central bureau. The

reference book had always to be carried by the holder and produced on demand, failing which the offender was liable to be arrested on the spot.

- *The 1952 Native Laws Amendment Act* provided that no African would be permitted to remain in an urban area for longer than seventy-two hours without a permit, unless born and permanently resident there. The use of labour bureaux was made compulsory so that nobody could look for work without permission of the local authority.
- *The 1954 Natives Resettlement Act* provided for the establishment of a resettlement board to assist the forced removal of thousands of Africans.

Although the movement and residence of Africans had previously been restricted to a certain extent, the new laws set up a rigid bureaucratic system to control where individuals could live and work. Their strict enforcement had an immediate effect on the everyday lives of millions of Africans. For many of those entering the workforce at this time it was their own experience of the operation of these laws which first brought them into conflict with authority, politicised them and turned them into active trade unionists and opponents of the National Party regime. The government was determined to keep Africans out of the towns and to control the supply of labour, using the labour bureaux to direct workers to where they were considered to be needed. Africans were equally determined that they would live and work where they liked, and they used endless ingenuity to get round the rules. However, in the eyes of the government this meant that workers became 'criminals'.

Industrial relations and political parties

In addition to its effect on the day-to-day lives of African workers, the government's apartheid policy had a direct effect on the organisation and effectiveness of political parties and the trade union movement. Apartheid laws were targeted at both the organisation of trade unions and the control of political opposition.

- *The 1950 Suppression of Communism Act* allowed the government to ban any organisation or individual deemed to be furthering the aims of communism, without the need for further proof. Individuals were banned from public office, from belonging to specific organisations, from attending gatherings, from leaving a prescribed area and, later, from standing for election to Parliament or Provincial Councils. Organisations could be declared unlawful and their property liquidated. Any organisation even suspected of furthering the aims of communism could be investigated, its premises searched and its documents seized. The Act was used extensively against progressive trade unionists. By 1955 fifty-six leaders, including nine of the progressive minority on the

Executive Committee of the Trades and Labour Council, had been banned and driven out of their positions. Trade unionists were also prominent among the 156 defendants at the Treason Trial of 1956-61.

- *The 1953 Native Labour (Settlement of Disputes) Act* was also targeted at so-called 'communist agitators' within the trade union movement. Under this Act all strikes by Africans were made illegal, as were sympathy strikes or any actions that might instigate strikes. Disputes were to be dealt with by a system of local and national conciliation dominated by a white bureaucracy consisting of Bantu Labour Officers, Bantu Labour Committees and a Bantu Central Labour Board.

- *The 1956 Industrial Conciliation Amendment Act* further tightened apartheid industrial relations legislation. It enforced further racial divisions within registered unions with both white and coloured members, prohibited the affiliation of unions to political parties and gave the Minister of Labour the power to declare any industry or occupation an essential service and to prohibit workers from striking. In addition Clause 77 gave to the government the right to reserve any job for members of a given racial group – explained by the Minister, De Klerk, as necessary to safeguard the standards of whites against 'exploitation' by the lower standards of other racial groups.

Life under Apartheid Laws

When the war ended in 1945 a number of those who were to become prominent in the trade union movement were just entering the workforce. The majority of black trade unionists came from poor families and struggled to educate themselves.

Like the majority of Africans at that time, Sam Pholotho came from a rural background. He was born in 1930 in the Transvaal.

> It is where my forefathers lived. My grandfather had a little plot. He was staying there and it was where I was born. I attended primary school until I passed Standard 6. My father was a mineworker in the area. After I passed Standard 6, life being very hard, they couldn't take me further than that. I think that was just after the war, 1948/49, and I started working as a hospital clerk in a mine belonging to Anglo-American. I worked there and I wasn't satisfied, of course, with the salary that there was. We used to get 15 shillings (R1,50) a shift. I then went to Premier Mine. I applied for work there as a clerk, also. That was in 1950.

Conditions also didn't satisfy me there so I came over to Johannesburg in 1951.[4]

Archie Sibeko was born two years earlier in the village of Kwezana, close to Alice in the Eastern Cape where his family owned some 12 hectares of land and a number of livestock. His father died when he was very young and his mother struggled to provide an education for him, his brother and two sisters by working in Cape Town (about 1 000 kilometres away). He completed Standard 6 and then, in 1948, his education was interrupted for a year while he went to work in Cape Town in order to earn enough money to complete his Junior Certificate. He later obtained an agricultural diploma before returning to work in Cape Town again in 1953.

Billy Nair came from a different background. He was a member of an Asian family in Natal, but his story also illustrates the difficulty experienced in acquiring educational qualifications:

> I was born in Sydenham, Durban, on the 27 November 1929. I am one of five children. When I got through my primary school I was unable to go to high school because my parents could not afford to send me to high school. I, together with my two sisters, began to work but I did do part time studies in the evenings. You went to what they call the night school and I completed my Matric through dint of hard work while working.[5]

For each of these leaders it was the experience of entering the workforce and the conditions which they were subjected to there which turned them into trade unionists. Archie Sibeko provides a graphic description of the treatment of those Africans who travelled from the Eastern Cape to work in Cape Town in the early fifties:

> When we reached there [Cape Town] we were treated like cattle. The train pulled into a side platform and we had to get out and form a queue. I did not see the relevance of this, and was amazed to find that we had to strip naked and put all clothes and blankets into 44-gallon drums filled with DDT powder. While the drums were being stirred we had DDT powder pumped all over our bodies. Then we were allowed to collect our crumpled belongings, dress and climb back into the train. This was a shocking experience for me, confirming that I was indeed entering a different and dreadful world.[6]

---

4.   Interview: S. Pholotho, Johannesburg, November 1997.
5.   Interview: Billy Nair, Cape Town, October 1997.
6.   A. Sibeko, 1996, p. 13.

Many of the migrants were black labourers transported from the Eastern Cape and destined for the dock labour compound in Cape Town.

> The dock compound was huge, there were literally thousands of workers there, but it was more or less hidden. Probably most of the white people didn't know anything about the whole thing. You know, you go to the docks through a gate but at that time you couldn't just go in unless you had business there. There were police there preventing people from going in, you see. Also, you may have noticed that when you get to the docks it's dug in – So when you drive along the road you don't see what's down below. But there were these huge buildings, open buildings like storage sheds. What do you call them? Warehouses, that's it – those warehouses that weren't being used for goods were used as compounds.[7]

Archie Sibeko describes how the dockworkers in the labour compound at Cape Town harbour had no work permits, which meant that they could be removed and deported back to their rural areas in the event of any unrest. Those who had no pass were generally exploited for low wages by unscrupulous employers, often with the connivance of the police:

> Bad employers wanted workers with no work permits or tied permits so they would be frightened to protest or strike. If they did, they knew they could lose not only those jobs, but also the opportunity to work anywhere.[8]

To be without a pass was to break the law, so Sam Pholotho, like so many black people, forged a permit (which he still carries to remind himself of those times):

> First of all my problem was, because I was born outside Johannesburg, I've got to have a permit to work in this area, so it was really a struggle. No company would hire me because I don't have proper documents. Those days we used to carry two types of document. One – they called it Dom-pass – that's the one that you carry. The other one is left at your employer's place where it ties you up so that you can only work in this area provided you are employed by this company
>
> I didn't have a permit to work in Johannesburg, so I and my cousin, we sort of forged this. I still use this but it is forged. The trouble is that nowadays it poses a problem because I've got to pay 300 rand to convert it into my proper names![9]

---

7. Interview: A. Sibeko, Manchester, 1998.
8. A. Sibeko, 1996, p. 15.
9. Interview: S. Pholotho, Johannesburg, November 1997.

31

Illegal workers were in constant danger of arrest and spent their time avoiding the police. Apartheid law in action had a profound politicising effect on those who experienced it. Samson Ndou moved from his village in the Northern Transvaal to Alexandra township, Johannesburg, in 1955.

> Coming into Alexandra threw me into a new situation. It was far different; life was very fast and many things were happening around and I then realised that life is not like in the rural areas, because in the rural areas we used to produce food ourselves. We never depended on buying from the shops. We made our own mealie meal, we had our own way of doing things in a traditional way but here now you live by buying, you must have money to have food.
>
> There was this thing called the pass raids. Every day you would see police collecting people in the township, and taking them to the police station for pass offences and so on. That had a great mark on my entire life. Because to me people were suffering. For what reason? There were no reasons, as far as I was concerned. These people were being collected daily to police stations where they were charged under the pass laws and were taken to farms to work there, under terrible conditions. And that changed my life greatly.
>
> About 1958 I attended an ANC meeting which was called on Africa Day in June. It was addressed by leaders like Oliver Tambo. Anti-pass campaigns were going on … It was after the bus boycott which really also changed my understanding. As a young person I was starting to be politically active but not as a card-carrying member. Then came 1960. I remember the pass campaign organised by the Pan African Congress and also the killings at Sharpeville, Langa and other areas and the call by the then President of the African National Congress, Chief Luthuli, to burn the passes. You can imagine, we as youth, the part we played burning passes and so on.[10]

The following account, from trade union activist Magwaza Maphalala, gives a first-hand illustration of the kind of harassment to which Africans were subjected. Originally from a small town in Zululand, Maphalala avoided the contract labour system and travelled to Johannesburg to find work for himself, but the pass system meant that the employment on offer was mainly casual and temporary and he was frequently arrested.

---

10.   Interview: S. Ndou, Cape Town, October 1997.

At that time the pass laws were very strict. You could not travel from one point to the other the way you wanted. Most of the people I grew up with and those who were there before me, my father included, used to go to Jo'burg on a contract. A company would send their representatives to Bergville and word spreads around, particularly from the labour office, that there will be a contract of employment on such and such a date. Everyone would flood into Bergville town seeking that employment, and that is how people got from Bergville into Johannesburg.

But I did not go through that route. Through my colleagues I just went to Jo'burg. I found it difficult. I found employment but I could not be registered; I could not be authorised to work in Johannesburg and I could not get legal accommodation in Johannesburg for that reason. Nevertheless I worked. I think I worked about one or two months and then I got arrested. The first time I got arrested because where I was staying – it was a mine compound, Shelter Number 5, City Deep, in Johannesburg – there was special police called Black Jacks. They invaded the place at about three o'clock in the morning. We were fast asleep. We were sleeping on the concrete beds, beds that were made of concrete, exactly like shelves. They come in and they demand payments from each one of the occupants. So I got arrested in that way.

I landed up in the police station. I was charged. I can't remember how much I was fined. I think it might have been ten rands. I spent the day and night there and the following day my colleagues came and rescued me and paid that fine, so I went back to work. A few days later, again, on our way to work there was a very big truck, a big truck called *Umgqomo.* There was a footpath from City Deep No. 5 to the central areas so we used to take that footpath because it's a short cut to the factory. We go through a stream and across and emerge into this street on the other side. Well, as you can imagine, in the street the truck was waiting there to check reference books – pass books! I produced mine but it was denied because it did not have the permit for me to remain in Johannesburg so I was arrested again – back to prison again! I can't remember how much time I spent in prison for that second time. So that went on, I got arrested, I got out and went back to work, got arrested again and so on. Eventually I lost that work, after being employed for about six months.

Later, he applied for a job as a seaman on a merchant ship sailing from Durban but, again, the bureaucracy of apartheid made life very difficult.

I passed the medical test so I was given a paper to go back to Bergville to have my documents endorsed. Employment was promised to me here. At that time it was fashionable to be a seaman so I was very excited. You know – 'I'm going to be a seaman!' I went back to Bergville to have my documents ready but when I went there they said, 'No, we can't give you the permit unless it is completely stated that you have that employment. Here they are saying that you must get a permit so that you are able to go and *seek* employment.'

I returned back to Durban, to the offices there. They said, 'No, we can't give you that authority unless you prove to us that you have a place to stay, that you have a residence.' I said, ' I'm staying with my auntie,' and they said, 'Go to the township manager. You have to have permission from the township manager that you are staying there.' I went and my auntie took me to the superintendent in L section and he said, 'No, I can't give that authority unless there's the proof that he has got work.'

So where they are supposed to give me permission to work, they say they can't give me permission to work unless I've got somewhere to stay; and where they are supposed to give me permission to stay they say they can't do it unless I've got permission to work! It was that kind of situation until in the end I went to bribe those guys in Durban. I bribed them and then at last they gave the authority for me to come and seek employment in Durban and that is how I finally got employment as a seaman.[11]

Trade Union Organisation and Political Opposition

One of the main aims of apartheid labour legislation was to make organisation by African trade unions as difficult as possible. The government rejected the report of the Industrial Relations Commission of Inquiry which proposed that black trade unions should be recognised and controlled. It believed that

> If we give that incentive to workers to organise … and they should become well organised … they can use their trade unions as a political weapon and they can create chaos in South Africa at any time.[12]

In the event, however, it was not so much the existence of organised trade unions that promoted political opposition as the attempts of the government to suppress them.

---

11. Interview: Magwaza Maphalala, Durban, November 1997.
12. Minister of Labour, B. Schoeman, quoted in B. Bunting, 1964, pp. 265-266.

At the beginning of the 1950s trade union opposition to the government was weak. Black trade unions had been dealt a blow by the failure of the 1946 miners strike, and between 1946 and 1950 the number of African trade unions affiliated to the CNETU had declined from 119 to 53. The progressive white unions were also under attack and although they opposed the 1953 Native Labour Act they were in a minority. The Trades and Labour Council, which might have been expected to have co-ordinated the protest, was no longer willing to oppose the government. Long bedevilled by conflict between conservatives and progressives, the TLC had begun to move to the right when its conference rejected a motion to press the government for the recognition of African unions in April 1944. The defection of a group of six right-wing unions to form the Co-ordinating Council of South African Trade Unions in 1948 and of a further sixteen unions to form the South African Federation of Trade Unions in 1951 was the beginning of the end for the TLC. A 'Unity Committee' was set up to discuss means of maintaining the unity of white trade unions and in 1954 the TLC was dissolved and the South African Trade Union Council (later known as TUCSA) was formed, with a racially exclusive 'colour-bar' constitution.

The continuing failure of the Trades and Labour Council to mount an effective opposition to the new government's proposals meant that it was left to an alliance between African trade unions, the ANC and the CPSA to organise African opposition to anti-trade union and apartheid legislation. This alliance was something new. During the inter-war years, despite some overlapping membership, there were tensions between the different organisations. For much of the time the mainstream of the Communist Party had put its faith in the potential of a revolutionary white working class. It dismissed both what it saw as the bourgeois nationalism of the mainly middle-class ANC and the ability of the infant African trade unions to organise and mobilise the relatively small number of 'semi-proletarianised' black workers. At the same time, as noted in the previous section, Clements Kadalie, the leader of the ICU, the major African trade union in the 1920s, pursued an anti-communist policy, forcing prominent members such as Thomas Mbeki to resign their membership of the Communist Party, and expelling others from the union.

Both Kadalie and prominent African communists such as JB Marks were also members of the African National Congress. This became an arena of struggle between the two camps, in which anti-communist supporters predominated for most of the time. Apart from the brief period of Josiah Gumede's leadership in the 1920s, the first sign of change came with the defeat of the mineworkers in 1946 when the ANC conference voted overwhelmingly against a motion by the anti-communists Kadalie and Msimang proposing a petition to parliament and in favour of one introduced by Moses Kotane, General Secretary of the Communist Party, urging Africans to struggle for full citizenship rights. It was, however, not until the election of the National Party on an apartheid platform that the influence of the radical wing, represented by the ANC Youth League, came to the fore.

At its 1949 conference the ANC approved a programme of direct action and for the first time set about building a mass support base in the rural areas and townships. The programme rejected segregation, apartheid, trusteeship and white leadership and undertook to consolidate trade unions into an industrial wing. Although leaders like Mandela were originally anti-communist, relations with the CPSA became closer and a number of African trade unionists and CPSA members took up positions in the ANC leadership. Trade unions were central to this alliance because the mass action demanded by the mainly middle-class ANC Youth League had to be rooted in the urban proletariat to stand any chance of success. The African trade union movement, which was itself radicalised by members of the Communist Party, went on to radicalise the ANC and put it at the centre of the non-racial liberation movement.

The Growth of SARHWU

We know little specific about the fortunes of SARHWU during the war years other than that, despite harsh conditions and government and Railway Administration hostility, the union survived the war intact. SARHWU came, however, to be in the forefront of growing militant anti-apartheid activity for three reasons. It was an established union with strong links to the Communist Party and the ANC; it was a public service union and railway workers, as government employees, were immediately affected by government wages and industrial relations policies; finally, it was a railway union and the railway was unique as a stronghold of apartheid and Afrikanerdom.

Working conditions of SARH workers

Housed in dirty, ill-lit cold and crowded rooms the workers had no freedom of movement and numerous restrictions were placed on their ability to hold meetings and carry on discussions. Food was provided but was of poor quality. As soon as a railway worker lost his job, for whatever reason, he was evicted from the compound ... Another source of resentment was the Administration's policy of transferring workers from one department to

> another and from city to city, making it impossible for the maintenance of any semblance of family life. If a worker had a house in one city, upon transfer there was little chance of getting another in the new location; the worker would be forced into the compounds and the family left to fend for itself. [13]

The working conditions of black railway and harbour workers continued to be among the worst in South Africa. The introduction of apartheid reinforced the discrimination against black workers which had begun in the 1920s and 1930s. By the end of World War II most unskilled Afrikaners had been promoted from the special white labourer grade which had been created for them. Unskilled work was now left to black employees – but without the promotion ladder which had been put in place for whites. By 1962 African workers made up nearly 100 000 of the 218 000 workers employed by the South African Railways and Harbours Administration. Of these more than a third were officially 'casual workers', originally hired for a specific construction job but often retained on casual terms for many years. This meant that they were subject to dismissal at 24 hours notice, paid a daily rate, had no leave or pension rights and were given no marriage allowance. The rest were 'temporary workers'. These could theoretically become permanent after five years but in reality most were held on temporary status.

Temporary and permanent workers were eligible for fifteen days leave pay and permanent workers for marriage allowances and pensions at the age of 60, but these benefits were considered to be privileges rather than rights. If workers left before the end of a year or if service was interrupted they were withdrawn. Workers continued to be accommodated in special compounds. They were also often suspended from their jobs for several months over minor misdemeanours, unable to take other work because their passes had not been signed off. Black workers were routinely subjected to racist abuse and ill-treatment but if they complained or quarrelled with a supervisor they would be reported to inspectors who assigned them to lower paying jobs as a punishment.

The Railway Administration had its own special police and could call upon troops to enforce discipline on its workforce. Trade union organisers were targeted and victimised. It is not surprising, therefore, that SARHWU struggled to recruit members and that the majority of railway workers remained un-unionised. Furthermore, although SARHWU was a national union, because of

---

13. K. Luckhardt and B. Wall, 1980, p. 171.

government restrictions it was forced to operate with a separate leadership in each of its areas of strength.

Organising SARH workers

As Archie Sibeko points out, the railway industry was particularly difficult to organise:

> A structure did not yet exist at national level. Every province had a regional structure, usually located in big towns, and they all called themselves the South African Railway and Harbour Workers Union but had no national officers or office. Our only links were when we met comrades from other regions at Trades and Labour Council national meetings. We always found it helpful then to exchange ideas – for example, we learned from Johannesburg the idea of negotiating the right of a worker with a grievance to call for an interpreter of his choice to go with him to meet the boss and making sure a SARHWU officer was that interpreter. We also picked up the idea of the value of letters of complaint being written by sympathetic lawyers or other people of standing, liable to frighten generally ill-educated railway officials. If necessary, we should write such letters ourselves.[14]

In the Cape, the union was led during the war by John Noako, a railway worker from the Salt River Works, and in the early post-war years by Johnny Mtini (a founder member of the union and member of the first executive committee), followed by Greenwood Ngotyana and Archie Sibeko. In Johannesburg the union was led by Lawrence Ndzanga and in Durban by Billy Nair and Moses Mabhida.

Cape Town

Archie Sibeko remembers the qualities of his predecessors well:

> Johnny Mtini was the chairman of the railway workers union when I first arrived. He was also a member of the ANC and the Communist Party, in Elsie's River, north of Cape Town. There's no doubt about it, he was a tough old man. When I came in he was just about to retire. He had never been to school, not at all, but he spoke English and Afrikaans and he could write. He didn't have a complex about it because once you are politically mature your complexes disappear and you help anybody

---

14.   Interview: Archie Sibeko, Manchester, April 1998.

that comes. He was that sort of person – even after he had retired he was at the office to help other people. Also politically, at his home, he was very influential. So that area, Elsie's River, produced a lot of activists who came from Mtini's hands. He was a big man as far as I am concerned. He taught me a lot.

Greenwood Ngotyana was a Transkei comrade who was the general secretary of SARHWU before me. He was a political animal too – all of these people were political animals. It's not surprising because it was a hard job. If you didn't mix it up with the political struggle that was taking place inside South Africa at that time you wouldn't survive. Ngotyana was a comrade who fitted in everywhere – with old people, young people, women and so on. He was always happy and laughing. He was an amazing person because his time wasn't an easy time, in fact it was a very difficult time. You would think that people wouldn't laugh at all but he was that sort of person. He related stories of his upbringing. You know most people then were lucky to get three or four years at school because of all kinds of problems. Fathers would go to the mines and they would die quickly so then you have to take the flag and go and be the breadwinner. It was the same for Ngotyana.[15]

Archie Sibeko was exposed to the message of the ANC while a student at high school but did not become a member until he returned to Cape Town in 1953. Here, while looking for work, he met up with Oscar Mpetha who was the General Secretary of the African Food and Canning Workers Union and a prominent ANC activist. Through Oscar Mpetha he also got to know Ray Alexander who still played a dominant role in Cape Town trade union affairs. Ray and her husband Jack Simons were both banned under the Suppression of Communism Act in 1950. This meant that they could not hold office in any trade union or attend any gathering but it didn't stop Ray from working tirelessly for the trade union cause and continuing to train and politicise up-and-coming leaders.

The first encounter between Archie Sibeko and Oscar Mpetha took place at the trade union offices in Plein Street, the same offices set up by Ray Alexander in 1936, still going strong as the headquarters of a number of different unions.

Early in my quest, when I went knocking on office doors asking for vacancies, I came across a trade union office in Plein Street. I knew nothing about trade unions but knocked on the door. A man came and introduced himself as Oscar Mpetha. He wanted to know my name and work. I told him I was looking for a job. He said that he would ask his

15. Interview: A. Sibeko, Manchester, January 1998.

comrades if they knew of any work and I heard the word 'comrades' used for the first time … Someone said that he thought that there may be jobs at the railway station soon.

Oscar Mpetha invited me to visit the office from time to time to help with the backlog of paperwork. At the same time they would prepare me for working in town and give me a general idea of what a trade union was all about … I was asked to copy records of workers' subscriptions. I listened to their discussions and, while doing so, got interested … Every morning they would discuss a certain area and how to organise workers there, forming an area committee and taking up the grievances of the workers … Oscar Mpetha took me under his wing and gave me mini-lectures on trade unions and how they were run. He covered the duties of members, shop stewards, factory and area committees and even full-time officers. He also took me along with him when he went to meet workers.

I was taken by Oscar Mpetha to see a white woman at a house up by the mountain [Table Mountain]. It turned out that this was Ray Alexander but I didn't know her at the time. This was to become my routine, once, perhaps twice a week, to go there for what I call tutorials. She talked first of all about what is a trade union and the way in which trade unions in South Africa were initiated by her and comrades like Bill Andrews. I knew nothing about the Communist Party, not much about the ANC for that matter. Ray had to explain to me the differences between them and that it was important for organisers, people like me, to join these organisations because it was easier to organise the workers at home [i.e. in the villages or townships] and it made things easier if they knew you were a member of the ANC because when you are addressing an ANC meeting you also talk about the unions and explain why members of the ANC need to join the unions.

She taught me other things too about how this business of Africans being put on this earth by God to be inferior was just a lot of nonsense and it was just an accident of history, and about how to conduct negotiations. She pointed out how the workers depended on being paid so it mustn't be easy for you to just strike, strike, strike so that they lose their jobs. You must talk first.[16]

---

16. A. Sibeko, 1996, p. 26.

It was not just the political arguments which Jack and Ray put forward which carried weight with the black trade unionists but also their warmth as human beings and the way in which they lived up to their ideals in their own lives:

> Ray was a warm-hearted person who worried about other people. When you come to her place the first thing she'd say was, 'Have you eaten today? Did you eat?' Before talking about anything she'd offer you food. She was a mother, she was everything to us. Jack too was a wonderful person. My house in Guguletu was built by Jack and me! And the materials and so on were organised by Jack and Ray. They treated us just like people and that sort of thing goes a long way with oppressed people, not only me. When a person says, 'I am a communist', we judge him by what he has done and that's why in South Africa we can't just reject communists because at that time communists were the only white people who recognised black people as human beings. I had never seen a white man speaking to a black man as an equal human being but Jack did that to me and that helped me.[17]

Ray Simons (Alexander) with her husband, Jack, veteran fighters for trade union rights.

Xola Tshabalala, CDC

---

17. Interview: A. Sibeko, Manchester, January 1998.

Trade union activists of the time saw themselves as part of a wider struggle with a mission to organise workers whatever industry they were employed in. Sibeko soon became involved in the meetings of the local branch of the ANC and in helping to organise trade union activities in the area.

> I was told of a job vacancy at the railway station and was taken along to see the foreman. He said I would start at 7.30 a.m. and work until 4.30 p.m., Monday to Friday. My wages would be £4 a week ... My job would be to help carry goods being delivered to or collected from the station. By now I was not just going for a job, I was also thinking of helping to organise railway workers ... I continued going into the Plein Street offices to help out on Saturday mornings [and] ... I got to know Johnny Mtini, chairperson of SARHWU in Cape Town. One day he arrived at the station at lunchtime, looking for me. He invited me to a stretch of beach at Paarden Eiland where he was to meet the area trade union committee ... I accepted the invitation and went with him to be introduced to the committee, who asked me to join them at lunchtimes in going around the area and having small meetings with workers from different workplaces. I agreed at once.
>
> Railway officials were not pleased with my union work and eventually I was sacked [but] ... Johnny Mtini had a plan in mind. SARHWU had never had a full-time organiser and he wanted me to take this on. He managed to raise some funds from the union and other sources to cover a small wage for me and minimum office expenses. I did not always get that small wage and we had no office of our own. We begged the use of one corner in the office of the Laundry Workers ...[18]

Another of Sibeko's co-activists was a young member of the Communist Party the same age as himself, Ben Turok. Turok was a member of a relatively wealthy Jewish family but he abandoned his chosen profession to work in the trade union movement.

> Ben was a surveyor but he decided to come and work for the trade union movement. I don't know who it was who organised him but he was a member of the Communist Party and he was definitely a revolutionary! He was even banned before me. He organised me to become a member of the Communist Party. I was with him all the time and we were together in one unit in Cape Town when the Communist Party was banned. It was Benny Turok, me, Sonia Bunting and Reggie September

---

18. A. Sibeko, 1996, p. 30.

in one unit. He was very very good indeed, very clever. Benny was a
real leader. In fact he led me into organising the factory that belonged
to his father, *Boston Bag*. It was run by his brother and there was a strike
there.[19]

As Ben Turok tells it he and Sibeko formed an organising team.

Archie had a very tough job but he was very good at it. Being a migrant
worker himself from the Transkei and being a rather down to earth kind
of chap he communicated very well with the railway workers, in
addition to which we had a system of African representatives in Parliament and the Provincial Council. First Sam Kahn was the MP for the
Western Cape and ultimately I became the African representative in the
Cape Provincial Council so we used those two platforms to take up cases
from the railway workers. What would happen is that Archie would go
out on site and walk up and down the railways and travel to talk to
railway workers all over the Cape Peninsula and even beyond. He would
take up grievances and problems, come to the office and we would work
it through then he would raise it with the MP or the provincial MP and
that was one way of solving problems.

The atmosphere in Cape Town was extremely difficult from a security
point of view. The police were very hostile. The special branch were
extremely vigilant. For instance what would generally happen is that
around 10 or 11 o'clock Archie and I would leave the office in my car
and as soon as we were driving we would notice the tail behind us. It
got to the point where we knew every police car and we produced a list
of number plates of all the police cars. And we circulated this throughout
the movement. So everybody had a list of all the police number plates.

The whole thing was under cover – more so on the railways than in
the other unions that I worked in. After a while I was banned and Archie
was banned so we couldn't address meetings. Archie was even more
clandestine than I was because if he was seen on railway property the
chances are that he would be arrested. That's why he donned this
uniform, the brown overalls and he indeed looked like a railway worker.
Also it was almost impossible for him to take up cases with the
management. It wasn't a registered union, it wasn't a recognised union,
it was really illegal so he had to find all sorts of other ways of taking up
cases.

19. As above.

The leaders of the ANC in Cape Town were proletarians, migrant workers, like Archie. He was an archetypal ANC leader from the Western Cape; a migrant worker, not very well educated, very deeply identified with his origins in the Transkei. In the Cape there were people like Greenwood Ngotyana for example, who was very similar to Archie in many ways. So the party here was in a way the left wing of the movement.

You have to remember that the state apparatuses were solidly behind repression. Some of the private employers were more liberal than the state sector so the state sector unions were up against a bastion of repression and anti-unionism. It was easier to organise in the private sector. In the public sector white workers were cushioned by the 'civilised labour' tradition. They were able to get concessions from the state more easily because they were voters, and in 1948 when the National party started to campaign seriously they were able to buy off the white workers in the state sector with all kinds of perks – a large degree of job security, and even if the pay of a railway worker wasn't all that great, he often had housing, medical insurance and other perks which gave a certain stability and loyalty to the white workers in favour of the government. But of course none of this applied to the Africans. Their pay was terrible, they were supervised by unskilled white foremen who were often very repressive, so the white unions in the public sector were not progressive.

Strikes did take place in the railways but they were mainly spontaneous actions and didn't last long because the unions had no power and no money so they were occasional flash points rather than solid strikes, although in 1973 when strikes began in Durban the railway workers union and the dockworkers union were quite central. Internal organisation was pretty rudimentary. Archie was more a kind of sea lawyer [i.e. unconventional] than a shop steward or conventional trade union leader. There was very little systematic organisation. There were meetings and there was an executive, but it was not very stable, much more fluid than in a registered union. The workers were migrant and always changing and the union had to organise underground – they couldn't have branches, officials etc. It was a union of a special kind.

Being a trade unionist was far more dangerous than being a member of the ANC. Trade unionists were being picked off left and right. The state was much more hostile to union officials and shop stewards than they were to leaders of the ANC. The state understood very well the dangers of unionism and the ANC was sort of semi-respectable because it caused no real threat. It was a lobby and the police allowed it to continue and sometimes welcomed it because they had identified leaders and they knew who was who. The threat of the ANC only arose when mass action came on the agenda. The trade union movement was a different matter because people would go on strike, sabotage production and be really troublesome. So to be a trade union leader or shop steward was a much more difficult thing than a politician or a leader of the ANC. The state understood the menace of unionism far better than even the employers.[20]

Black trade unionists had considerable problems negotiating with white employers or government officials, who frequently refused to recognise them:

I went to negotiate [with management] with Ben Turok. The leader of the negotiations was me but when we arrived at the negotiating table at the Labour Department the officials were looking at Benny Turok. I started talking but this chap said, 'We don't talk to you. We want Mr Turok to say what's happening.' But Ben said, 'No. He's my leader,' and there was a deadlock immediately with that! There had to be a strike for me to even talk as the leader. That was South Africa. There was no way a black man was going to address white people. Particularly with another white person there. [21]

Although he was dismissed from his railway employment, Archie Sibeko continued to organise both railway workers and those in other industries.

When I left the railways I still had my uniform which continued to do a lot of good work for me! ... Outsiders are not allowed in so to organise the workers was very difficult. We had to trespass all the time. Because of my overalls I could go straight through the guard box without any problem, straight to the workers ... I carried a Bible in my pocket in case I was challenged. The railwaymen knew me and welcomed me to join them and talk at lunchtime. We discussed their grievances and many joined the union. If a foreman came to see what the noise was about he found the Bible open and us talking about biblical texts. Because of my uniform I could also go inside the Head Office and fetch railway forms for complaints ... then I would sit down with the workers and later draw up a list of demands to submit ... Many complaints were solved this way. [22]

20. Interview: Ben Turok, Cape Town, October 1997.
21. Interview: A. Sibeko, Manchester, January 1998.
22. A. Sibeko, 1996, pp. 30-36; Interview: Manchester, January 1998.

45

Johannesburg and Durban

The organiser of SARHWU in Johannesburg was Lawrence Ndzanga (who was killed while in jail in 1976). Lawrence was assisted by his wife, Rita, who came to work for the union as a typist. As she recalls:

> I attended school in Sophiatown up until 1952 when I left. The first job I did was to work for the Railway Workers Union, SARHWU, in 1954. I was looking for a job and I met an old man called Caswell Mukeke. He was a Lesotho citizen who was working on the railways and he asked me if I can do a little bit of typing. I said, 'Yes I can,' and then they gave me the job. During that time trade unions were not allowed under the government of the day but my late husband, Lawrence Ndzanga, worked for the union as an organiser.

The work of an organiser was hard, as the authorities were constantly on watch:

> My husband used to work for the railways. There was a time when he went to organise in Bloemfontein, in the Free State. He was wearing a railway overall, the overall he used to wear at the railways, but he forgot to take off his tie. He went on to the railway line, organising workers. He was busy there with a spanner, working alongside the people, but somebody notice that that man has got a tie. Then they asked, 'Who's that man there?' Then they started rushing. But someone told him that, 'Hey, you'd better run. It seems to me there's going to be trouble!' During that same time there was a goods train coming; it was moving out. So they rushed him, bundled him into the goods train. The police were coming, and they were shouting, 'Get that one with the red tie!' They wanted to arrest him but the workers had bundled him into the goods train and the train went with him and they couldn't get him. He got off at the next station and bought a ticket and came back home. So you see how difficult it was! [23]

In Durban, as in Cape Town, security was particularly tight because of the role of the railway and harbour workers on the dockside. As was noted in the previous chapter, industrial action in the docks tended to be militant and government reaction harsh. In the period immediately following the war Billy Nair and other progressive unionists began to organise in earnest:

> In the late 40s, early 50s we – that is, communist and other highly conscious leaders – began to organise [dock and harbour workers] into trade unions ... We wanted to maintain the secrecy of their membership

23.   Interview: Rita Ndzanga, Johannesburg, October 1997.

for fear of victimisation. [The police] would just single out a few individuals who are at the helm, shop stewards and so on, and turf them out of the area so, although members carried cards, we made sure that they were not exposed at all.

Initially the dockworkers helped to organise the railway workers and therefore we formed a single union. But the Executive Committee was kept secret and we separated our meetings with the dockworkers and the railway workers because we didn't want them to fall foul of anyone talking loosely and the information leaking. Not that we didn't trust our own members but we wanted to keep them separate so as to maintain our organisational strength there.

The union itself began to grow apace within a short while because the workers were working in a common area. You had the shunting yards and the ships docking all in the same area so that they were able to organise each other. But soon it became necessary to separate them because the issues were quite different, the dockers largely dealt with loading and unloading of ships whereas in the case of the railways the work was quite different.[24]

Despite the secrecy of the operation, many trade unionists in Durban were arrested and banned and at one time in the early 1950s Billy Nair was forced to take over the running of sixteen unions!

It meant working day and night. I literally slept in the office, did the typing, correspondence, everything, there was no help whatsoever. Fortunately, we were able to train some of the other comrades into helping. I trained the shop stewards to do the books. They used to come weekends and write the books and present the financial statement and everything. We were able to get, within a short space of time, nine full-time trade unionists, largely from among the workers. [These included Curnick Ndlovu who later became leader of the union in the region.] It is during this period also that we organised the separate Railway Workers Union.[25]

Moses Mabhida was recruited to assist with the separation of railway workers from the Dockworkers Union. He already had a reputation as an organiser:

He was working for a co-operative in Pietermaritzburg and, of course, he was already involved in organising workers. He was also a member of the [Communist] party and quite an active ANC member. I suggested

---

24. Interview: Billy Nair, Cape Town, October 1997.
25. As above.

to him that he attends a summer school, that we had in Johannesburg, just for two weeks, taking leave from the co-operative – because he was earning well there. But I said, 'Don't leave your work because we would not be able to pay you if you became full-time.' So he then took leave – he was quite a revolutionary, Mabhida, as you know. He came down to Durban, we put him on the train and he went over to Jo'burg. Now after two weeks of the summer school he comes back all fired up. Then he informs us that he resigned from his job the day he left!

Now comes the problem. How are we going to maintain Mabhida? At least to give him somewhere near the equivalent of his wages of £20 or £25 a month. Then we went around hunting all the [sympathetic] doctors and lawyers we've got all over, to put in £2 each and I was able to get £25 for him a month and he became a full-time functionary. He did not even go back home to Pietermaritzburg. He began addressing meetings and what not, firing on all cylinders. This is Mabhida!

What happened is that he became full-time organising Secretary of the Railway Workers Union. That is how he gets his baptism in fire. You wouldn't believe this – he didn't have to go to the dockyards or the railway shunting yards and so on to recruit the workers. He was in the office – the workers come there! Queues were forming throughout the 1950s – massive queues. We were on the third floor of a building. This queue used to go down from the third to the second to the first – they are all standing in a queue. We used to call mass rallies. If you call a meeting of the Dock and the Railway Workers it used to be like a mass rally. The YMCA and what was called the Bantu Men's Social Centre used to be flooded.

There were thousands of workers who joined. The union itself was not confined to Durban. It expanded, had branches in Pietermaritzburg and in outlying areas, Greytown, Ladysmith, Newcastle and so on. The workers heard about it because many of the workers used to travel by train. They worked on the goods train. They passed the message and they used to recruit from the outlying areas. Those who are on passenger trains, the bedding men and waiters and so on, they also began to recruit. So you had the union developing into a fairly expanded one within a short space of time. [26]

---

26. As above.

Political Unionism

Given the politicisation and level of militancy of its leaders, it was natural that SARHWU should be closely involved in the ANC and SACP and that it should become one of the founding unions of the South African Congress of Trade Unions (SACTU) when this was established in March 1955.

The South African Congress of Trade Unions

> The organising of the mass of workers for higher wages, better conditions of life and labour is inextricably bound up with a determined struggle for political rights and liberation and from all oppressive laws and practices.[27]

SACTU combined the unregistered African unions affiliated to the CNETU with the fourteen registered unions that had refused to support and join the racially exclusive TUCSA. At first membership was relatively small (around 20 000) but by 1961 there were 46 affiliated unions (36 black) with a combined membership of around 53 000 (nearly 39 000 black) and 63 permanent organisers.[28] From the beginning it recognised the connection between trade union and political aims and action and allied itself explicitly with those political groups that opposed apartheid. Less than three months after its formation it participated in the adoption of the Freedom Charter at the Congress of the People in Kliptown. Later in 1955 it joined formally with the ANC, the SA Indian Congress, the Coloured People's Congress and the Congress of Democrats to make up the Congress Alliance.

The Statement of Policy submitted to SACTU's first Annual Conference in Cape Town in 1956 enshrined the principle of non-racialism and proclaimed that the fights for economic and political rights were one and the same. Other resolutions dealt with opposition to the Bantu Education Act and the forced removal of Africans from their townships near Johannesburg by the Western Areas Removal Scheme.

In its ideology, organisation and practice SACTU was a clear example of a form of 'political unionism' which saw social transformation and the improvement of the conditions of the workers as two necessary sides of the same coin. SACTU members played a leading role in the parallel organisations within the Congress Alliance and affiliates supported Congress campaigns, but its major preoccupation was, inevitably, the struggle for the rights of African workers and

---

27. SACTU, Statement of Policy, March 1956, quoted in K. Luckhardt and B. Wall, 1980, p. 97.
28. R. Lambert, 1985, p. 250; J. Haarlov, pp. 42-43.

their trade unions. This took the form of an active push to organise unorganised African labour on the one hand, combined with a boycott of the official industrial relations machinery on the other. The CNETU had campaigned against the passage of the 1953 Native Labour Act; SACTU now took that campaign forward by distributing pamphlets urging workers to have nothing to do with Native Labour Officials and to demand direct negotiations with employers. All African trade unions refused to operate within the Act and when Special Branch police arrested workers and charged them with incitement to strike or participation in an illegal strike (both offences under the Act) SACTU assisted with their defence.

SACTU supported the use of the strike weapon, not only as a means of backing up economic demands but also as a challenge to the unequal social order which underlay everything else. It saw action as the most effective way of mobilising workers and solidifying the trade union base. In the years 1955 to 1964, therefore, it gave organisational support to a wide range of strikes and industrial action by affiliates and to political campaigns such as the 1957 Alexandra bus boycott, the 1959 potato boycott and the 1960 anti-pass campaign, as well as national stayaways initiated by the National Co-ordinating Committee of the Congress Alliance.

SACTU operated by establishing factory 'cells' of politically conscious activists who were given a thorough training in Marxist ideology as well as in organising strategy. These were co-ordinated through a series of provincially-based Local Committees (LCs) and industry-based National Organising Committees (NOCs) which took responsibility for recruiting workers, setting up new unions and co-ordinating national campaigns. These were linked to the community struggle in the townships by cross-membership of the organisations making up the Congress Alliance. In this way they were thoroughly integrated with the wider political activity.

In Cape Town the SACTU regional committee and a number of its affiliates, such as SARHWU, shared the union offices in the Plein Street building where the Food and Canning, Laundry and other progressive unions were. Organisers like Archie Sibeko saw themselves as belonging to a wider movement and worked together with those from other unions to build up grassroots structures:

> SACTU's policy was for industrial unions, with one union to cover all the workers in one industrial sector, such as the railways, textiles, food etc. We encouraged the formation of local branches as soon as there were 50 members in any industrial sector. The workers were then asked to meet and elect their own chairperson, secretary, and other officers for their branch. In this way a strong layer of grassroots trade union leadership grew.

Another policy we developed in the Western Cape was to set up informal committees of shop floor leaders ... including local leaders of both SACTU affiliated unions and other unions. These committees by-passed union bureaucracies and built real workers' solidarity at grassroots level. They were able to raise financial and other support for strikes as well as mobilise workers for wider issues like bus boycotts...

Under the notorious Industrial Conciliation Act Africans were allowed to form African-only trade unions if they wanted to but those unions could not carry out basic trade union functions. They could not become registered unions, and only registered unions were allowed to negotiate with employers on behalf of their members ... These laws made it difficult to organise black workers, because there was little chance of quick gains being made. The only practical approach was to raise the political level among workers so they would accept a long-term strategy.[29]

SARHWU and SACTU

The organisers of the railway workers played a prominent role in the activities of SACTU. Billy Nair and Caleb Mayekiso became members of the founding National Executive Committee. In Cape Town, Archie Sibeko became Secretary of the Local Committee (LC) and in Johannesburg, Lawrence Ndzanga became national co-ordinator for the railways in the Transport National Organising Committee (NOC) that was established in 1958. Together with the docks, the railway was considered to be one of the most strategically important areas to organise – largely because the railways and harbours administration was directly owned and controlled by the government. Workers were denied even the minimal rights obtained by those in other industries and any action to improve working conditions and wages in that area posed a direct challenge to the apartheid regime.

In Durban, as Billy Nair testifies, the railway and dockworkers continued to be at the forefront of activity throughout the 1950s:

You could say the base of SACTU, the major component of SACTU at the time from the 1950s onwards, were the Railway and the Dock Workers Unions. We had strikes in the docks, strikes in the railways; and because the railways is a state owned enterprise the authorities took very stern action. But because of the numbers involved they were unable to act against the workers, as they would do with an industry or a

---

29. A. Sibeko, 1996, p. 34.

51

particular factory coming out on strike. All strikes for African workers were illegal because they were not registered in terms of the Industrial Conciliation Act. And because they were not registerable they didn't have any rights whatsoever. What we relied on was the absolute strength of the workers. We only pulled out workers on strike in various industries of African, Indian and coloured workers when there was sufficient strength. And, of course, the workers were politicised; they knew what to expect.

Hundreds or thousands of workers used to be just taken, locked up for the night or the weekend and then taken to court, charged and prosecuted. Now what used to happen was that the workers chose to go to be prosecuted, got themselves detained, went into detention for a day or two. Then when they were brought to court the technique that we used was to get the workers to go one by one into the witness box to actually give evidence on their own behalf as to why they stopped work and after about the third or the fourth worker the prosecution would decide to withdraw. [30]

The Treason Trial and state repression

Throughout this period state repression against both ordinary trade union members and trade union organisers was intensifying. Police raids were carried out on the offices of SACTU and its affiliates and minutes of meetings, conference reports, correspondence, leaflets and other trade union literature were seized. Then, at 4 am on 5 December 1956, 156 people, thought to be supporters of the Congress movement, were rounded up from addresses throughout the country, flown to Johannesburg and charged with High Treason.

Among them were more than 23 trade unionists including SARHWU leaders Archie Sibeko, Caleb Mayekiso, Lawrence Ndzanga and Moses Mabhida, and other SACTU national and local leaders like Billy Nair, Ben Turok, Wilton Mkwayi, Frances Baard, Stephen Dhlamini, Aaron Mahlangu, John Nkadimeng, Mark Shope, and Leslie Massina. The government sought to prove that the defendants had all participated in a violent 'communist' conspiracy but although the trial continued for fifty months – until 1961– it was unable to win the case. The accused were all finally discharged but the state only redoubled its persecution of those who opposed its regime.

---

30. Interview: Billy Nair, Cape Town, October 1997.

Workers who demanded improved wages and conditions were confronted by a combination of anti-trade union legislation, employer victimisation, police harassment and a variety of other restrictions on their freedom and mobility. In a contemporary article on railwaymen in SACTU's newspaper, *Workers Unity*, Lawrence Ndzanga described the tactics used against trade unionists by the railway administration:

> As soon as a worker is known as a shop steward or active member of SARHWU (in all centres) he is immediately transferred to a remote area. His wages are reduced and in this way attempts are made to punish him for his trade union activity and immobilise him for future activity ...[31]

If these methods failed, strongarm tactics would be resorted to, and organisers would be beaten up. If they were found on railway property they were prosecuted for trespass. The railway administration did all in its power to stop African employees from joining the union. Workers were frequently dismissed, suspended without pay with their passes not signed off for several months, or demoted to work at lower rates of pay. The administration refused to reinstate those who won their appeals at the appeal board and those who found other jobs were victimised by the Special Branch forcing their new employers to dismiss them.

Nevertheless, SARHWU managed to infiltrate its organisers, to recruit members and, with SACTU assistance, to organise industrial action. In Port Elizabeth, railway and dockworkers went on strike early in 1957 in support of a demand for an increase in wages from 11s 6d (R1,15) a day to 25s (R2,50) a day. The strike is described by Ken Luckhardt and Brenda Wall in *Organise or Starve*, the history of SACTU (using contemporary accounts by Govan Mbeki in *New Age*). The strike began at the end of February.

> The railway officials and shipping companies called on the state for assistance and the full range of its resources were mobilised to defeat the workers' actions. In addition to the normal representation by the Labour Bureau, the Department of Native Affairs officials, police and Special Branch, the army was called in and placed on standby orders ... Armed police guarded the ships ensuring that there was no contact with strikers ... On 5 March railway workers were locked out and replaced by prison labour. A recruitment drive brought in workers endorsed out

---

31. Quoted in K. Luckhardt and B.Wall, 1980, pp. 170-71.

TREASON TRIAL

The **ACCUSED**

DECEMBER 1956

The Treason Triallists, 1956. Among those arrested were Archie Sibeko, second from the right, 7th row from the top and Ben Turok, second from the left, 6th row from the top.

of major cities … and also large numbers from the Transkei and Ciskei where food production had fallen …

Militant leaders like Vuyisile Mini, Caleb Mayekiso and Alven Benny led the campaign to support the harbour workers within the

SACTU Local Committee [but] the companies were clearly in a stronger bargaining position with the state organising a large army of surplus labour … The workers decided that … they should return to work …

Stevedores were accepted back because they were relatively skilled and would ensure greater efficiency at the docks. The unskilled railway workers however were dismissed, their work-seeker permits withdrawn and their reference books left unsigned as a means of punishment. The re-employed stevedores were subsequently paid at the rate of the railway casuals, 9s 6d (95c) for married men and 7s (70c) for single men, thereby cutting the workers' wages by between 2s (20c) and 4s 6d (45c) per day. [32]

Popular protest and the political struggle

Throughout this period mass resistance to apartheid was beginning to manifest itself through spontaneous demonstrations such as the Alexandra bus boycotts (protesting against increases in the cost of transport) in early 1957. SACTU used the opportunity to mobilise workers around a national campaign for a legal minimum wage of £1(R2) a day, focusing on the state as the key determinant of the low level of wages paid by employers. The campaign also acted as a focal point for a recruitment drive to enrol a target of 20 000 new trade union members.

As a public service union SARHWU was crucially involved in these campaigns. The Transport National Organising Committee, which SACTU set up in May 1958, co-ordinated the campaign in the transport industry, distributing leaflets and collecting funds to pay organisers in the Transvaal and both the Western and Eastern Cape. A memorandum on railway wages and working conditions was submitted to the Minister of Transport and other MPs and legal action was taken in support of workers subjected to the arbitrary action of the Railway Administration.

The campaign was widely supported and by 1960 total membership of SACTU affiliates had risen to 52 583. Some wage increases were gained but the main achievement of the campaign was its success in raising the awareness by workers of the role of the state and the link between economic exploitation and the government's policy of apartheid. This was to prove the key factor in the development of the use of political strikes and stayaways by the Congress Alliance.

---

32. As above, p. 282.

Previous attempts by the ANC to harness the strike weapon in the fight against apartheid had met with limited success – largely because there was no organisational connection made between the employees' struggle in the workplace and the wider struggle for freedom and political rights. SACTU was a founder member of the Congress Alliance and trade union membership overlapped widely with that of the ANC and other Congress partners, but it was not until the keynote speech to the 1959 SACTU Conference by the ANC President, Chief Luthuli, that the role of workers in the struggle was fully recognised. His declaration that 'SACTU is the spear, ANC the shield' laid the foundations for a closer partnership between the two organisations in planning a joint campaign to recruit thousands of new trade union members and tie their demands to action in support of political freedom.

The anti-pass campaign

A major vehicle for this alliance was the campaign against the hated pass laws, launched by the ANC at the beginning of 1960 and planned to lead up to the burning of all passes across the country on 31 March. The Pan Africanist Congress (PAC), which had broken away from the ANC, was anxious to attract support and to appear more radical. It led premature demonstrations to police stations to burn passes on 21 March. Police fired on demonstrators at Sharpeville and Langa and a total of 71 people were shot dead. The ANC called for a mass stayaway from work on 28 March and thousands of workers responded.

> In Cape Town, strikes spread from one factory to the next, beginning on 21 March and continuing for a week. In Vereeniging and Vanderbijl Park a similar reaction occurred. On Monday, 28 March, the day of mourning called by Chief Luthuli, African workers throughout South Africa stayed away from work to protest the massacres at Sharpeville and Langa. In many cases they extended the one day … into a prolonged strike and organised marches through the townships and into the cities. Tension was high and violence flared in several areas. The workers were demonstrating that they were prepared to act collectively and extend their opposition beyond the original call.
>
> Strikes continued in Cape Town until 4 April, with 60 000 workers out on strike on the peak days of 30 March and 1 April. A significant aspect was the solidarity of coloured workers … In Durban … Cato Manor workers, representing approximately 20% of the workforce, stayed on strike for ten days, causing major difficulties in industry and

commerce. Lamontville workers clashed with police who fired shots killing one person and wounding two others.[33]

On 30 March the government declared a state of emergency and arrested many leaders, including most of the original Treason Trialists and a large number of trade unionists. Under the Unlawful Organisations Act, passed a week after the declaration of the state of emergency, the ANC and PAC were both banned.

SACTU and its affiliates were not banned and were able to continue functioning for a while as a legal platform for opposition to the government, but activists such as Moses Mabhida and Archie Sibeko were forced to operate underground. Mabhida then left the country and went to Prague, where he stayed as representative of SACTU at the World Federation of Trade Unions (the federation to which most of the Eastern Bloc trade unions belonged). Sibeko stayed underground until the ending of the state of emergency some five months later. Opposition to the government was organised using what was called the M (Mandela) Plan to build up networks of cells to ensure a secure basis for communication and mobilisation. Sibeko was put in charge of a seven-man cell co-ordinating all ANC activities in the Western Cape and helped with the organisation of a national stayaway strike at the end of May 1961 in protest against the establishment of the Republic of South Africa.

During the course of the strike, compound workers in the railways, docks and mines were marched to work under armed escort with more soldiers standing by, and these industries continued to function. In other areas, however, the strike was again a great success, as this contemporary account testifies:

> The Nationalists huddled in the rain in Pretoria to install their new President in a South Africa in which all gatherings but their own were banned; where martial law has been proclaimed in all but name; where for three days past a large proportion of the country's industry had slowed to a trickle; where empty lecture theatres and classrooms were an eloquent testimony to contemptuous rejection by the youth of the 'Republic' … By passing from words to action [the African people] dramatically exposed, as nothing else could have done, the people's rejection of state forms decided on by a minority in its own interests.[34]

Immediately following the strike a law was enacted giving police the right to detain people without trial for twelve days without the need to bring them to trial, and Archie Sibeko was immediately arrested, along with many other trade union and ANC activists.

---

33. As above, p. 363.
34. Alan Doyle, 1961, quoted in K. Luckhardt and B. Wall, 1980, p. 364.

Trade unions and the armed struggle

State repression brought an end to the policy of non-violence to which the Congress Alliance had clung throughout the 1950s and on 16 December 1961 Umkhonto we Sizwe (MK) was formed as the military wing of the ANC. Although under a banning order, Archie Sibeko became commander of one of the eleven MK units set up in the Western Cape and became involved in planning a programme of sabotage against government and industrial buildings.

The police used spies and informers to infiltrate union offices to gather information and trap unionists. In December 1961, soon after the formation of MK, the SARHWU offices in Johannesburg were raided after infiltration by an informer. As a result of the raid, individual membership cards were seized and members were subsequently intimidated by threats of dismissal and actual transfers to lower paid jobs. Rita Ndzanga recalls the incident:

> I remember there was a man who came from the Northern Cape to come and work in Johannesburg as a messenger. He used to have a messenger's suit and he would come to the office in Kerk Street and stay there the whole day. This man was always there but I was wondering, 'When do you work?' – because he was always in this office. Then one day there was a man who had a complaint.
>
> When he came I started phoning. I phoned the railway about his case and I wrote a letter. The police went to this man at the railway compound and said, 'Where's the railway union card?' They started ransacking his room and then they started searching his body and they found the card. I said, 'How did they know this man is in the union?' Then I got a letter from another man who was a railway worker, a Mr Mambi from Kimberley who was also banned for taking part in the activities of the union. He wrote to tell me that this man was an informer of the security police of the railways and the police were using him; he was going from province to province. So he said, 'Please, when you get this letter don't keep it; just tear it.'
>
> Then I confronted this man and I said, 'When do you work? Why are you always in this office? When do you work?' Then from that day he didn't come to the office and the following day we were raided. It was a big raid. When I was coming in from the taxis from the station I saw the lights on in my office and I thought, 'There must be something wrong.' I came in and when I came in I saw the police coming. I rushed up the stairs and went into the doctor's surgery and sat there. And then the nurse said, 'They are raiding your office, everything is upside down.'

> They took all our membership cards, everything that we had; they took
> everything that we had. Immediately after, we found that it was this man
> who was an informer. They crippled the union because now we had to
> start making new cards.[35]

The work of trade unions was made extremely difficult by another new law –
the General Law Amendment Act No 76 of 1962, popularly known as the
Sabotage Act. The Act prohibited and laid down penalties for the act of sabotage – which it defined in such broad terms as to cover even the writing of slogans
on a wall. All strikes and most normal trade union activity were potentially
classifiable as sabotage. The maximum sentence for sabotage was hanging and
the minimum five years imprisonment. The normal laws of evidence were
reversed so that those charged were assumed to be guilty unless proved innocent,
and if acquitted defendants could be re-tried on another charge even for the same
action. Publications opposing the government were already liable to suppression
under the 1950 Suppression of Communism Act, and this power was now
extended to allow for the levying of a fine of R20 000 for every offence.

Section Two of the Act also widened the already very extensive powers of the
state to ban organisations. Sweeping powers were given to the Minister of
Justice, among which was the power to ban anybody ever charged under the
Suppression of Communism Act from holding office in named organisations,
including trade unions (known as the 'blanket bans'). These 'statutory communists', who did not need ever to have been actual members of the Communist
Party, could also be put under house arrest for twenty-four hours a day without
trial, have their movements restricted by having to report daily to the police, and
even be prohibited from attending social gatherings.

In December 1962 a Government Proclamation listed thirty-six organisations,
including SACTU, and issued orders banning 432 persons from holding any
office in these organisations. Forty-five officials of SACTU and its affiliates,
including SARHWU, and many ordinary union members were thus forbidden
from belonging to or holding office in any of the SACTU affiliates or any of the
remaining Congress Alliance organisations which had not already been banned.
SARHWU continued to operate and in September 1962 the various SARHWU
regions came together to form a new national body with Lawrence Ndzanga as
National President. Resolutions were passed supporting the SACTU national
£1 (R2) a day campaign, permanent employment after three months, unemployment insurance, sick leave, improved workmen's compensation, full trade union
rights and three weeks annual leave. In the following year, however, more

---

35. Interview: Rita Ndzanga, Johannesburg, October 1997.

members and officials were detained without charge under new, even harsher, legislation such as the General Law Amendment Act Number 37, 1963, which allowed arrest and detention without trial for 90 days (extended to 180 days by GLAA 96, of 1965).

This legislation had a devastating effect on SARHWU and the trade union movement as a whole. Moses Mabhida had already left the country and had been replaced as leader of SARHWU in Natal by Curnick Ndlovu, one of the trade unionists trained in Billy Nair's night classes. Archie Sibeko managed to evade arrest and for a while continued his work as an organiser for SACTU and the Communist Party despite being under a banning order. He was detained again in 1962, and in 1963 he was sent overseas by the ANC for military training as a member of MK. Sibeko and Mabhida were the only senior leaders of SARHWU to escape, and had they not done so it is certain that they would have met a fate similar to that of their comrades left in South Africa.

The black trade union movement had been dealt a hard blow but the leaders of SACTU and SARHWU continued to fight against the apartheid regime – some externally as members of MK, some with the ANC in exile and others organising underground inside South Africa.

Summary

The introduction of apartheid in 1948 led to increased political oppression and economic misery for black workers. SARHWU survived the war but it was not recognised under apartheid labour legislation and was forced into political opposition to the regime. It continued its links with the ANC and the SACP (even after this was banned in 1950), became a founder member of SACTU and was involved in a number of national campaigns. Membership grew but officials were harassed by the company and by the state security police. Many leaders became involved in the setting up of MK and were finally forced to leave the country or go into exile. As a result the union suffered greatly from state repression.

3

Repression and Revival

Introduction

In the 1950s SARHWU emerged as a fully-fledged member of SACTU which was part of the Congress Alliance. The impact of apartheid legislation on the working conditions of its members and on the organisational capabilities of unions made it inevitable that, to pursue industrial ends, its leaders had to become deeply involved in political opposition to the apartheid system. As a result, by 1964 almost all the original leadership had been arrested, driven underground or forced into exile. The initial organisational structure of the union was destroyed. There was no local or national organisation, the rank and file members were left leaderless, and any form of industrial action was immediately punished by arrests and dismissals. For the remainder of the 1960s there was almost a complete absence of open trade unionism. However, the core of the union internally and externally continued to organise underground in support of the Congress Movement. In the early 1970s there was a revival of industrial militancy which, coupled with a revival of political militancy, provided a fertile recruitment ground for the trade union movement. New young activists were keen to join the fight against apartheid and now, at last, links between the movement outside and those who had remained were sufficiently re-established for recruits to leave the country for training and be reintegrated into the underground movement inside. Their task was to organise workers and lead them in the struggle for trade union and political rights. The SACTU veterans re-emerged, railway workers were reorganised through general unions at the beginning of the 1980s and SARHWU was eventually re-launched in 1986.

State Repression

Following the banning of the ANC, although SACTU and SARHWU were not themselves banned, trade union activity became impossible. As Luckhardt and Wall have recorded, during 1963 and 1964, every SARHWU official was either detained or banned. Arrests and harassment of SACTU Local Committees and affiliated unions occurred regularly throughout these years; union offices were under constant surveillance and workers were threatened upon entry. Caleb Mayekiso, Secretary of the PE branch of the union, was banned in 1963, detained under the 90-day law and upon completion of the first term he was detained again. He was again detained in 1969, but before being charged died in jail of 'natural causes'. Curnick Ndlovu, Secretary of the Durban branch, received a 20-year sentence in 1964 for 'sabotage'. In 1963, while working in the Port Elizabeth SACTU LC, Vuyisile Mini was arrested along with two other activists, Wilson Khayinga and Zinakile Mkaba. All three were charged with committing acts of sabotage and complicity in the death of a police informer in January of that year. Held in solitary confinement under the 90-day law, these three men were finally sentenced to death in March 1964; they were hanged in Pretoria Central Prison on 6 November 1964.[1]

Underground activity

Despite this repression rank-and-file members of the trade union movement organised openly for as long as they could, and when they were banned they continued their activities underground. Lawrence and Rita Ndzanga were both banned in 1964.

> My husband [Lawrence] was banned in 1964 under the Suppression of Communism Act. He was prevented from entering the trade union office, prevented from working anywhere where there's a group of people, prevented from leaving the magisterial area of Johannesburg without the permission of the magistrate. He also had to report to the police, I think it was Marshall Square, every Monday. On every Monday we had to report there.
>
> Then my husband couldn't get any job so Mr Levy [Leon Levy, then President of SACTU who was himself banned and forced into exile] arranged with a dry cleaning firm that they should take my husband as an agent. He had to walk round in our area, collecting dry cleaning by

---

1.   K. Luckhardt and B. Wall, 1980, pp. 176-77.

hand … But he was not just collecting … at the same time he was heading an underground unit of the ANC, organising the people. Then it happened that in 1964, the same year, in August, I was also banned and prevented from attending gatherings in the same way as my husband, reporting to the police at the police station every Monday. The banning order was also for five years.[2]

Sam Pholotho became President of SACTU in 1965 but, following his banning, he was also driven underground.

The leadership within SACTU was almost all banned, but people like us, rank and file, decided, 'No man. We can't just leave the organisation to die of natural causes without the state even banning it.' Then we took over. I remember I took over as Transvaal Metal Workers Organiser. We used to be together in the same offices together with the late Lawrence Ndzanga and his wife Rita. But they too were removed. They got banning orders and the unions were shaky because people who used to have experience of how to run a union were removed. We tried by all means, the skeleton staff who were there, to run the unions. But it was difficult. In 1965 we decided that we should hold SACTU's Annual Conference.

We went down to Durban and there it was where I was elected the President of SACTU. But, unfortunately, seven days after the Conference, I was issued with a banning order. We were fourteen, fourteen trade unionists that day. I still remember the date. It was 1 June 1965. I was issued with a banning order for five years. I can't go and work where there are more than 10 people in that establishment so I decided to sell some soft goods. I bought a motorbike, went to some wholesalers there and bought some goods to go and sell and make a living. So then started my underground activity. It was difficult, because we couldn't interlink with our comrades who were in exile. It was very difficult to get hold of the comrades outside so that we should work together.[3]

An underground ANC unit was set up to which belonged Rita and Lawrence Ndzanga, Sam Pholotho, Elliot Shabangu and Samson Ndou.

Ndou's story

I got employment in the Transvaal in 1960/61. While I was working there I met a gentleman by the name of Mashalela. He was a very active

2. Interview: Rita Ndzanga, Johannesburg, October 1997.
3. Interview: Sam Pholotho, Johannesburg, October 1997.

politician and there were meetings that took place in town during the evening. In 1961 an organisation was formed to deal with problems in the Transvaal area, particularly rural communities. A man by the name Elliott Shabangu used to attend these meetings. He was an ANC activist, secretary of the Coal Workers Union which was an affiliate of SACTU. This comrade shaped my political understanding. He showed me the policies of the ANC and introduced me to the Freedom Charter. By 1962 I was already an ANC activist. The organisation was banned at this point in time. There was no link between ourselves and the people outside. It was very difficult, but at the same time we never stopped organising ourselves, organising the workers into unions and so on. We formed groups, like a socialist group where we debated things, where we could exchange views and see who's who. And then out of these people we selected the ones who could work underground.

Around about then we felt that we should organise workers in a much broader, less isolated way. We then formed what we called the African Workers Consultative Council. Now at this level Shabangu brought in people like Aaron Mahlangu, Rita Ndzanga, her husband Lawrence Ndzanga and Pholotho – many people. We were growing in numbers but our groups were in different areas. We were organising our people into the trade union movement, into cells, into other organisations and so on.

Around '67 we were already well organised on our side. Winnie Mandela was organising other people so it was felt that we should work under one leadership rather than work under different leadership. We then decided to meet – the group which was organised by Winnie and ourselves. Winnie had organised young people and we had organised young people and seasoned politicians under Shabangu's leadership – Lukuthu and them. People like the late Malele. Now we brought these two groups together and we then put up what we called a sort of nucleus that all other cells operated around.

In the Transvaal we already had underground structures but we needed to organise elsewhere. I was personally tasked to form cells. You know, you form cells of three people and you then make them take an oath. That was my job. I went around doing that. I went to the Eastern Cape, in '68 I think, and Port Elizabeth, where I met the late Caleb Mayekiso. We formed a cell there which Mayekiso ran in that area. Then I went back to King William's Town to meet Sisa Mpendu there and also to organise cells in the area. Then I went to Langa, in Cape Town, but the work didn't materialise there because people were very afraid at that time. Then I moved to Durban where I went to Fatima Meer, trying to get people in the townships. We tried to get to know what was happening outside [the country] and tried to find people who could go out and find out but communications were very difficult during those days.[4]

The unit continued to operate until 12 May 1969 when the leaders were arrested under the Terrorism Act. About 240 people were arrested nationally on the same day. Twenty-two were eventually charged under the Suppression of Terrorism Act, seventeen men and five women. Among those detained was a young Englishman, Philip Golding, introduced to the group by Samson Ndou. Golding had been used as a courier to make contact with SACTU in London but later gave evidence against the others.

> Philip Golding [was] a young Englishman who just came within the country. He didn't like the conditions in which the people were living here and we befriended each other. I introduced him to my other trade union comrades who were banned, including Elliot Shabangu, Lawrence Ndzanga and others. He used to donate to us R100 every month. Just to carry on the underground movement.
>
> At a later stage the security forces infiltrated a spy within our cell and in the middle of '69 we were all arrested. It was a sort of a mass swoop. We had comrades from Eastern Cape brought in, comrades from KwaZulu Natal, comrades from Free State and here in the Transvaal. We were all detained, interrogated, including this young man. The British raised hell and said, 'Our citizen can't be treated that way. You can't just lock him up.' Eventually after, I think, about eight months we went on trial and he gave evidence. He gave evidence against the chaps he knows, particularly myself, that at one stage we sent him to our comrade Phyllis Altman, out in England and that we used him to do some underground work for the organisation. [5]

Rita's story

Rita Ndzanga was arrested together with her husband Lawrence and forced to leave her four children alone. She was taken to Pretoria Central Prison where she was kept in solitary confinement.

---

4. Interview: S. Ndou, Cape Town, October 1997.
5. As above.

65

Before my banning order expired in 1969, on May 12, we were all detained – that's my husband and myself and many others – Mrs Mandela, Sam Polotho, Shabangu, Samson Ndou and many others. When we were charged we were first twenty-two. We stayed in detention for seventeen months. When they came to fetch us my children were alone and they were very young during that time.

We were all in Pretoria, at Pretoria Central, a very horrible place. It was solitary confinement all the time. And, you know, when you are in solitary confinement, you really lose track of time. You never knew what time it is because we are just left alone there in a small cell and sleeping on a straw mat with dirty blankets and that's where you've got to stay. Sometimes they gave you time for exercise just for about half an hour and sometimes when they didn't feel like giving you exercise for the day, they didn't.

My first interrogation took place on May 16; I was taken to a room at the back of Compol Buildings. Major Swanepoel called me by my name. I kept quiet and did not reply. Other security police continued to question me. Day and night is the same in this room because of the thick, heavy planks covering the windows. I remained standing. It was late at night. One policeman came round the table towards me and struck me. I fell to the floor. He said, 'Staan op!' and kicked me while I lay on the floor. [6]

Rita Ndzanga, banned and arrested with her husband, Lawrence, for her work for trade unions and the ANC in the 1960s and 1970s.

Rita was interrogated for several days. During interrogations she was kept standing, made to stand on bricks without shoes and dropped on to them, pulled by the hair and doused with water.

Pholotho's story

I was accused Number One and Winnie Mandela was accused Number

---

6.   Interview: Rita Ndzanga, Johannesburg, October 1997.

Three. We had lost Comrade Caleb Mayekiso in prison, during detention. They killed him.

The case went on up until the court recess, the Christmas recess, and
we reappeared on February 16 1970. The Senior or the General Prose-
cutor or whatever it is came into courtroom that day and stated that he
was withdrawing the case because they have found new information
which they said they have gathered. Then the Judge said that he found
us not guilty, though it was only on what you call technicalities. We
were all discharged … but before we could move out of the courtroom
we were re-detained under section 6 of the Terrorism Act and put under
solitary confinement as happened earlier on. There we are – we went
back under solitary confinement – February 16, March, April, May, June
18 we appeared for the second time, now charged under the Terrorism
Act.

Now we were only twenty and they brought in the late Comrade
Ramotse. They brought him into our group, as Accused Number One.
I became Accused Number Two. They were making the case heavier
because this comrade was trained, military trained, in Egypt and the
Soviet Union. And he was bringing in cadres through Botswana – the
Gazangula Road it was called, in the northern part of Botswana. They
had built a truck which has a space at the bottom where he could put
two fellows there. They brought him there to strengthen their case. The
case went on from the 18 June up until the 14 September. But this type
of strategy didn't help the police because people who have been discharged can't be charged again on the same matter. The law does not
allow that so we were all discharged. In fact, although retrials were not
permissable, defendants could be tried for other offences. Presumably
the police used incorrect procedures, leading to the arrest of all those
charged, apart from Ramotse. Only Ramotse got 15 years' imprisonment. That was 1970. [7]

After their release, however, all the accused were banned again for another five
years.

Trade Union Revival

The next step in the development of the black trade union movement can be
linked to the economic growth that took place between 1960 and 1980. This gave

---

7.   Interview: S. Pholotho, Johannesburg, 1997.

rise to conditions that increased the importance to industry of black workers and therefore their bargaining power. First industry and then government became more prepared to make economic concessions. Between 1960 and 1980 the number of Africans working in manufacturing industry increased from 308 332 to 780 904 – a rise in the proportion of economically active Africans working in manufacturing from almost 8% to 14%. The total of all workers in the manufacturing sector rose by 124% between 1960 and 1982. South African manufacturing industry became concentrated in the hands of a few large conglomerates and by 1981, eight corporate groups controlled over 60% of all of the private assets in the country. At the same time there was an increase in the average size of each establishment from 58 to 82 persons.

The 1973 Durban strikes

Government repression of trade unions and political organisations continued throughout the 1970s but in contrast to the 1960s, when the state had virtually eliminated industrial action, the decade saw an outburst of industrial and political strikes. Dissatisfaction over low wages was the main cause of industrial unrest, which began in 1970 with strikes in the transport industry in Port Elizabeth and Natal followed by a strike of bus drivers in Johannesburg and action by 4 000 dockworkers in Durban and Cape Town in 1972. Between 1971 and 1973 the cost of living of an average black family rose by 40%, and in 1973 there was a major wave of 'rolling' strikes in the Durban area.[8] These began with stoppages by thousands of workers in the brick, textile and metal industries but then spread to municipal employees and workers in other industries. Action spread to other areas, including the mines of the West Rand where there were violent clashes, and continued into 1974.

The demands of the workers were primarily economic; workers were careful to avoid the election of representatives who could be identified as ringleaders and victimised, and most of the strikes appeared to be spontaneous. Nevertheless, they were clearly not unorganised and the size of the demands (for a doubling or tripling of wage rates) gave them a definite political dimension.

> The very high wage demands by the workers became a political manifestation against a system which could not offer a satisfactory standard of living. The strikes were also, *ipso facto*, a political act. According to the Bantu Labour (Settlement of Disputes) Act of 1953 the strikes were illegal, and the works committees, which the law intended to establish,

---

8. See J. Haarlov, 1983, p. 23.

failed to function according to plan … The system's lack of ability to stem the black workers' demands was clearly demonstrated. The strikes therefore represented a political demand to the government about revising the existing regulation of the labour market.[9]

The evidence of Samson Ndou suggests that SACTU bore at least some of the responsibility:

SACTU was working outside to build the unions at home, to reconstruct them. I remember that one of the progressives in the ITF came to meet the leadership of SACTU in Lusaka with money – I think R30 000 – to assist in the reconstruction of the unions. The money was distributed and we saw the first march in Durban for many years, when the railway and dockworkers marched down Rail Street carrying a red flag, demanding the legalisation of SACTU. From that attack in 1973 there was never a lull in the unions in South Africa. They started there from that time and it went on like a veld fire. Unions just started mushrooming.[10]

SACTU activists who had been working underground or had been released from prison were joined by new worker recruits, white and black intellectuals and some individuals from within the established white trade unions in building up new African trade unions. Following the 1973 strikes there was a virtual explosion of union organisation with many new unions being set up – often with overlapping membership. By 1976 trade union membership claims totalled around 40 000, although only a proportion of these members were paid up and the new unions were organisationally weak.

New unionism

A number of different organisations were involved in encouraging the development of African trade unions in different parts of the country.

- *In Durban* the General Workers Benefit Fund was formed in 1972. This was responsible for founding what became the Trade Union Advisory Co-ordinating Council (TUACC) group of unions including the Metal and Allied Workers (MAWU), the National Union of Textile Workers, the Chemical Workers Industrial Union and the Transport and General Workers Union.
- *On the Rand* there were three separate initiatives. The Urban Training Project (UTP), founded in 1970/71 by ex-TUCSA officials, grouped some existing

---

9.   As above, p. 13.
10. Interview: S. Ndou, Cape Town, October 1997.

unions expelled from TUCSA and formed a number of new unions. The Industrial Aid Society, set up in 1974, helped some of the TUACC unions to set up branches in the Transvaal. Finally, in 1977 a number of the TUACC unions, including the Transport and Allied Workers, Sweet, Food and Allied Workers, Building, Construction and Allied Workers, the SA Chemical Workers, the Catering and Allied Workers and Paper, Wood and Allied Workers established the Consultative Committee of Black Trade Unions.

- *In Cape Town* workers' committees were organised by the Western Province Workers Advice Bureau which was set up in 1972. This later changed its name to the Western Province General Workers Union which was the forerunner of the General Workers Union.

In addition the Black Consciousness Movement established the Black and Allied Workers Union (BAWU) in 1971.

Government Reaction

Government reaction to the outbreak of industrial unrest and trade union activity was to employ a combination of legislation and state violence and to pick on individual leaders in an attempt to eliminate opposition. The Durban strikes themselves led to an increase in wages of some 20% and there were few arrests; elsewhere, however, strikers were met with guns. Eleven were shot dead in the transport strikes in Port Elizabeth and Natal in 1970, twelve in the 'Carltonville Massacre' at Western Deep Levels Mine in 1973, and some 178 in violent clashes on the mines between 1972 and 1976.

Over 300 workers were arrested during the 1972 bus-drivers strike. Elsewhere, as at Natal Cotton and Woollen Mills in 1975, the whole of the workforce was simply dismissed. David Hemson and Halton Cheadle, officials of the Textile Workers Industrial Union and the African Textile Workers Industrial Union, were arrested and banned soon after the 1973 Durban strikes in that industry. David Davis, an official of the General Factory Workers Benefit Fund, was also arrested.

At the same time, the state looked for new ways to control the activities of the trade unions by co-optive legislation, aimed at absorbing black unions into the state's industrial relations machinery. The Bantu Labour Relations Regulations Amendment Act 1973 legalised the use of strikes by African workers but it did so only within a restricted framework of regulations which still made the majority of stoppages illegal. An elaborate industrial relations machinery involving liaison and works committees was set up as a substitute for the granting of genuine trade union rights. In the liaison committees half the members were management representatives and half were selected from the workers. Works committees were made up exclusively of workers. Liaison committees were purely consultative. The role of works committees was to convey workers' demands to employers. There was, however, no legal framework for reaching and implementing agreements and works committees were unable legally to represent workers in individual cases. In addition the legislation made it possible for the Minister to set wages by issuing Wage Orders at the employers' request.

Employers' preference was for liaison committees and they took the initiative in setting up 2 503 by 1977 (a ratio of 8:1 compared with the number of works committees). However this failed to stem the development of trade unions which, although fragmented and organisationally weak, could call upon large numbers of workers to take militant action.

The strike by MAWU at Barlow Rand's Heinemann Electrical plant in 1975, described here by Jeremy Baskin, illustrates the way in which unions defeated the object of the 1973 Act:

> After four months the workers felt strong enough to make a move. They persuaded the company-appointed liaison committee, most of whose worker members had joined the union, to resign. Workers then boycotted management's attempts to hold further elections and presented a petition calling for union recognition. [11]

At that time only one company in the whole country had recognised an emerging African union. The management at Barlow Rand refused the union's demands and dismissed 400 workers, only re-employing them on an individual basis provided they agreed to support the company's liaison committee.

The Soweto strikes

The following year the Soweto student uprisings in protest against the government's imposition of Afrikaans as the medium of instruction triggered mass demonstrations and 'Stay-at-Home' strikes. These were not organised by the trade unions, were not linked to any specific economic demands and were openly political. They were, however, most successful in areas with the highest percentage of trade union organisation, where there was co-operation between the ANC and SACTU supporters. They were least successful when called by students acting alone, who tried to intimidate workers into taking part. In all some 75-80% of all workers in the Johannesburg area participated in the second strike (23-25

---

11. J. Baskin, 1991, p. 22.

71

August) with the 13-15 September strike being even more comprehensive and bringing out workers in Cape Town as well.

In response the government reverted to its former tactics: 500-1 000 people were killed during the period of the uprisings and in November 1976 twenty-six trade unionists were arrested and issued with five-year banning orders. These included the organisational leadership of NUTW and MAWU in the Transvaal and Natal, officials of the Urban Training Project and students involved in the Western Province Workers Advice Bureau. Nine others were tried for reviving SACTU in Natal. Five of these received life sentences and four were given sentences from seven to eighteen years imprisonment.

The death of Lawrence Ndzanga

Luke Mazwembe, Lawrence and Rita Ndzanga were among those arrested, accused of recruiting activists to join MK and organising for them to leave the country for military training. Lawrence and Luke Mazwembe both died in detention before being brought to trial. Rita Ndzanga was charged but found not guilty.

Lawrence Ndzanga, first national president of SARHWU, who died in detention.

Like many veteran activists, Rita is still reluctant to talk about her experiences:

> During that time nobody would tell any other person, 'I am doing this.' When work came then you had to do it but I didn't have to stand on top of the roof and tell everybody what I am doing! I knew what I was doing and I knew with whom I was working. The thing is, most unfortunately, a group was arrested in Zeerust before they got to Botswana and that was how I was arrested. Before that a lot of other groups had gone through without being apprehended but this last group was the one that was picked up by the

72

police and we were all arrested. I was fetched from where I was working in Kliptown. They collected me and they brought me home and then they collected my husband at the house and we were driven to John Vorster Square and then we were detained there.

That was the worst period during all my detentions because it was when my husband died. I remember it was a Sunday in the evening. The Matron came to my cell and asked me, 'What is your husband's name?' I told her and she asked me, 'Where is your husband?' I told her, 'He's in the men's section.' Then she left. And after a few minutes the same Matron came back again and now she was accompanied by an African Matron and she said to me, 'Rita, your husband collapsed and died.' Then I asked her what happened. She said, 'He was taken to go and get food and then he just collapsed and died.'

I had to go home to then bury my husband, but I couldn't. All the arrangements were made by my children and my family – and my children were very young then. I was taken to court where arrangements were made for me to get bail so that I can go out. The court decided that the bail would be R5 000 and that it should be paid in cash and I was taken to another cell in John Vorster where I had to wait for bail and I waited there, Saturday, the whole day, nobody came, I was just on my own until in the afternoon … so my husband was buried while I was locked up and I was only released after the burial, which was on a Monday. [12]

At the end of the decade trade unionism stood at a crossroads. A number of African unions had been formed or revived but they were not recognised for the purposes of negotiation. In contrast, there were some 2 600 liaison committees and over 300 works committees established under the Bantu Labour Act. Unions were, however, gaining ground in two different directions. In 1979 the successful use of a consumer boycott by the revived Food and Canning Workers Union (an original SACTU affiliate) showed the potential strength of a political alliance between community and workplace organisations. In the same year talks between the TUACC group of unions based in Natal, the Consultative Committee of Trade Unions in Johannesburg and a number of coloured unions in the Cape resulted in the affiliation of twelve unions to form a new union federation, FOSATU (Federation of South African Trade Unions) which represented about 50 000 workers. [13]

---

12. Interview: Rita Ndzanga, Johannesburg, October 1997.
13. Estimates of total membership vary between 20 000 and 50 000.

On the government side, the failure of the 1973 Bantu Labour Relations Regulations Amendment Act (amended again in 1977 to include the setting up of Industrial Councils) led to another attempt at incorporating black workers into a controlled system of industrial relations. In May 1979 there came an apparent change in government policy towards African trade unions with the publication of the Wiehahn Report recommending the recognition of the right of African workers to form and belong to trade unions.

The Wiehahn Commission and the 1979 Industrial Conciliation Act

The Wiehahn Commission was set up by the government in 1977 to look into the scope and content of trade union rights and other employment issues. In May 1979 the Commission delivered its substantive report and in July 1979 a new Industrial Conciliation Act was passed. The Wiehahn Report was based on the principle that in order to control African trade unions they should be registered and incorporated into the current industrial relations machinery. The government rejected this and tried to impose conditions that contract workers and foreign workers should be excluded, but it was forced to retreat by union opposition.

Under the Act black trade unions could apply to the Minister of Labour for registration and then, if recognised by employers, could negotiate stop-order facilities and legally binding wage agreements. There were still, however, a number of restrictions. Job reservation was eliminated but closed shop agreements between white unions and employers were retained; government employees were excluded from the Act and trade unions were forbidden to have any connection with a political party or to take part in political activities. The Minister had the power to refuse or withdraw registration on those grounds.

The impact of the report drove a wedge between the two wings of the developing black trade union movement that was already divided into rival groupings. CUSA (Council of Unions of South Africa) had been formed in 1980 by former members of the Consultative Committee of Trade Unions who had opposed the formation of FOSATU. Affiliates believed in black leadership and in the separation of trade union and political struggle, and all of them applied for registration under the 1979 Act. The FOSATU unions recognised that trade union struggle involved political issues but steered clear of direct political connections which they saw as harmful to their chances of recognition by employers and their ability to negotiate for improved wages and working conditions. They also decided to register and to use the influence that that gave them within the system to fight the ban on racially mixed unions and to work for gains for their members.

In addition to the FOSATU and CUSA unions there was a group of general 'community-based' unions representing around 80 000 workers that had been formed by SACTU operatives in close touch with SACTU in exile. These allied themselves directly with the political struggle and saw registration as a deliberate attempt to control and incorporate unions inside the existing system. They identified themselves closely with the ANC and took a leading role in community and township based organisations, being closely involved in the foundation of the UDF (United Democratic Front) in 1983. It was through these unions that railway workers were recruited and SARHWU was finally revived to be re-launched nationally in 1986.

SACTU and the Community-based Unions

The role of SACTU in exile was to provide financial assistance and publicity for those South African trade unions that supported the ANC and the struggle against apartheid. There were committees in both London and in Tanzania. Archie Sibeko was actively involved first in Tanzania and then as Western European Co-ordinator based in London.

> In London there were leading SACTU people. John Gaetsewe, who was the last elected General Secretary, Phyllis Altman, the former Assistant General Secretary and other people like Mike Harmel who were Communist Party people close to SACTU. JB Marks would also come there from Africa. They decided to form a committee there to explain the trade union part of the struggle in South Africa. John was very good at doing this. He was the initiator of the outside SACTU. Then people like us who were in Africa were consulted. It was decided that there should also be something in Tanzania because we weren't always occupied with military things (in MK camps). A committee was set up there with the SACTU people like myself who were in the military wing of the ANC.
>
> There were two committees but it became obvious that the London committee was more powerful. They were concentrating on doing solidarity work. That grew and then we decided that we should have a conference to co-ordinate the work in Africa and Europe. A delegation was sent from London to Maputo and we had a conference. That conference wasn't only people from Europe and Tanzania; it included people from home. That was when we decided that our HQ can't just be in London. It must be in Africa so that we can co-ordinate what is happening inside South Africa. In the end the General Secretary stayed

75

in London and Eli Weinberg was the co-ordinator in Dar es Salaam with other people like Alven Benny. There was also a co-ordinating committee inside South Africa. discussing strategies – people like Sydney Mufamadi, Samson Ndou, Sam Pholotho and Sisa Njikelana were all on that committee at various times. We also decided to have a conference every year.

In spite of all that, though, London was still the source of everything. It was very important because London is the centre of all forces in the Western world – money forces, technical forces and even trade unions were not excluded. People from South Africa went there. It was easy. You couldn't invite a person to go to Zambia or Tanzania but you could invite a person to go to London. The London office was delegated to collect money, produce leaflets, attend meetings and they did that very well.

The question of money was important. Among the international trade union community there were some who said, 'We'll give you money and you can do what you like,' but there were those who said, 'We'll give you money but we need a report,' and those who said, 'We'll give you money for specific things.' We agreed to all that and we suggested that when people came from South Africa they must go to sister organisations, linking up. That would lead to them giving money to the unions, sometimes above ground and sometimes underground. Also money was given directly. Organisations like UNISON (then NUPE) sent people inside South Africa. They would go openly to attend a conference and pass the money on for underground work. In South Africa there were people in each of the unions who were SACTU people. The money was given to them to use to support the struggle. The trade unions in the west contributed a lot to the underground work at home. That SACTU office in London was the paymaster of the underground people.[14]

SACTU actively promoted the setting up of the community-based unions to act as a counterweight to the non-aligned policy of the two federations, CUSA and FOSATU. The largest unions in community-based grouping were the Food and Canning Workers with 25 000 members and three general unions – the General Workers Union, with (approximately 12 000 members), the Black Municipality Workers Union, (later to become the Municipal and General Workers Union) with 11 000 and the South African Allied Workers Union (SAAWU) which had

---

14. Interview: Archie Sibeko, Manchester, January 1998.

around 20 000. Smaller but still important were the Motor Assembly and Component Workers Union (MACWUSA) and the associated General Workers Union (GWU), the General and Allied Workers Union (GAWU) and the National Federation of Workers (NFW).

Apart from the Food and Canning Workers Union and the GWU, the community-based unions were all formed at the beginning of the 1980s. Most were regionally based. Two grew out of specific industrial disputes – MACWUSA out of a strike by Ford workers in Port Elizabeth in 1979 and the Municipal Workers, led by Joe Mavi, out of a massive strike in Johannesburg in 1980. SAAWU, GAWU and the NFW all had their origins in the black consciousness union, the Black and Allied Workers Union (BAWU).

The Black and Allied Workers Union was taken over by SACTU activists in the late 1970s as a power base from which to launch a new organising drive and, following a confusing number of splits and breakaways, the three community-based unions emerged leaving only the rump to continue into the 1980s. GAWU was formed in 1979/80 by a group based primarily in the Transvaal, which was led by Rita Ndzanga, Samson Ndou and Sam Pholotho:

> In the early 1970s, in Durban, trade unionism started to wake up but we on the ground, we didn't know how to get hold of our leaders. We'd hear a lot about people going outside the country but we couldn't get in touch exactly. We also were worried that here in the Transvaal it was quiet, nothing is happening. So in 1979 or so a few comrades regrouped and analysed the situation that, 'Now, it seems now we must start. We shouldn't just wait for the authorities to give us that chance or the Wiehahn Commission to come and allow the African people to form their own trade unions.' Then we said, 'On our own we are weak so let us join the existing trade unions and get into them and see how things develop.'
>
> We were all doing underground operations and establishing our smaller groups. Then we agreed to go, as a block, into the Black and Allied Workers Union. That was in 1978/79. We went into the Black and Allied Workers Union which was organising a National Conference and we were able to put our people into the National Executive Committee. But there was a power struggle because we were not of the same political school of thought as the people in BAWU. The Black and Allied Workers Union was a black consciousness type of union and we were not from that school of thought. We were different people altogether.

Also, to them it was an issue of bread and butter, whereas our aim was to unite the people towards freedom. We were not only involved within the workplace but also outside it because if a particular worker leaves the factory gates and goes to the township that particular person is still going to be confronted with problems in the location.

A power struggle emerged and by 1980 a split occurred and we could not work together. We then regrouped and discussed things. The BAWU members in the Transvaal were all under our leadership. We needed to do something with this membership and we formed the General and Allied Workers Union, GAWU.[15]

At the same time two other groups broke away. The first, led by Thozamile Gqweta and Sam Kikini, formed the South African Allied Workers Union which soon built up a stronghold in East London. Then Mathews Oliphant and Magwaza Maphalala who had become, respectively, General Secretary and National Organiser of BAWU also split off to form the National Federation of Workers that had its main base in Natal. At this stage contact with SACTU was still difficult and after consulting Sam Kikini, Oliphant and Maphalala left for Swaziland to ask for advice.

Both of us did not know where we are going to! We just went there. We arrived in Swaziland and couldn't trace anything until we went to Manzini. We finally traced the people we were looking for in Manzini – that was Jabu and Nzima, Jabu was a SACTU activist, uNzima was more on the MK underground activities there. We met them and we related the story. Then the comrades told us that we need to come back and transform BAWU from a black consciousness organisation and we need to move away from a general union into organising industrial unions. So we came back. That was the mission. We put that as a proposal to the executive of BAWU – that we need to industrialise and BAWU must be a federation. It was agreed and accepted that that is the direction we need to go in.

We started organising people in that fashion but whilst we're doing that process then a meeting was organised in BAWU and we are expelled! It was clear that the main reason for our expulsion was that we were digging into issues and we are introducing a non-racialism in BAWU, those were the main reason for our expulsion. We had already expanded into Mpangeni area, back to Ladysmith and Newcastle, so when we were expelled we quickly ran around to all these areas and

---

15.   Interviews: S. Ndou, Cape Town, October 1997; S. Pholotho, Johannesburg, October 1997.

informed workers that this is what is happening. They stood on our side and they moved away from BAWU with us. Then the National Federation of (initially) Black Workers was formed, NFBW, until shortly thereafter we said, 'Remove this "Black",' and it became the National Federation of Workers.[16]

Although there was no formal alliance, the community-based unions shared a political philosophy. They acted in co-operation rather than in competition with each other and in areas like East London even held joint general meetings.[17] Workers flocked to join and a wave of strikes and demonstrations was organised. In 1980 there were 207 illegal strikes involving a loss of 175 000 working days. Many of these were quasi-political but they built on real economic grievances that stemmed from a fall in real wages of some 13-15% between 1977 and 1980.

The state replied by urging employers not to recognise the independent unions and by using the security police to harass their members.[18] In 1980, 298 striking textile workers were arrested and the leaders of the GWU and BMWU were held without trial during the meat workers and municipal workers strikes. SAAWU was banned by the puppet government of the Ciskei 'homeland' and during the first six months of 1981 over sixty activists were detained. In May of the same year three leaders of MACWUSA were imprisoned for terrorism without any detailed charges being laid against them.

The death of Neil Aggett

Early in 1982 Sisa Njikelana the Vice-President of SAAWU, Samson Ndou (GAWU) and a number of other union leaders including Neil Aggett, leader of the Food and Canning Workers Union, were arrested and taken to the police station in John Vorster Square, Johannesburg. On 5 February Neil Aggett died. Sisa Njikelana remembers him well:

The memories that come up about Neil – I've never seen such a dedicated cadre, soft spoken but resolute. You know, uNeil would come, we'd meet in the morning and he would say, 'Look, can you handle the workers? Because I'm drowsy.' He was working at Baragwanath the whole night. Neil Aggett was a qualified doctor but he never wanted to be called Dr Neil. He used to tell those workers, 'Don't call me Dr Aggett, I'm Neil Aggett.' He used to sleep on the bench. He was drowsy

---

16. Interview: M. Maphalala, Durban, November 1997.
17. SARHWU, 1997, p. 2.
18. J. Haarlov, 1983, p. 41.

but he still has to go and do union work. He only went to work in Bara at night to earn a living to have money for food and clothing and rent. He worked on Wednesday nights and Friday nights because it was easier. In short, the thing that Neil did there reflected his ideological vision and ideological commitment. He was a doctor but he was working two nights a week – not two days but two nights – to earn a living in order to carry on with the trade union work. I think he was arrested before me. Barbara Hogan went down to East London and Grahamstown and came back and got arrested and Neil got arrested too. Down the line we all got arrested. We were brought in here. I was asked a lot about what I did with him. I wrote everything – there was nothing to hide. I knew that I wasn't selling him out; he would just say the same thing and that was fine. We used to see each other. Sometimes he would be going to the bathroom and I was still running up and down or going to the district surgeon. That was shortly before he was murdered.

He was murdered, as far as I'm concerned. Neil was damned tough. He said he wouldn't be conscripted. I said to him, 'Neil go to the army,' and Neil said, 'No,' and he told me that it was going to be six years hard labour but he was prepared to face it. You dare tell me that a comrade of that strong personality would kill himself! No way, not Neil. Neil was even more militant than me, I must confess. What Neil did when we met – there was a room about this size, he came in. I was already there. We couldn't talk to each other; that was the rule but he pointed on his right wrist. He had a triangular shaped mark, very red, and I picked up the signal that was that things were bad, 'I'm being tortured.' It was a point where there were electric shocks. I knew because I myself, when I got electric shocks, I discovered two weeks after that I had marks here where they put the metal on the inside of my biceps on both sides.

That was the last time that I met him. The night he was murdered there was a noise past my cell. You could see that there were a couple of guys and what was striking was that they were not moving in the normal direction. They were moving toward the left and down the passage. At the end of the passage there were other entrances that were always locked. In the morning we heard that Neil was dead. If he'd died of natural causes or if he'd hanged himself as they claim, they could have called the police and checked everything and taken him by the normal route. [19]

---

19. Interview: Sisa Njikelana, Johannesburg, November 1997.

Unity talks

The community-based unions had the advantage over FOSATU and CUSA affiliates of being able to organise extensively across occupational boundaries and to bring thousands of workers on to the streets in support of their demands, which were both economic and political. They had the disadvantage, however, of being structurally weak, divided from one another and having a dangerously high profile. Membership increased at the time of strikes but waned again afterwards without a network of local workplace organisations to sustain it.

In order to organise effectively against the employers and the state it was necessary to build on the strengths of both kinds of union – to develop more workplace-based structures but at the same time to link these to the wider political picture and to unify the opposition to government policy. The next step in SACTU's strategy was therefore to encourage the splitting up of the general unions into industrially-based unions such as SARHWU, and to sponsor 'unity talks' between the 'political' community-based unions, FOSATU, CUSA and other trade union organisations, including a new 'Africanist' grouping, the Azanian Confederation of Trade Unions (AZACTU).

Talks about the formation of a new broad trade union federation began in August 1981. The talks were often bitter and were marked by deep divisions between the two sides, particularly on the issue of registration. Seven of the community-based unions set up their own loose co-ordinating group, known as the Inter-Union Project. This stood out against the terms proposed by FOSATU and its allies and at the beginning of 1984 the talks broke down. MGWUSA, SAAWU and GAWU walked out and the other unions agreed to continue without them.

It was important to SACTU and the ANC that the new federation should not take a narrow anti-political line but should become a partner in the struggle against apartheid. The SACTU community-based unions were, however, negotiating from a position of weakness because, unlike the FOSATU unions, their membership was widely spread. They had difficulty in collecting union subscriptions and could not, therefore, demonstrate a large paid-up membership on which to build power within the new organisation.

Sisa Njikelana was one of those involved in the talks on behalf of SAAWU:

> From the very outset when SACTU gave us a directive to form SAAWU it was on the understanding that we were going for a single federation which would do its level best to unite workers as much as possible into a trade union movement not just a body. So when we set up our small localised or regionally-based trade unions it was on the basis that we

81

were moving in that direction. We saw ourselves as a conglomerate leadership – Sydney Mufamadi, Samson Ndou, Louis Ramono, Sam Kikini, Ngcobo and others. Our objective was nothing less than to revive progressive trade unionism in South Africa. We got together – SAAWU, GAWU, Food and Canning, MACWUSA, the Municipal Workers and then, later on, NFW too – to discuss the super-federation, as we called it.

Well the history is that in '83 there was very little progress. There were a lot of meetings and debates and summits but it was debating mainly around principles. At that stage there was a lot of ideological difference between us and other unions. It was not just a matter of the issue of registration, but also questions of international links – Do we take money from the ICFTU? – And how we take up the revolution? – Do we just organise workers, for example?

I remember there was a lot of rage (what was formally known at Witwatersrand as fierce debates!) about the participation of UDF structures in trade union locals. That was the time when UDF was very strong and we were saying that there was nothing wrong for the community-based organisations and other structures to come to trade union meetings because they need to be exposed to what trade unions are doing. But we didn't only discuss broader politics and defend UDF principles. It went beyond that because we also participated actively in the struggle.

Simply because we [UDF unions] were linked to Umkhonto we Sizwe, it immediately struck a chord in us – that there's something beyond this damned trade union thing we've got to do. Comrades disappeared one after another. We knew that cadres were recruiting and the comrades had gone into exile and then were coming back to undertake MK activities. Politically we could interpret that and we saw ourselves as handling the labour department of the broad spectrum of the struggle. That was the difference between us and the others. They said, 'You touch guns, limpets [mines]? Good Lord!' The militancy was at its height and that obviously impacted on our attitudes towards them. We were thinking, 'Who do you think you are? I can just be arrested when I'm going out of here and I don't know whether I'll have to talk about the MK activities. You don't know anything about it.'

That got us bogged down until 1984. There were manoeuvres, fights, debates. We weren't very strategic. We had no time to study. All there was to do was to fight as much as you can before you go back into detention – because we knew that we would go back to detention. So you fight as much and you organise as much as you can; set up as many structures, make as much political rhetoric as you can, before you go back.

But finally we had to compromise. Later down the line, at SACP Congress, we realised that the thrust of our struggle is actually to ensure we've got the support of the workers and to organise the workers into a federation. We also had the guidance of SACTU through our underground linkages. In January 1985 we went to Harare to a meeting organised by the ILO [International Labour Organisation] through SACTU. They influenced us to be more strategic and work out things properly and also they were able to use ILO linkages to bring other unions there too so their leadership was able to go and get exposed to SACTU's point of view.

At the end of the day you can pick up a few things which were a compromise. We compromised on registration. Registration is a tool for control but we needed funds and hand collections were just not good enough; we needed the stop-order facility. In that context we had to compromise about registering – very reluctantly. We also changed terminology, like from 'Workers Committee' to 'Shop Steward Committee' because, even at that level we saw that terms like 'Workers Committee' were actually revolutionary.[20]

In the opinion of Archie Sibeko, SACTU played an important role in bringing the different sides together by keeping open lines of communication with the leaders of different unions.

Probably if SACTU wasn't there COSATU wouldn't have been formed at all. They negotiated for four years. We insisted that it was no use to form another centre in South Africa if you are going to exclude some people – that's just the same old apartheid. We were talking to our own people but also to that young element that came in from universities. There was a mixture of people. The South African union movement was divided up into three. There were those that were attached to SACTU and in alliance with the ANC and CP. Then there were those who although they were progressive didn't dare come close to the ANC. Then there were the reactionaries who were police and nothing else. They did come abroad and we worked very hard so that they might be isolated. When we heard that they were around we worked hard to see that they never came again or were never accepted.

---

20. Interview: S. Njikelana, Johannesburg, November 1997.

> During the talks we made a point if anybody was coming here that
> they should phone us from home and we would meet them at the airport
> and explain to them who they were meeting. Some of them didn't want
> to come to us but it worked very well. The TUC had a school at Crouch
> Hill to which many South African trade unionists were invited. The
> TUC received money from the British Foreign Office and it was not
> sympathetic to us, but we had people inside the TUC who were, and
> they arranged for people to come to our offices in the evening. We would
> discuss things and we never slept until midnight. Sometimes we had
> meetings actually inside the TUC College.[21]

In the course of 1984 political developments in the country at large began to
impinge on the unity talks. Community organisations and the community-based
trade unions began campaigning against the elections for the new, racially-based,
tri-cameral parliament which were scheduled for August and September. Violence and unrest spread and the government responded with the declaration of a
state of emergency. Workers and unionists of all persuasions were drawn into
the conflict and it became clear to FOSATU that it would be counter-productive
for a new federation to cut itself off from the liberation movement by excluding
the community-based unions. Talks were reopened and an agreement was
reached to form a new federation that included the UDF unions but excluded
CUSA and a number of smaller unions. Attempts were made by the UDF unions
to postpone the launching conference until they were better prepared but these
were defeated and at the end of November 1985 the Congress of South African
Trade Unions (COSATU) was born.

One industry one union

The formation of the new federation reinforced the impetus to disband the general
unions that had acted as a 'holding pen' for the mass of workers recruited at the
beginning of the 1980s and to redistribute the membership into industrial unions
along the lines of the 'One industry one union' policy adopted by SACTU in the
1950s. It was necessary to form new industrial unions both to act as a power base
within COSATU and to consolidate organisation at the grassroots. Mike Roussos, a young white South African of Greek extraction, had become involved with
the community-based unions through his work on a trade union education
programme:

---

21. Interview: Archie Sibeko, Manchester, January 1998.

The unions that I was involved with were all the emerging political unions. None of them, at that stage, had any kind of access to the workplace. It was pretty much political – from the *outside* type of thing – and so there wasn't much of the day-to-day stuff. Obviously there was a concern that the new federation should be a vehicle for advancing the broader aims of the struggle and not getting lost in a kind of narrow trade unionism within it. So there was a lot of concern that when we consolidated, when we joined these other unions, were we going to have the organisational base? Were we going to demonstrate enough clout to consolidate certain areas that would build on what we had done in the past or would we just kind of be sucked in? Because most of our guys were not paying on stop-orders; we didn't have audited membership figures so it was hard to demonstrate our relative strength with the others.[22]

Sisa Njikelana was involved in the process of creating these new unions from the combined membership of a number of the general unions.

From the very moment when SAAWU was set up we said, 'Because there has been a break in the history of the labour movement in South Africa we are starting from a very unfortunate position where people fear to be organised into trade unions and where there was no infrastruc-ture of progressive trade unionism.' There were TUCSA, the FOSATU unions and a number of other independent unions, so there was a sizeable labour movement in South Africa in the late '70s to early '80s but not a progressive one in our view. We set up a general union, but part of our programme and structure was to start categorising workers internally with the ultimate aim of forming industrial unions.[23]

One of the first industrial unions to be set up was SARHWU.

---

22. Interview: Mike Roussos, Johannesburg, November 1997
23. Interview: Sisa Njikelana, Johannesburg, November 1997.

The revival of SARHWU

Then we set about saying, 'Well, we want to consolidate a number of industrial unions,' and one of the ones we wanted to focus on was SARHWU. Here was a union that we had the only substantial base within; there was obviously the history of what SARHWU had been in the past and the name and so on. In a way, it was territory that we could legitimately claim for ourselves. So we said, 'We are going to form this industrial union; we want to integrate all the workers from the different general workers unions, bring together any railway or dockworkers or whatever anybody has into it; we are going to revitalise SARHWU and we are going to re-launch it properly.' [24]

The consolidation of a single railway union was an important part of the strategy of creating industrial unions and building up the strength of the SACTU unions within the new federation. It was also vital to the ANC's political challenge to the government. The South African Railways and Harbours had become reconstituted as South African Transport Services (SATS) on 1 April 1981. The new body, which included South African Airways and a road transport division, virtually monopolised the transport sector and occupied a strategic position in the South African economy. In 1984 SATS contributed 77% of the transport sector share of GDP and employed more than two-thirds of the total employed (240 237, of which 110 160 were African, 109 710 white, 18 377 coloured and 1 990 Indian).[25] Unlike other state corporations such as ISCOR (the Iron and Steel Corporation) and ESKOM (the Electricity Supply Commission), SATS remained a sub-department of the government and its general manager was directly responsible to the Minister of Transport. Although there was a regional management structure, policy was highly centralised and labour relations were rigidly controlled.

Living conditions

Although the wages of SATS African employees were not significantly worse than those in private industry, working conditions were very poor. The majority of workers were contracted migrant workers who lived in railway hostels and labour compounds. Conditions in the hostels were primitive. Delmore hostel near Germiston held 7 000 inmates housed in three different kinds of sleeping quarters –

---

24. Interview: M. Roussos, Johannesburg, November 1997.
25. P. Green, 1986.

buildings contained 50 four-man and 20 five-man and four-man rooms, each containing a single stove and iron and wire bedsteads. There was no hot water and lights remained on at all hours because there was only a single light switch, and there was no privacy or creature comforts. Food was prepared in one big kitchen and was the lowest quality mealie-meal (maize), badly cooked in unhygienic conditions. Although monthly deductions of R39-59 were made for food and accommodation, hostel inmates were required to carry a hostel permit and refused entry if they could not produce it, and visitors were not allowed.[26] Those who complained could find themselves transferred to remote rural depots where conditions were even worse.

> Our people were sick and tired of being subjected to dehumanising conditions, living in these corrugated huts. That was part of the strategy – to remove our people to those distant places. Once or twice a month you could get a train and go to a town, pay debts and come back. Later on they even levied rent for those places. It was men far away from their homes in those compounds with no women.[27]

Working conditions

Almost all African workers were still confined to the grade of general labourer and classified as casual or contract labour, liable to dismissal on 24 hours notice. Strikes were forbidden by the Conditions of Service (SATS) Act, 1983 and disputes were referred to a joint Conciliation Board appointed by the Minister of Transport. Workers were controlled by special railway police and those who stepped out of line were subjected to arrest and intimidation or transferred at short notice to other depots. Racism was rife and individuals were treated in a humiliating fashion by white supervisors, especially if their standard of education was relatively high.

Derrick Simoko, Bonakele Jonas and Charles Ntlangula began working for SATS at different times but the conditions they experienced were strikingly similar. Derrick was following in the footsteps of his father and elder brother when he went to work for SATS in 1963:

> At home it was me, my brother and my sister. We are the only three. I went to school but the conditions were bad because my family was poor. I lived at home and then I come here to Johannesburg in 1963 to start to work on the railway. My father was also working on the railway, but

---

26. Jabu Matiko, 1987 (a).
27. Interview: Johnny Potgieter, Kimberley, October 1997.

Whatever their standard of education, black SATS employees began work as general workers or sweepers.

he started in 1953. He was a labourer. Even if you were doing skilled or semi-skilled work, as far as the railway was concerned you remained as a labourer. Most of the railway workers were casual. When I started I was sweeping the floor of the black station and then from there I made an application to be a sorter. They always called us a sorter. The white people were called a checker but we were doing the same work. My brother died in 1967 but we got only something like R30 and that was the end of it. [28]

Bonakele Jonas was also the son of a railway worker. He began working for SATS in Bloemfontein in 1981:

I was born in Bloemfontein in 1963. My father comes from the Transkei but because of the migrant system he settled in Bloemfontein. He was a railway worker for twelve years in the permanent way inspecting. I left school in 1980 as a result of the student uprising and the riots and then in 1981 I moved to SATS. We used to queue at the railway hostel.

28. Interview: Derrick Simoko, Johannesburg, October 1997.

There was this white woman who would come and look at your face and then appoint you and send you to various areas. You never had a choice to say where you were appointed. When I queued I was picked up and sent to the mechanical workshops. First I worked in the black-smiths' workshop where they made the parts for the locomotives. Subsequently I became a messenger and I finally became a crane driver.

Initially there was a limit on jobs. You could work up to a certain category. In our case it was a striker, who used to take the hot iron from the ovens to the steam hammer to be panel beaten. In some other areas the highest job was a shunter. It was very bad. The wages were very low. When I first started I earned something like R136. You would move on until R307. Initially wages were determined by parliament and the Minister had to say how much would be offered. There were benefits like travel, sick leave, etc., but they were bad. Some of them were only for whites. It was the policy of the government that we were not permanent residents of South Africa and we must go back home when a job was over.[29]

Charles Ntlangula experienced similar conditions:

I was born in the Eastern Cape. My father was a postal worker. I came down to Kimberley with my mother and I went to school in Kimberley and the Cape up to Standard 9 before finally coming back to Kimberley to find work because things were bad at home. I was the only man in the family as they say in my culture so I had to fend for my sisters. I started working for SATS as my first work in Beaconsfield in the locomotive depot as a general worker (labourer). My responsibility was to get rid of the weeds and clean the yard then I was promoted to cleaning the sheds inside and scrubbing the floors with a hard broom! I was still a casual because you had to work about two years before you became a member of the pension scheme. I was again promoted and went to work shifts, starting at six, knocking off at two or ten until two, two until six as a 'spanner boy', carrying the bosses' tools and so on (though most of the time we were the people who were doing the job). I was earning R137 when I started in 1981, R137 a month. I worked shifts for about three or four years (without any allowance). [30]

---

29. Interview: Bonakele Jonas, Johannesburg October 1997.
30. Interview: Charles Ntlangula, Kimberley, October 1997.

These poor conditions were experienced by workers in all parts of SATS. Justice Langa, who became the first President of SARHWU, was employed by South African Airways.

> In SAA we had a lot of problems which we didn't know how to solve. We experienced terrible oppression from our superiors. For instance you were only allowed to be a labourer and there were no opportunities at that time because SATS was a company which was a special area for whites only – where the whites were protected whether they had knowledge or nothing. It was their own island and that's why it was impossible for a black person to get a job which he wants. It didn't matter about qualifications; you just got offered a job, take it or leave it. Even the uniforms were bad ones; you had to have what they gave you, whether it was big size or small size; you can't complain. When it comes to the uprising of the workers, we were blind as to what was happening because we were not unionised at that time. We didn't have proper medical care, we used to have railway doctors who were giving us the same tablets: whether you had arthritis, bronchitis or what they give you the same tablet. They were acting to encourage you to go back to work. In fact they were not even conducting any check-up at all.
>
> Most of the people who worked on the railways at that time were not local people. At that time they employed people from rural areas, Venda and so on. They would bring them in a coach, maybe 500 people with one ticket, like an ordered convoy. I think they understood that people from rural areas aren't in a position to challenge management about the things that are wrong, and that's why they tried to avoid people from urban areas. Because of the suffering at the time they had no choice as they had no future. For example, if you leave for a pension you only get maybe R800 and then its finished. That was a problem, and people didn't understand why it was like that. They were easy to fire. As temporary workers you had no rights, nothing.[31]

Disciplinary procedures

Most resented of all was the arbitrary use of disciplinary procedures that led to many unfair dismissals.

---

31. Interview: Justice Langa, Johannesburg, November 1997.

If a worker on the railways came late by two minutes he was fined something like two or three days salary. There were no proper disciplinary hearings. We were just called into the boss's office and given a letter and told, 'You are out of a job now.' That was the way people were treated. You had no right to say anything or you would just go to jail. If you said anything they would club you and call the police and you were branded as a communist. The railways then had a court. You were tried by an officer and he took all statements and sent them to the systems officer who would read the statements and reach a decision. That system was very unfair. You never had justice in it; never had an opportunity to mitigate your sentence or to argue your case. In most cases people were dismissed. At that time the country was faced with racial tension. Most of the people presiding were Afrikaner, always white, and there was no way they would have mercy.

The disciplinary system was a mockery. The system in SATS at that time was based on South African criminal procedure. The people who presided at appeal hearings were retired magistrates and they were historically antagonistic to the trade union movement, especially as represented by black people. So you had no chance of ever receiving a fair hearing. Within the internal hearings our biggest fight was a campaign that was taken up to do away with the SATS disciplinary code. It was notorious. [32]

Organising railway workers

In the confused situation at the beginning of the 1980s there were a number of different unions operating in the transport sector and some marked regional differences.[33] In all areas, however, attempts to obtain recognition were met by harassment and intimidation. In Natal railway workers were organised by SAAWU and in the Transvaal by GAWU. In East London and Port Elizabeth SAAWU organised outside the docks but railway workers in the docks belonged to the General Workers Union (GWU) which was led by David Lewis.

In 1982 the GWU attempted to obtain recognition for a Works Committee in Port Elizabeth harbour but this was rejected by the management which stated that it would only recognise its own staff associations or internal unions. The leader of the committee, Jeremiah Tolwana, was dismissed with twenty four hours' notice, despite having worked for the railway for 15 years. Workers began

32. Interviews: Bonakele Jonas, Justice Langa, Johannesburg, October 1997.
33. P. Green, 1986.

a go-slow but they were evicted from their hostels, rounded up and transported by lorry back to their 'home' areas. Some 400 were dismissed and not reinstated.

Eric Ngcingwana and Sello Ntai worked in the electrical department of the railway in Durban before they both became active in SAAWU.

> We were organising workers for SAAWU. We read from our comrades at SAAWU how to make a union and we started organising. Then the Security Police pulled in Sello. When [he was] released after two months the management transferred him. So then Sello resigned and went to work in the office and we worked together [on building the union]. How we organised at that time was to go to see friends, some people we know in the station, maybe ticket collectors, and talk to them so those people would at least get an idea of the politics of our country – of the people who were oppressed in this country at that time. Then we would take those people as individuals and bring them down to the office and explain that there is a need to build a union. Then they were clear. We started to make some paper or sort of like cards so that if you joined somebody then you could give them like a temporary member-ship card. [34]

Organisation of railway and harbour employees on a regional basis and by different unions was clearly a weakness. The community-based unions therefore agreed that these workers should be combined to form a relaunched SARHWU – not simply in order to form an industrial union but also, as Njikelana explains, to provide a link with the past history of the trade union movement and the political unionism practised by SACTU and its affiliates.

> The linkage between handing over SAAWU membership and organis-ing the struggle in the transport industry for SARHWU wasn't just a matter of handing over bodies, numbers, members, it was also ensuring that we were handing over a history of trade union revival from the late '70s and 1980s so we could actually say that this was part of a continuum. This meant always pulling in other unions, mobilising them, educating them, lobbying them into our school of thinking and the style of unionism that we're propagating.
>
> The good relations between SAAWU and SARHWU were replicated throughout the country, particularly in areas like Durban and Bloem-fontein where SAAWU was relatively strong. It was a matter of sitting down and saying, 'Where are you getting formed? When do you want

---

34. Interview: Eric Ngcingwana, Durban, November, 1997.

to take over the membership?' That kind of thing. 'How many of the organisers from SAAWU are you going to take over?'

The same is applicable to GAWU. Where they were strong one would assume the same thing. We are subscribing to the same school of thought when it comes to the labour movement. In the struggle generally we were regarded as UDF unions, but the bond between us went beyond being just UDF unions. There was an ideology pulling us together and SARHWU was revived within that culture and simply handed over. [35]

In the Transvaal Rita Ndzanga, Ndou and Pholotho collaborated with Joe Mavi, whose Black Municipality Workers Union (later the Municipal and General Workers Union of South Africa, MGWUSA) also organised railway workers, to re-establish SARHWU structures. Pholotho was put in charge of reviving the union, and on Joe Mavi's death he asked Catherine Mavi to act as the Secretary for the organisation in the region.

Rita Ndzanga was Treasurer here in GAWU and immediately after it was formed the comrades gave me the task. They used to call me the President of SARHWU but I wasn't elected, I used to chair the meetings when we had SARHWU business. They said, 'Okay Com. Now try to launch this union.' We brought in Johannes Ngcobo as an organiser. It was crucial to have funds for distribution of pamphlets for going out to other areas but it was a problem because we didn't have anything. We started with Ngcobo, Mike Roussos and others, a team. We were quite weak, but eventually we picked up quite a few members because railway workers were very ill-treated and their salary was little.

Immediately after that Joseph Mavi died in a car accident. We had his wife – that is Catherine. We were a poor union and we could not help her. Both unions had no money. We could see that this is a rural young woman, but we felt that she has got potential, leadership potential. In the reviving SARHWU we then said she must act as a Secretary. She wasn't chosen through elections, we were reviving an organisation. That is how we started that, the revival of SARHWU which becomes a very big and powerful union. So SARHWU is from our hands. It's not just from anywhere. We revived it. That was Lawrence Ndzanga's union earlier on, but we revived it and we are very proud of that. [36]

Mike Roussos played a key role in combining the railway membership from the various general unions into a well-organised single union.

---

35. Interview: S. Njikelana, Johannesburg, November 1997.
36. Interviews: S. Pholotho, Johannesburg, October, 1997; S. Ndou, Cape Town, October 1997.

My involvement was then with a committee which included Sam Pholotho, Rita Ndzanga and some other people and the thrust was basically, 'Let's get our branches sorted out; let's get our elective structure sorted out; let's get a constitution sorted out; let's get the symbols; let's create some sort of momentum that this union is established.' Then, when it has legal structures, we can jack up our attempts to put in place systems that allow us to claim formal status within the Federation Committee. Subs, even if it's by hand, demonstrating that we've got the fees and, therefore, we have a legitimate membership; servicing our members; making sure we are starting to cope with dealing with their needs. [37]

Catherine Mavi acted as interim Secretary but stepped down once a conference was held in the Transvaal which elected Johannes Ngcobo as Provincial Secretary. Catherine remained as office administrator while Mike Roussos and other members of the organising committee, travelled throughout the provinces, visiting the Northern Cape, Free State, Durban, Eastern Cape and Western Cape recruiting more members. Interim Branch Executive Committees were set up in a number of places including East London, where SAAWU provided SARHWU with an office. [38]

It was a long process of building structures. It changed, over a period of a couple of months, from a situation where the organisers pretty much did whatever they liked and weren't answerable to anyone, to a situation where we set up structures, workers were elected and people were called to account. So there were all sorts of tensions in the early days. But we kind of bulldozed or found our way round a hell of a lot of those and got to the point where we, after an enormous amount of work, set up the basic infrastructure to launch a national presence.

A number of regional structures were actually in place, we had drawn up a constitution and we had got some people to draw up the big SARHWU logo. That was actually created at that time. Obviously we drew as much as we could from the past, building on history, but the point is that we had to reintroduce it to people. We had to say to people, 'Here we are, and this is now the way you are going to recognise people.' We made T-shirts, so that people could wear them and identify themselves with it. It was a hell of an important thing to build an organisational commitment amongst our people, particularly in the light of what

37. Interview: Mike Roussos, Johannesburg, November 1997.
38. Chairperson, S.Vumazonke; Secretary, N. Dubula; Vice-Chairperson, T. Majalisa; Organiser, Xola Nodikane.

was happening within the Federation because of all these tensions and these attempts to try and dissipate things. And it worked very well. [39]

SARHWU affiliated to the UDF and to COSATU when it was formed in December 1985. It was essential, however, to re-launch the union formally, with an agreed constitution and elected officials. SACTU was now able to operate from an office in Lusaka, the capital of Zambia. Unlike other 'front-line' African states such as Angola and Mozambique, Zambia was not under direct military attack by South Africa. It was possible for SACTU operatives to keep in touch – sometimes using white supporters who could travel and sometimes sending messages via Swaziland and Lesotho, which, although surrounded by South African territory, were formally independent.

External finance was provided to organise a national conference and pay the expenses of delegates from nine regions. This was held at the Stonedrift Hotel at Grahamstown in the Eastern Cape in October 1986. The meeting was chaired by Sam Pholotho with Jay Naidoo, the General Secretary of COSATU, as guest speaker. By then the recommendations of the Wiehahn Commission had been accepted by the government and black trade unions had more scope to function. Nevertheless there was some harassment. Pamphlets were distributed announcing that the Grahamstown Conference was postponed, and delegates were photographed by security police. When the conference began there was quite a lot of tension but enough momentum had been generated by the preparatory organisation to enthuse the workers. Sello Ntai was elected as General Secretary and Justice Langa, a worker from Jan Smuts Airport, (now Johannesburg International) as President. There was a committee for the first time and, in the words of Pholotho, SARHWU was given back to the workers.

Summary

During the course of the 1960s the remnants of SACTU and SARHWU were harassed and imprisoned. Trade union activity became impossible and the leadership turned to underground political activity as the only means of working for the overthrow of the government and improving the conditions of workers in the long term. Increased economic growth and industrialisation improved the bargaining strength of African workers and at the beginning of the 1970s African trade unionism revived. General unions such as SAAWU, GAWU, MGWUSA and the NFW were set up at the end of the 1970s under the auspices of SACTU

---

39. Interview: Mike Roussos, Johannesburg, November 1997.

and began organising key workers in the docks, railways and factories. At the same time other unions formed the rival federations, FOSATU and CUSA.

Government repression of trade unionists continued and a number of key figures met their deaths in police custody. Eventually, however, at the beginning of the 1980s, the Wiehahn Commission recommended the recognition of black trade unions. A rift developed between those unions which decided to register, and the SACTU-linked unions, which were community-based and opposed registration. Unity talks began between the different trade union groupings and the general unions agreed among themselves that they would consolidate their position by forming industrial unions from among their joint membership. The re-launch of SARHWU was an important part of this strategy as the railways and harbours played a key role in the political economy of South Africa. In November 1985 COSATU was formed, and in October the following year the first national conference of the re-launched SARHWU was held at Grahams-town.

4

Strike!

Almost as soon as SARHWU had been re-launched it became involved in industrial action. At the end of 1986 a campaign of protest began against the conditions in railway hostels and compounds. A full-scale strike followed rapidly, beginning in March 1987, which was to last nearly three months and spread to over 20 000 workers, mainly in the Transvaal but also in other areas.

The foundation of the United Democratic Front (UDF) in 1984 and of COSATU in 1985 were signs of renewed political activity among the black population – activity which was met by increased government repression and the declaration of a State of Emergency in June 1986. Springing as it did from SACTU and the community-based unions politically aligned with the UDF, it is not surprising that SARHWU adopted the line that unions should take a lead in the political arena as well as in the workplace.

For both strategic and symbolic reasons South African Transport Services was an important target. SACTU had long considered the organisation of SATS workers to be a fundamental part of the liberation struggle in South Africa because, as well as playing a political role as the major employer of unskilled white Afrikaner labour, the railways also played an important economic role. The company controlled the ports, all rail and air traffic and a section of road transport too. About 80% of the freight in the country moved by rail (including much to and from neighbouring territories) and most of the African workforce depended on trains to travel from the townships and 'homelands' to their place of work. In addition, the rail network was militarily very important in the movement of troops and supplies, particularly during the State of Emergency.

Over 180 delegates, representing an initial membership of some 10 000, attended the re-launch but all was not plain sailing. SARHWU was a national union but its strength varied in different parts of the country. It was strong in the Transvaal (where organisers claimed 8 000 members) but it was challenged by three other unions. These were the African Railway and Harbour Workers Union (ARAHWU) which was a former AZACTU affiliate, the National Union of Railway Workers (NUR) which was based on local workers committees in East London and Port Elizabeth, and the Transport and General Workers Union, which argued that railway workers should be organised in the same union as workers in other parts of the transport sector. In addition, it was faced with the need to replace the SATS 'sweetheart' union, the Black Trade Union (BLATU).

SARHWU had an ideological commitment to the philosophy of 'One industry one union' which went back to its affiliation to SACTU in 1955. SACTU had been determined to avoid the ICU's mistake of forming a loose general union and had set up National Organising Committees to organise separate unions in key industries. The launching conference of COSATU followed a similar policy, resolving to merge all affiliates into ten broadly-based national industrial unions within the first six months. The decision of the conference was that the SACTU-linked general workers unions would distribute their membership into these new unions. SARHWU (which had affiliated with 8 220 members) was to merge with the Transport and General Workers Union (which had affiliated with 11 000) to form one big union in the transport sector.

What in fact happened was that GAWU and SAAWU allocated their organis-ers and railway members not to the TGWU, which was a former FOSATU affiliate, but directly to SARHWU, with which they felt most politically at home. COSATU accepted the argument that it was too difficult for SARHWU to reorganise and merge with the TGWU at that time. Both continued to be represented on the COSATU council and both continued to pay lip service to the idea of merger but it was not a priority for either. The unions were not rivals because they organised in different sectors of the transport industry, SARHWU in the public sector and the TGWU in private firms. Therefore it was not until the late 1990s when conditions changed, that SARHWU became interested in the idea again.

SARHWU's objective was to monopolise the organisation of SATS workers in order to be in a position to disrupt essential services and exercise maximum influence on management and the government. In order to do this it had first to fend off attempts to organise railway workers by its rivals. Both ARAHWU and the NUR had pockets of local support but the major threat came from the 'company unions', BLATU and TATU.

Company unionism

The interests of SATS and the government lay in preventing workers from organising collectively and acting independently. Control over white workers was achieved in the 1920s and 1930s by destroying the power of the craft unions and incorporating others through a privileged relationship with management. The attitude of the SATS management towards any form of independent labour organisation by black workers was one of total repression.

The 1973 Labour Relations Act, which legalised the right of black workers to take strike action, deliberately excluded the railways, and black railway workers had no legal right to form a union. In the 1970s the company tried to divert the impetus towards black trade union organisation by setting up Liaison Committees, and following the report of the Wiehahn Commission in 1979 it fostered a number of internal 'unions', or Staff Associations, which were organised and controlled by management. At the beginning of the 1980s it set up its own Black Staff Association.

According to Vic van Vuuren (who became a member of the company's first Industrial Relations Department), up to 1987 there was nobody inside SATS at all qualified to deal with industrial relations matters:

> Although there were numerous unions that existed in the company at this time there was no form of collective bargaining. That which existed could rather be termed as collective begging. The recognised trade unions that did exist were in fact originally categorised by management and allowed to develop within those determined boundaries.
>
> The unions were firstly divided into black and white and thereafter the white trade unions were divided into broad job bands. The black trade unions were however only divided into black, coloured and Indian. The categorising of the trade unions was done many years before … with some of the first unions appearing as early as the 1920s. The unions used to conduct the collective bargaining on the basis of holding meetings with the Minister responsible. He would listen to them and tell them that he would do what he could to assist them in resolving those issues identified by them. [1]

In all there were eleven 'in-house' SATS staff associations representing different grades and racial categories. Most of these were converted into registered unions following the recommendations of the Wiehahn Commission and the enactment of the 1979 Industrial Conciliation Act.

---

1. Notes on the relations between SARHWU and Transnet by Vic van Vuuren, April 1998.

The only black union recognised by SATS was the Black Staff Association, later renamed the Black Trade Union (BLATU), which was formed in 1981. By 1982 membership was claimed to be some 60 000, out of 95 000 black employees – largely as a result of a unique form of company recruitment. All employees were automatically assumed to be members of BLATU and subscriptions were collected by the company through stop orders on workers' salaries. Office premises were provided and workers were offered inducements to become officials. It was not a democratic trade union even in the sense that leaders were properly elected, and the choice of representatives to act as shop stewards or to sit on the Joint Conciliation Board was normally made by supervisors rather than by the workers themselves.

> The Labour Relations Officers appointed organisers or officials who were their puppets or stooges. The so-called *indunas* (supervisors) were instructed to persuade workers to join BLATU. They were promised R600 as a reward if they could bring more workers into these staff associations. Workers were told that the black staff association would fight for their rights. There were many ways used to organise workers into BLATU, such as promoting BLATU members and better treatment to attract non-members. There was police harassment of other workers and people joined BLATU because they wanted to be on the safe side but things didn't go that way. There was no protection. Workers were disciplined and BLATU did nothing to defend them. [2]

A number of workers who were selected as shop stewards became disillusioned with the system. James Phera was a representative for the Black Trade Union in Cape Town before he resigned to join SARHWU:

> The staff association came about because of the divide and rule system. The management didn't want political people to represent people or didn't want people who have been enlightened to sit with them whenever there is a meeting. They knew that if they had people who are chosen by them, then they won't understand what's going on. So we represented people. We were actually told what to do for that person. We knew the lines that had to be toed.
>
> It seemed to me, 'I'm not representing the people because I feel that this person is wrong or is right. I have to be told what to say to this person or I have first to beg this management.' There was one manager – whenever he came to see me he used to call me kaffir. It hurt me. I

---

2.   SARHWU, 1997, p. 2.

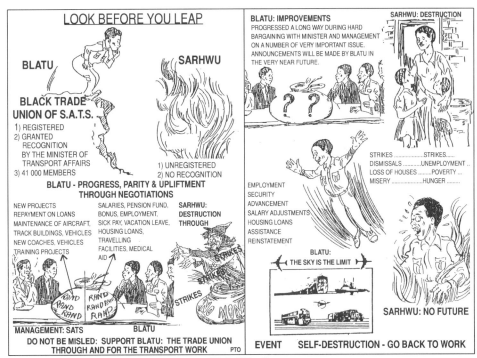

BLATU leaflet

had to laugh because I was going to represent somebody. I had to behave that way so as to have that person released or free. But on the way somebody hurt me and I thought, 'What can I do? To that man I will remain a kaffir until doomsday. I will never change. I will remain in that position and he will make me remain there for ever.' So I just decided, 'I'm going to resign and join SARHWU.'[3]

Other workers also began to realise that the company union was not the real thing.

We were tired of the liaison committees. You could speak to the manager and it ends there. If he says, 'No,' it's a no; if he says, 'Yes,' it's a yes. We thought if we had a staff association, it would be much better. I will tell you how foolish we were! But at that time we thought it was better. So we went on and we formed a staff association and we formed some sort of a union. That union finally became BLATU. That is how we formed BLATU. Then I started to notice something. We were being given a company car to organise people. We had been given an office inside the company premises. Somebody was writing our constitution

---

3.   Interview: James Phera, Johannesburg, October 1997.

somewhere. We had stop orders; we had everything. Then I said, 'No man. We cannot be helped by this company to form a union and be given a car. There is something wrong here. I am not going to go with this any more.' [4]

I was a shop steward of the staff association, chosen by the supervisor – not elected by the workers. You had to call them baas, not Mr van der Merwe. One day the Labour Managers called us and said, 'Don't join those people,' [i.e. SARHWU]. I just kept quiet because in those days just to mention the names of COSATU or the ANC meant that you would go to jail. On the depot level we had a problem. I started to recruit the comrades underground, gave them the forms and they filled them in their break. People joined very fast but they didn't want me to speak out because they feared losing their job. [5]

The staff associations were used as an essential part of labour control. It was in their interests not to oppose management but to support it. Workers who resisted joining were harassed by railway police, and their job security and promotion prospects were threatened. Those who were discovered to have joined SARHWU faced instant dismissal.

The railway administration saw SARHWU as being both militant and political. It was clear from the outset that recognition would not be won without a fight, and 1987 provided a clear opportunity. It was the 75th anniversary of the foundation of the ANC and activists were determined to mark this with an escalation in opposition to the regime, which had extended the vote to Asians and coloureds but still excluded Africans. In the last six months of 1986 over 29 000 people had been arrested. The struggle in the townships was at its height and workers were already mobilised and willing to recognise the need to use their industrial power for political ends in order to improve their economic position.

Organising the union

Because of the hostility of SATS, the union was forced to operate in a more or less clandestine manner within the workplace:

It was a problem for us. We were not recognised and it was difficult to get into the railways and organise the workers. We had to take the overalls and the uniforms of the workers and organise them, but if you

---

4. Interview: David Moeti, East London, October 1997.
5. Interview: Eliphus Fosi, Pretoria, November 1997.

were found then you would be arrested. The way the union operated was as an underground organisation. People would just meet five people, discuss the issue and say what's happening. Fortunately people at that time understood the real issues. I mean, people would not take ten minutes arguing the merit of the issue; everybody would be informed about the situation and you would take note. If you wanted to understand anything else you would have to go to a SARHWU meeting outside the depot. But in the work environment it was a three-minute talk system – what has happened and this is the decision – and you accepted that and abided by it without questioning the merit and rights of it.

Management had picked up that there was a union called SARHWU and then they had a policy to say that, 'We don't speak to an unregistered union, a communist union,' – that was the attitude. An ordinary manager would not want to see you if you were saying you were in SARHWU. So then what happened was that there was no communication.

The only communication was between workers. They'd say, 'This is the problem and we're not going to work.' Management would pick it up because Jo'burg would inform other areas but nobody on the ground would go to his manager and say 'On Monday we are not going to work because of a, b, c, d.' [6]

Recruitment was very tough and there was severe pressure. If you were found with the forms of the union you were fired on the spot. What I did, I had a friend who helped me because I was a target and if I was found with anything they had an excuse to get me out of the job. We worked like that. We used to go to the toilet – many people used to wonder why we were going to the toilet every now and then – but we were signing people during that time! We signed so many people in a short space, and we explained to them the whole thing. I managed to take 90% of them. I won them and they joined SARHWU. In a short space of time the whole department was unionised. [7]

Lack of recognition and lack of communication between the workforce and the employer fostered both an uncaring attitude on the part of management, which spread from supervisors right to the top, and a festering discontent among the workers that would occasionally break out in short-lived wildcat strikes. Spontaneous unrest began in this way in the single-sex railway compounds and hostels

---

6.   Interview: Nelson Ndinisa, Johannesburg, October 1997.
7.   Interview: Justice Langa, Johannesburg, November 1997.

where many of the workers were crowded together in conditions little better than those described in 1936 and 1950.

The compounds campaign

Immediately after the re-launch SARHWU began a campaign to persuade workers to resign from BLATU and join SARHWU.[8] Because of the difficulty of organising in the workplace the campaign centred on the railway hostels where workers lived in appalling conditions guarded by compound security guards. At Delmore hostel members of the union elected a hostel committee of ten workers.

> Recruiting at work was difficult due to the way management organised our work. We don't spend most of our time together. We are doing different jobs and in small numbers, except workers maintaining the railway tracks and electric cables, but even then we did not have contacts in those sections. The other problem was [that] management imposed the Staff Association which pretended it represents the interests of workers, and due to the absence of an alternative organisation in the past it was difficult for workers to believe that SARHWU was different from the Staff Association.
>
> After work, most workers spent time at the hostel's beer hall as there is nothing else to do except sleep. Our energy was concentrated on this beer hall. We used to go there and started singing workers' songs. People would join in the singing and others would stop and ask what all these songs meant. Discussion would take place. In fact, within three days we had already recruited twelve workers and today membership is approximately 4 000 out of 7 000 hostel residents.
>
> Our first activity centred around organising workers as members of SARHWU ... We had to show them that it is SATS who creates problems which they were confronted with. The main issue we focused on to develop this understanding was the bad quality of the food. On 8 November 1986 a general meeting was called by the committee. The compound manager was also invited to this meeting. Workers' grievances about the living conditions were raised; the question of food was also included. The compound manager's response was that he was going to raise those grievances at a top management meeting and feedback would be made on 1 December 1986. After he left the meeting the committee requested workers to stay. This opportunity was used to

---

8.   Led by SARHWU stalwart Simon Mulumone.

explain further about SARHWU and the need to join hands together; union pamphlets were also distributed.

The compound manager never fulfilled his promise. His attitude to the committee changed. He claimed it was consisting of union instigators. Following that one of the committee was evicted from the hostel. Workers response to this development was a boycott of food. A demand that monthly deductions be stopped was made. Failure of the compound manager to do this was met with workers' anger; the kitchen was looted and the authorities responded by closing it down …

A decision was made by workers that expired meal tickets should not be handed in for renewal. The authorities' solution was to send in dogs and police at the hostel to pressurise them to hand in the meal tickets. Only 55 workers responded to the authorities' call. On 19 February 1986 the whole committee was called to the Germiston charge office where they were questioned for one day in connection with the food boycott. After their release a meeting called at the hostel was interfered with by the police … [9]

The food actions stimulated interest in joining SARHWU to the extent that workers were queuing round the building and filling the corridors of COSATU House, where the union's offices were based. There was a huge growth in the number of members – all looking for further action to improve their conditions – and by the end of 1986 some three-quarters of the railway workers in the Southern Transvaal and a substantial number in Southern Natal had joined the union.[10]

Workers were taking action by themselves and the momentum generated by the [re-launch] Conference and the work that led up to it took on a life of its own. In different parts of the country people started taking action around food. It was an issue at the time, quite a big one. We were organising the hostels and people started coming along and saying the food was terrible and we had to take action. It was one action that just happened. The workers decided by themselves that they were going to boycott the kitchens. They're not going to eat there any more. And they just closed the kitchens down, literally. Started cooking in their rooms. It was a very important blow against the railways management because for the first time they couldn't keep control.[11]

---

9. Quote by Jabu Matiko, 1987 (a), p. 3.
10. Interview: Mike Roussos, Johannesburg, November 1997.
11. As above.

Sello Ntai, the new General Secretary, was active in bringing things under the union's control, but the management refused to accept that SARHWU represented its employees and refused to talk to it, preferring the non-elected representatives of BLATU. In February 1987 Sello Ntai and a number of SARHWU shop stewards were arrested for their role in the compound protest; they were not to be released for another four months. The intention of the state was to weaken the union by removing the leadership, a tactic successfully followed in the 1950s and 1960s.

On this occasion, however, the tactic failed. On 8 March 1987 SARHWU called a rally at COSATU House which was attended by around 1 000 workers representing committees at Delmore, Kaserne, New Canada, Central Rand and Lanwen hostels. Resolutions were passed condemning the migrant labour system, supporting the COSATU living wage campaign, and urging that all hostel committees should meet to discuss the food boycott. The meeting set a deadline of 15 March for SATS to stop deducting the 50c membership subscription for BLATU and resolved that members would stay away from work on May Day and 16 June (the anniversary of the Soweto Uprising) and would take industrial action if leaders were not released from detention.[12]

Johannes Ngcobo, then Provincial Secretary of SARHWU in the Transvaal, was one of those trade unionists who had been recruited by SACTU to work within South Africa to further the political ends of the liberation movement. It was clear to him that the workers were ready for a strike:

> There was a fever among the workers that united them. They had managed to find a home and managed to win their struggle in the compounds so now they were looking for something to happen. Our shop stewards weren't recognised as SARHWU – the management were saying, 'No, we're not going to recognise you.' So towards the end of that year we took a decision that we are now going to face them head on, come whatever may. [13]

Strike action had already been discussed earlier in 1986, at a meeting of ANC and SACTU underground activists in the front-line state, Mozambique. It had been decided that there should be a strike to celebrate the 75th anniversary of the foundation of the African National Congress. Somehow either the state or the Railway Security Police got wind of SARHWU's plans, however, and the management was alerted.

---

12. Jabu Matiko, 1987 (a), pp. 6-8.
13. Interview: Johannes Ngcobo, Johannesburg, October, 1997.

Transnet [i.e. SATS] knew about it before the recess time in December because in the early days of December there were already pamphlets flowing up and down saying that whoever goes on strike, action will be taken. The first meeting we had was in January, at Wits University, where we also called Winnie Mandela. We started outlining what we wanted to do. She agreed with us and said, 'There is no way you are going to win recognition by means of just organising people because SARHWU is banned, the objectives and aims are of a communist nature in terms of what government will say. They will not accept that. And also you are pushing the aims and objectives of the ANC, which is banned. So you will face a very serious opposition.' The decision of that meeting in January was that we will have to bring Spoornet [the rail sector of SATS] to a standstill. So we were looking for anything that would bring us to an action, but Spoornet started to be very careful of what they were doing, not to harm anybody, because of the momentum our discussions were gaining.[14]

The 1987 Strike

The strike began at the City Deep container depot in Johannesburg following the sacking of a delivery driver, Andrew Nedzamba, over a relatively trivial incident – his failure to pay in cash-on-delivery receipts because he returned late to the depot at the end of the day. Workers at City Deep went on strike on 16 March. On 21 March a mass meeting of some 4 000 railway workers was held at COSATU House to demand the reinstatement of Nedzamba. The hall was surrounded by police and at the end of the meeting workers were escorted away in groups of twenty guarded by armed police.

On 23 March other depots in the Transvaal including Germiston, Braamfontein, Boksburg East, Vereeniging and Standerton voted to strike in solidarity. At a further meeting held on 25 March workers elaborated their demands to include unconditional reinstatement, the elimination of racism, the establishment of grievance machinery, full pay for time on strike and no victimisation. They agreed to return to work provided that they were allowed to elect their own representatives to negotiate with management.

Management failed to respond and the number of strikers grew from some 8 000 on 25 March to over 20 000 by the first week in April. The NUR and ARAHWU both pledged support for the strike and pressed for inclusion in a joint

---

14. As above.

107

Xola Tshabalala, CDC

Marching SARHWU members fill the streets of Johannesburg.

strike committee. In contrast, BLATU urged its members to continue working and not to break the no-strike agreement that the union had signed in 1981. The response was overwhelming. Railway workers flocked to join SARHWU. BLATU was ignored and the NUR and ARAWHU which announced support for the strike were excluded from strategy discussions by SARHWU leaders who wanted to keep control in their own hands.

The SATS management applied for a court interdict to stop strikers from disrupting the operation at City Deep, but the strike succeeded in bringing the container depot to a complete halt with 751 containers at the terminal waiting to be delivered and 458 still on trains and unable to be unloaded.[15] The Minister of Transport published a special *Government Gazette* giving SATS the right to dismiss the strikers without notice, and workers were sent notices warning them that they were in contravention of the 1983 SATS Conditions of Employment Act under which any employee taking part in a strike would be deemed to have terminated his service. After a month, an ultimatum was given to strikers that they should return to work by 22 April or lose their jobs.

When this was ignored some 16 000 railway workers were dismissed and police violence was stepped up. Meetings and demonstrations were attacked,

---

15. Jabu Matiko, 1987 (a), pp. 9-14.

workers were killed, and offices bombed. There were mass arrests and detentions of union leaders. The strike did not end until more than two months later following international pressure and the intervention of COSATU, church leaders and members of the business community. The workers won a partial victory. Those workers who had been dismissed were reinstated without victim-isation or loss of benefits, and permanent employment status was granted for the first time to black railway workers with more than two years' service.

The account of the strike by SARHWU members who were personally involved in the events makes it clear that it was not solely an industrial dispute. There were three associated reasons for the development of unrest among railway employees. In the first place, as we have seen in previous chapters, the conditions of work imposed on employees by the railway administration, SATS, were among the worst in the country. In the second place, the political atmosphere of the mid-1980s was highly charged and workers were spoiling for a fight. Finally, the SACTU unions and the external command of the liberation movement were looking for a trigger which could be used to spark off industrial unrest which would weaken the South African economy and put pressure on South Africa's Western allies to encourage the Pretoria government to make political conces-sions.

The strike at City Deep

On hearing of the dismissal of Andrew Nedzamba workers downed tools and asked for a meeting to discuss reinstatement, but management refused to talk to anybody associated with SARHWU. As the following account by Jonas Makhavhu shows, the scene was one of confusion, common enough in any large workplace, with no clue that this was to grow to be a major strike.

> Mr Berndt [was brought from] Kimberley to negotiate. He called us next to the gate and said, 'I would like all of you to go back to work and then I'll need some people to discuss things with and they'll give a report back to you.' We said, 'No, we're going to wait here but we'll give you the shop stewards so you can go and negotiate with them.' That's when we told him we were going to elect other people to go with the [management-appointed] shop stewards in order to strengthen the team and we elected a couple of people to go with them …
>
> During that time, while we were busy down there at the ablution block, they went collecting some white workers. They gave them trucks to start moving the goods so, in order to reinforce the strike, we decided to come over and close the gate. The trucks that were coming from

outside couldn't go in and the ones that were from inside couldn't go out. Mr Berndt came down and asked for the perishable goods to be delivered and we said no.

That raised the spirit of the workers and they said, 'We're not going to leave here; we're going to stay.' We stayed for the whole day and at about five o'clock we decided not to move, to sleep there, because if we moved they are going to come in and move the containers. We slept there and at about three o'clock in the morning the police came with Mr Berndt and a court order which they had arranged during the night – I don't know where! They read it to us and said they were giving us five minutes. All of us should have handed in the truck keys and vehicle keys and we should leave the gate.

We gave them the keys and went down to the changing rooms ... We stayed there for three weeks. The first night we slept in the ablutions block but after that we used to come in [from outside]. We used to leave home as if we were going to work and have meetings and discuss. The first week – the first three days – we were staying in the changing rooms. The second week there were not much negotiations and management was trying to look for other ways; maybe getting other white people to come and drive trucks, so we started saying, 'We need to intensify the strike. We need to go to other depots.'

I was elected to go around the depots, going to brief them on what's happening and asking for support from the others. So I went to depots like Kaserne and then I moved over to Jo'burg and I also went to Braamfontein to the bus depot and Germiston to discuss with them. The third week was when they gave us the final warning that we must move and leave the depot. We were dismissed from City Deep and then we started functioning and organising everything from COSATU House. [16]

The dispute escalated rapidly because of the intransigence of the management, the militancy of the workers, for whom Nedzamba's dismissal was symbolic of many other instances of unfair treatment, and the decision of the union to use it as a means of confronting the state as employer and forcing recognition. The stoppage at City Deep was supported by a meeting of the general council of shop stewards in the Transvaal and then by the 23 March meeting of all depots which agreed to extend the strike.

---

16. Interview: Jonas Makhavhu, Johannesburg, October 1997.

The strike spreads

The objectives of the strike went far beyond the Nedzamba case which had sparked the dispute:

> [It was] a *national* strike, in solidarity with that one worker but linking up with all other unfair dismissals throughout the country. We wanted an entrance into halting Transnet. It was not the salaries or the wages we were most interested in but the recognition of the union, then the reinstatement of this worker, then improving the working conditions and then the salaries. Salaries were somewhere around demand number five or four.
>
> We used the dismissal as a mobilising point but as the problem developed people realised that there were other pending issues such as the question of money, working conditions and the recognition of the union. In the end the recognition of the union became the central demand – for it to be recognised, in order for it to negotiate for us as members of the union – and that was the major stumbling block of the whole affair.[17]

Shop stewards were given the job of explaining the issues to members and motivating them for a strike:

> We all went to a central venue at the railways where we started to debate the issue; to say, 'This is the problem. This is why we are doing what we are doing.' Because we found that some people were still working because they didn't actually understand. Some people were just in-formed in the morning that, 'Today we are not working,' and they did not have the opportunity of understanding. So it was at that time that we started to openly debate the whole issue and also to put another flavour on it – to say, 'What is the situation in South Africa? How are we going to overcome this problem?'
>
> Immediately we pulled people out the first problem was that the police were always there, and in order to sustain the strike you needed to put it in context so that people understood that the decision we had taken of not working was quite simple but the implications were quite drastic. At that stage the railway was purely a department of the government, so the government took it as a pure and open challenge from the communists. We had to start to say to people what the

---

17. Interview: Johannes Ngcobo, Johannesburg, October 1997.

implications were, so that we could motivate them to expect that it will not be an easy burden. [18]

Vic van Vuuren confirms this impression:

> From my observations it was not the management of Transnet (SATS) that dealt with the strike but rather senior government officials, particularly the Minister of Defence and the Minister of Police. Meetings were held at the Spoornet offices led by these high-ranking officials wherein the management were told what to do. The company and government stance was that the union movement was directly linked to the struggle associated with the ANC, the UDF and suchlike other organisations. It was this aspect that led to the matter being managed at governmental level. The company stance, although not always so communicated, was to ensure that SARHWU was not successful in obtaining recognition. In my opinion the strike was managed strictly according to politics and legal procedures …
>
> Opposition to the apartheid era obviously was the centre of SARHWU's role in obtaining 'freedom' for the people. It was clear that SARHWU was strategically placed to assist the bigger players in obtaining their objectives of overturning the status quo in the country and that future action was going to be focused on this. [19]

SARHWU attempted to initiate discussions with the management but SATS continued to argue that BLATU represented the majority of the workers and that all negotiations should be conducted through that union. This attitude proved counter-productive, however, in that, according to Johannes Ngcobo, workers saw management's reluctance to recognise the union as confirming that the SATS objective was to prevent the development of structures which could be used to question management control. By 16 April the strike had spread as far as Bloemfontein and East London where the Vice-Chairperson, Thembekile Majalisa, and 200 others went on strike. [20]

> When we heard the news we said, 'Enough is enough.' It was time for us to stand up and be counted. We discussed in our general meeting and we decided that we are going to support them. At that time we were not recognised by SATS. We felt that we cannot leave them alone and that we need to support them. Our membership in East London at that time was 500, and 200 of them embarked on a strike. Within three days we

---

18.   Interview: Nelson Ndinisa, Johannesburg, October 1997.
19.   Notes by Vic van Vuuren, April 1998.
20.   Jabu Matiko, 1987 (b), p. 1.

were dismissed. As you know, when you are on strike you need to do something … We were banned from entering the company premises so we used to hold meetings outside company premises. We tried to pressurise the company to take us back and the comrades from Southern Transvaal used to come to us and encourage us.

At the port I was alone on the strike. The other workers in the port refused to embark on that action so I was together with those from Spoornet. I didn't want to breach the decision and I wanted to show the management that we wanted to change and I wanted to change the attitude of management because all along they took us as their babies. I was dismissed in 1987 with the other 200 but fortunately we were reinstated after three months. They refused to let me work on the ship again. They put me on the shore and they didn't want me to mix with other workers. I was working alone the whole year. They sent me up and down, one day to this place, next day another place. It was a sort of harassment.

I wasn't afraid that I would be arrested. I was tortured already, there was no need to be afraid. From 1985-86 we were tortured after we launched the union. We launched the union publicly to expose the fact that we were members and no longer in secret so there was no need to fear the management. They must know that we are members. I went on strike to show the others that there was nothing the management could do to me and after that I came back and organised them to show that I'm still alive. I learned the lesson that you must be together. [21]

Mike Roussos, who as National Education Officer played a major role in running the SARHWU head office following the detention of Sello Ntai, saw the management approach as being a result of government pressure:

Obviously we were wanting to use it as an opportunity to get some official status with them and get them to acknowledge the fact that we were increasingly representing more and more of the workers. It was at the time when a State of Emergency had been declared and everyone was supposed to be calm and controlled, under the leash as it were. It was very clear from the beginning that management were under enormous pressure from the government not to deal with us at all because we were seen as these politicos who were just attempting to stir up a lot of trouble during a time when the State of Emergency was supposed to

---

21. Interview: Thembekile Majalisa, East London, October 1997.

keep control, and, of course, the election was during that period too, the May [parliamentary] election. [22]

There were indications that the strike was beginning to have an effect in the townships. Trains were set alight in Soweto, and by 18 April, 50 coaches were reported to have been damaged by fire. SADF troops were brought in to guard all strategic depots and railway property. [23]

Under attack

SATS management refused offers of mediation by COSATU, accusing it of being an organisation dedicated to overthrowing the status quo. At first SATS agreed to meet a negotiating committee, but then attempted to undermine elected representatives by packing the meeting with representatives selected by the management before refusing to consider a neutral arbitrator and unilaterally dissolving the team. It attempted to break the strike in a number of ways: bringing in unemployed white workers and students to act as scab labour, cancelling workers' bonuses and giving notice of its intention to evict workers from their hostels. When all else failed it called upon state power to put down the strike by force.

The rapid escalation of the strike placed a great strain on the organisational capacity of a union that was just a few months old:

> [There was] lots of confrontation with the police. They had huge meetings of workers. People were very, very upset and were wanting to assert their rights … We [officials] had an enormous amount of work. We started creating structures as fast as we could, electing shop stewards. We set up a Communication Committee on the one level and a sort of Executive Controlling Committee for the strike on the other level. These included a lot of people who were on the Exec anyway having been elected by the Conference but expanded to include representatives from a range of different workplaces around Johannesburg. (This was obviously at the beginning when it was centred pretty much around the old Transvaal area. At a later stage when things spread to some of the other areas we had representatives from Committees there that had been set up as well in Bloemfontein and Eastern Cape.)
>
> It was just complete chaos in COSATU House. Our guys would just flood the building, and they'd take over the halls, you know, and also

---

22. Interview: Mike Roussos, Johannesburg, November 1997.
23. Jabu Matiko, 1987 (b), p. 6 .

the halls in the basement and some of them took over the [basement] garages as well because there was no place to put people, there were thousands of people just coming in!

From the beginning, we said to people, 'Stay at work,' (as in 'Stay on the work premises'). 'Meet there. It could be a place for you to gather, so don't come here. Meet there, have meetings, be at your workplace but don't work and use it as opportunity to make your presence felt to talk to other workers.' And it worked for a while. We had a person who was a kind of representative from there, on this Communication Committee. At Executive Co-ordinating Committee level we would have discussions about what's going on and we'd try and feed it through the Communication Committee and the Communication Committee would, through representatives, take it up to all the different workplaces.

That was the theory and it worked reasonably well, I mean, bearing in mind the complete chaos of the circumstances plus the fact that by that stage probably 60% of our membership had been recruited in the couple of weeks prior to that. People were new. The shop stewards had been new anyway, because it had been just a few months since the Conference, and they did not really have any organisational experience. And the Executive Committee members were completely new to unions![24]

For its part, the management was perceived by the union to be little more than the tool of a government which could see the writing on the wall and had little to lose by going hell-bent to destroy all opposition.

The government, or the company initially, knew that people wouldn't be able to survive, so what they did was to start and play delaying tactics. Firstly, in order to prolong the strike, to become so arrogant as to say they won't talk to SARHWU unless everybody goes back to work. They also indicated that when people did go back to work they would select them [for re-employment] so if you go back to work voluntarily you will be selected. Then suddenly, when they could see that they could not win they started to play dragon rules, like starting to intimidate workers and withholding salaries. Finally the worst straw was when they started to put a deadline. The government put a deadline and also a condition to say if by April 21st people are not back at work, firstly they would forfeit their bonus and also they would be dismissed. Fortunately people had a better understanding now because the

24. Interview: Mike Roussos, Johannesburg, November 1997.

management were not just arrogant, they were doing things which made the people stronger like sending police, sometimes beating workers and all sorts of things. So now the atmosphere began to pick up. [25]

SATS claimed that it was willing to talk to strikers' representatives, but not SARHWU, on condition that they returned to work. Come 21 April, nobody went back to work; so on 22 April the government started to take drastic action. Over 16 000 workers were deemed to have dismissed themselves and were threatened with instant eviction from the railway compounds and hostels.

The result was not capitulation, as the government had intended, but a further strengthening of the determination of the strikers. Unlike the skilled and semi-skilled workers who were members of the factory-based unions registered and recognised by employers after the report of the Wiehahn Commission, the SARHWU membership was made up for the most part of unskilled, semi-literate labourers, toughened by the harsh conditions in which they worked, and embittered by years of unfair treatment by the railway administration.

Their leaders spoke of them with pride and not a little awe, and struggled to control the genie that had been let out of the bottle. Strikers looked on their struggle as a war and on those who stayed at work (many of whom were members of BLATU) as traitors and enemies to be dealt with accordingly. Many decided to seek retribution and, although they were officially discouraged by the union, it is clear from the following account that some shop stewards also took part.

By the time we were in COSATU House we changed the strategy. There was no need to go and ask for support because SARHWU had already told all the workers in the region that we were on strike. We still had teams of shop stewards but now those teams used to go and collect workers, no longer to ask for support but to bring them over to COSATU House. We used to have a big hall in the basement and we had a stage there so when the collectors brought the people back we used to parade them so people could see them and ask them, 'Where were you? Why weren't you supporting us?' And then they would be told they must join with us. We found the collectors were coming back with the same people time and again! They would be warned that the next time they would be punished, then they were brought again. There was a sort of kangaroo court there and they would be given some punishment, like scrubbing the steps from the top of the building all the way down, with a marshal checking that he's doing the job. [26]

---

25.   Interview: Johannes Ngcobo, Johannesburg, October 1997.
26.   As above.

When this strategy failed harsher measures were employed:

> There were those still working. Black people were still working, so at
> the meeting we started saying, 'No, for us to win the struggle we must
> make it a point that nobody's working.' We went out and we went to
> the PWI depot, which dealt with the rail installations and all that. We
> took trucks and went into each and every depot where we knew blacks
> are working and we loaded them on to a truck.
>
> In the East Rand we were meeting in Springs. So we took them there
> and we called them one by one to come and account seriously: 'Why
> are you working when others are not?' And if you didn't give a
> satisfying explanation you would get 50 lashes. Others got very seri-
> ously injured; others are damaged even now. Some, even before they
> reached the place, they were already bleeding profusely. It was because
> of anger or excitement and the likes. [27]

On the government side police harassment was commonplace:

> We had easily between 16 000 and 22 000 people out on strike.
> Increasingly there were conflicts between groups of workers and groups
> of strikers and people still at work; clashes with the police on a regular
> basis and white workers attacking individual members of ours. We
> ended up with a few people in hospital and they just kind of took it out
> on our guys because they felt that we were getting too cheeky. [28]

At the beginning of the strike, on 9 April, the union claimed that approximately
400 workers had been arrested under the state of emergency regulations or the
Intimidation Act. Over 300 were later detained in one police action at Ogies and
it became commonplace for workers to be detained because they had 'gathered
illegally'.[29] The union's offices in Germiston and COSATU House were frequently raided:

> The office [in COSATU House] was always open but the only thing that
> was happening was that we were confronted by the police by that time.
> Sometimes they surrounded the building or sometimes they came in the
> office and told us to stand against the wall. At the time we were busy
> collecting the subs for the members who were still coming to pay those
> subs. Some of the members were joining at that time. You find that the
> police, when they come in the office, they said, 'You must leave what

---

27. Interview: Robert Mashego, Johannesburg, October 1997.
28. Interview: Mike Roussos, Johannesburg, November 1997.
29. Jabu Matiko, 1987 (b), p. 3.

you are doing,' and we must open our drawers, because they needed the information (I don't know what kind of information they were actually looking for), and tell us to stand against the wall and not look at them; to face the wall. And some of the police were busy opening the drawers, not knowing what they wanted from the drawers. We'll stand there maybe about three hours. Sometimes if they came tomorrow they would tell us to go back and stand as we were standing. In the afternoon they would tell us that they don't need people in the building; we must move out of the building. So we would find out the police are standing with their guns, ready to shoot. By that time we are not allowed to use lifts; we must use steps to leave the building. [30]

There is also, more sinister, evidence of possible involvement by the clandestine Third Force which was secretly funded by hard-liners in the white security and military establishment.

The Germiston Massacre

On 22 April a violent clash took place between strikers, police and members of BLATU at Germiston (near Johannesburg). During the confrontation three workers were shot dead and many injured. Robert Mashego became involved in this event, which later became known as the Germiston massacre, on his way from his depot to a protest meeting with a trainload of dismissed railwaymen.

The area [of the depot] was full of soldiers ... We were told that if we cannot start working then we must leave because it is railway premises. It was in the morning about eight. So then, I then said to them, 'Can I be allowed to talk to these people that they should go back to work?' They agreed. They stepped aside and I started addressing them that, 'Comrades, we are told to go to work but because we don't want to work we are walking to Springs Station [instead] and then we are going to meet our comrades in Germiston.' I told the soldiers, 'Everybody doesn't want to work and therefore we are going home, as we are dismissed.' So they escorted us to a main road and we walked to Springs. It is a quite a distance; I am sure it's about 10 kilometres. We walked those kilometres, singing, with the soldiers at our back with horses and all that.

---

30. Interview: Bukie Motloung, Johannesburg, October 1997.

We got into a train at Springs Station. On our arrival at Germiston Station, to our surprise – because normally the trains don't come together at the same time – there were a lot of people at the station. When our train stopped, four canisters of tear gas were thrown into our coaches. When you [tried to] go out somebody hit you. There was a squabble of fights; others were just stabbing us with knives. Of course, we also, we knew that it is not going to be smooth on our way so we had others carrying knives. It was very rare for people to have guns by then but we would carry knives, knobkerries, assegais and the likes.

We believed it was BLATU. We thought, 'BLATU is retaliating.' (Because they announced earlier on that if we want to take over they will resist that.) So then a very serious war erupted. As this tear gas was thrown at us, before it exploded, we grabbed it and we'd throw it back to those people. I am sure there was a war for about two hours, a serious fight, and trains were just stationary there. I don't even know today as to what happened, why were those trains made to come at the very same time, waited for such a long time, and the police were there.

Nobody was arrested up until when people saw that now there is a serious deal that is taking place and then they started releasing dogs on us. [People fled] but we – some of us who believed that we have got the responsibility to lead the constituencies that we brought in – remained

Mopping up blood after clashes between security police and striking railway workers.

119

and started identifying the people. There were a lot of people who died; a lot were seriously injured. People were dying inside trains, on the platforms – one, two, three and four – on the other side of the station and others even right on the road. SARHWU people were simply identified because they were wearing red, red T-shirts of SARHWU. But some of our members, when they met somebody that they knew was a BLATU person, they picked him up, ran away with him, killed him wherever they are going to kill him and so I can't give an exact number of those – but it was a lot of people.

But the big surprise was when we went out to identify these people at the station. I still remember exactly, that out of the people that we picked with overalls of the railways and who were blacks, earlier on, when we wanted to identify them we found that four of them were whites but they were painted black! And inside, inside their overalls, they were wearing South African Police uniform. Up until today really I do not have answers of what was the motive. But I can debate, and I believe that it was a well-calculated attack which was aimed at us on that particular day. [31]

At mid-day a further confrontation took place at Doornfontein station which left three dead and many injured. Later on the same day about 200 members of the security forces invaded COSATU House, attacking and beating those inside and arresting many more and forcing out members of SARHWU who were holding a meeting there.

We took a decision to join the West Rand people at the Freedom Square. There we were surrounded by the police. They were saying to us that we should disperse within seconds but we could not disperse because they were closing our way out to the station and they were also closing our way out into town. So we would have to take a direction where they will push some of us into the Caspirs [armoured cars]. There were a lot of Caspirs and also video machines and the likes.

Then something automatic just happened. I do not remember anyone giving instruction, but I just saw people entering those shops where you see hacksaws, big knives, and pangas being sold and everyone grabbed whatever was in front of him and we faced these white soldiers. They were shooting but we were coming. Of course, our people died but a lot of soldiers also died. A lot of people were also injured, hundreds of

---

31.   Interview: Robert Mashego, Johannesburg, October 1997.

people, our members and also soldiers and police. Because if we saw police we just hacked on them. [32]

Increasing violence

Following these killings government repression increased and the strike rapidly reached a level of violence on both sides remarkable even in a country noted for the violence of its political life. 'A situation was very rapidly developing where the railway dispute was becoming the focus for a broad upsurge of the South African people fighting for an end to apartheid rule.'[33] Africans throughout the Transvaal began boycotting buses and other forms of transport and the whole community was rapidly becoming involved. To some extent, however, this meant that the union began to lose control of the strike.

> Everything started to go wrong. Firstly, the venue where we were meeting was destroyed. The police came to Germiston on the 23rd and shut everything so we didn't have our own place and they started to detain most people. We started to regroup people and send out people who had been informed what was happening and everybody started to be angry. Everybody started to be quite violent because there was nowhere we could meet and start to tell people that, 'This is right,' or 'This we'll not do.'
>
> [The massacre] turned the strike quite ugly because now people felt that they had no alternative. They'd been dismissed, they had been killed, so now they started to vent their anger against people who were the cause of the problem, like people who were still working. Now the strike became quite violent. The government started it and the workers automatically responded because they felt that if they don't do anything then it means they won't be able to go back to work because their aim was not to go back to work without their demands being addressed. [34]

The strength of the union – its militant membership and strong grassroots organisation – was also its weakness. As SARHWU's national leaders were forced underground the influence of the militant shop stewards committee grew, and while Mike Roussos and Justice Langa issued press statements from the offices of SARHWU upstairs in COSATU House, something very different was going on in the basement.

---

32. As above. Among those who died in the strike were SARHWU members Joseph Mampuru, Christopher Jozana, Molahlehi Mohlakametsi, Moses Mokgopa, Jeremiah Diutlwileng, Zonwebele Mogubata.
33. NUR, 1987, p. 14.
34. Interview: Nelson Ndinisa, Johannesburg, October 1997.

> The shop stewards had their own committee apart; there was another room in COSATU that only the shop stewards could go into to discuss and come up with some ideas on how to strengthen the strike. When we came back from the negotiations we used to go to the hall and give a report. When the strike intensified the workers realised that management did not want to hear and they started coming up with other actions. But they were not discussed openly; the shop stewards used to discuss and then form some committees. [35]

These committees are likely to have been responsible for various acts of sabotage, including the burning of trains at Orlando Station, and for the murder of strike-breaking workers. Many of the shop stewards and ordinary members were poorly educated and unsophisticated. They were suffering genuine hardship as a result of the strike and they were extremely angry with the management and with strike-breaking workers. As Mike Roussos explains:

> What happened is our guys decided that they were going to retaliate and for a while there were kind of informal structures that I discovered much later had been set up. The workers basically decided by themselves that they had had enough of these bloody people. They were busy getting killed and their families were starving and these other guys were going to work. They were really angry and they set up informal gangs of people and they went round grabbing people and beating them up. A lot of our guys were from the rural areas and traditional influences were important to us. They called in a guy from the Transkei, who was meant to be a very powerful sort of witch doctor. It was all very secretive. They weren't going to tell the Executive Committee but I found out when I walked in on this huge meeting. There were fully 500 of our guys there, basically, stripped down to their underwear and there was a big ceremony going on. It turned out later that this guy was giving them *muti* [medicine] to protect them from bullets. (Remember our guys had been shot by then.)
>
> A couple of days later a group of guys grabbed some people who were working, scabs, and they brought them to a massive meeting in the basement. I mean, we were sitting upstairs doing various things not knowing that there's this huge meeting going on in the basement. There must have been fully 2 000 people and the guards bring the scabs up to the front, and they said, 'These guys are going to be killed because they're killing our families.' I was in the office at the time and the guys

---

35.   Interview: Jonas Makhavhu, Johannesburg, October 1997.

came to me and they said, 'Listen, we need a car, we've got to have some petrol.' Then off they went. I didn't know it but in fact they were taking those workers off to do them in on the side of the road near City Deep.[36]

Arrests of strike leaders

The deaths of the strike-breakers triggered a huge government response that spread to include COSATU and its affiliates as well as SARHWU. The first rally to launch the COSATU 'living wage' campaign was banned and many shop stewards and union officials were detained. In Kroonstad the COSATU offices (which included the SARHWU office) were closed down. SARHWU offices in East London were burnt out. In Vereeniging the state attempted to close down SARHWU offices using the Group Areas Act.

On 29 April armed police surrounded COSATU House. The occasion for the attack was a mass meeting of railway workers to discuss the next stage of the strike and the planned COSATU two-day stayaway to mark the 6 May elections. Nelson Ndinisa was present:

> After the police had discovered that people were slain [i.e. the scabs] they had one of their biggest operations. I have yet to see that type of operation again. They surrounded COSATU House; we had soldiers, we had police, we had a helicopter hovering above. When we got out we are all searched one by one – all of us. We were more than six or seven thousand but all of us were searched one by one; other people were arrested. It was one of the biggest events.[37]

Police moved through the building, seizing union materials. Workers were roughly searched and beaten up. At the end of the day the union had more members in prison, and many more injured.

Among them was Robert Mashego:

> We were surrounded by the police and we were called two by two to pass through a guard of honour made of Caspirs. In each of these Caspirs, there were two people wearing balaclavas and when you come, it is either the person shakes his head or he nods his head. If he nods his head you are jailed; if he shakes his head you are allowed to pass. My assumption of that action was that if the person shakes his head you are

36. Interview: Mike Roussos, Johannesburg, November 1997.
37. Interview: Nelson Ndinisa, Johannesburg, October 1997.

innocent; if he nods his head you are guilty. So, most unfortunately, on my way to pass, somebody nodded his head and we were taken. [38]

In the period following the mass dismissals almost all the union leadership were arrested, including the President, Justice Langa, the Transvaal Regional Secretary, Johannes Ngcobo, and the Education Officer, Mike Roussos. Johannes Ngcobo was arrested at his flat following a union planning meeting in the week before Easter:

I was picked up at my flat. I was staying in Johannesburg, in Hillbrow. I was coming from a planning session with the Provincial Organiser and the then General Secretary where we had been evaluating what the management were offering so that we can begin to sit down and say, 'How much gain have we won? Can we begin to discuss whether workers should go back to work?' I went home to see my woman because she was now panicking because this was the beginning of the strike and I was underground.

The police were monitoring our movements. As soon as I arrived at the flat at about 8.00 pm we watched the television. At about 9.10 when we looked outside – I was staying at the 17th floor – Pretoria Street was surrounded by police; it was blue. Then I said to a comrade who I was with in the house, 'We are not going to go out we are going to be arrested.' It was obvious! You know, we are, like, friendly with the security guards. They called to say, 'The police are at each and every floor. They want to come to your room and I am saying you are not there.' So we waited for the police to come. They only knocked at the house at about 2 and indeed we were beaten immediately when we were arrested. I was put in chains immediately and in handcuffs.

In the vicinity at the Highpoint area, all the shops, which are usually working 24 hours, were forced to close down. When we came out of the lift everybody wanted to see exactly who was this person. There we found some of the workers were already picked up. They were the ones who had pointed me out and said that I was assisting them logistically with whatever they needed. I was the taken from Highpoint to John Vorster Square [police station]. On my arrival there was a braai at 7th floor – police were celebrating. Then shortly, at about 3, they came with one worker ... We were then taken from John Vorster Square to Brixton Murder and Robbery Squad cells. It was where we were beaten up. We were questioned, of course, about the ANC's involvement in the strike

---

38.   Interview: Robert Mashego, Johannesburg, October 1997.

and all those sort of things. Then the following day we are taken to a doctor and we complained to the doctor that we had been beaten up and after that we were beaten up again and then went to Sandton where they were actually questioning almost all of us. [39]

At 3.30 a.m. on 7 May, one week after the police raid and immediately after the successful stayaway, COSATU House was once again the focus of attention when two bomb explosions effectively destroyed the building. The effect on SARHWU was disastrous. All the union's resources, including membership records, files and equipment, were destroyed or confiscated by the security police. At the same time, even more importantly, the union was deprived of its organising centre.

> When COSATU House was bombed that created a worse problem because after the Germiston problem everybody was able to come to COSATU House but when COSATU House was also bombed we didn't have any venue to meet. We had to start to meet and co-ordinate workers. That was the most terrible time. People were starting to lose faith, lose hope and direction, and people were being arrested. [40]

On the morning after the bombing Mike Roussos was picked up on suspicion of involvement in the murder of the strike-breakers (falsely said to have occurred in COSATU House). He was taken to John Vorster Square and held in solitary confinement:

> I was kept completely by myself ... The anniversary of the State of Emergency happened during that time. It was one year after they first declared the State of Emergency and they were due to either release it or renew it. In fact they renewed it and what they did when they renewed it they transferred all of us to Section 29 [of the Act] which meant that we had no access to lawyers; we were basically incommunicado. The Commissioner came to my cell and gloated as he took everything that I had to read and everything else. He said, 'Right. Now do you think it's funny to use lawyers against us? Now you'll sit you bastard!' and he took photographs of my family and with great glee stripped the cell and said, 'Right. Now you're under Section 29 and you're not going to see anybody else.'
>
> During the course of my interrogation during that time they kept on giving me statements that others had written, basically saying that I had ordered the other guys to get killed, that I had given orders that those

---

39. Interview: Johannes Ngcobo, Johannesburg, October 1997.
40. Interview: Nelson Ndinisa, Johannesburg, October 1997.

people should be killed and it was carried out by people within the union. Obviously their attempt was to try and find a way of implicating me as the central leadership figure within the union at that time, certainly the most visible one ... If they could link me then they would link the union, officially. [41]

To avoid capture the strike leaders moved from address to address, sleeping in cars or wherever they could find a bed. Everyone the police could find who they thought was on any of the strike committees or in any sort of national leadership in any form was arrested. The strike continued but under conditions of severe difficulty.

In London SACTU, under the leadership of Archie Sibeko (known there by his MK name, Zola Zembe) was mobilising international support, both financial and political, from trade unions and other sympathetic organisations. A strike fund was set up and events were organised to publicise the plight of the strikers. The British NUR set up an organisation called Rail against Apartheid, organised a petition for the release of detainees and invited strike leaders to England. When they were arrested it dispatched its own fact-finding delegation. The atmosphere of the time is caught by their report which comments on the power of the mass marches of strikers accompanied by singing and toyi-toyi dancing to inspire and to motivate.

> Arrangements were made for us to meet SARHWU leaders who had so far avoided arrest. During our first discussions with them, we came to understand how during the dispute the relationship between the leaders and the strikers was maintained in spite of all the difficulties. Whilst we were actually talking to them, we suddenly heard hundreds of voices singing freedom songs. This was coming from the streets of Johannesburg and it was the strikers coming in for the daily report from their stewards. They packed into a meeting hall and those who couldn't get in went to the nearby blacks-only parks and squares. When the first mass meeting finished and reports from the stewards had been heard, the mass meeting would then send runners to the parks to bring in those who could not attend the first meeting. These rolling mass-meetings were another example of the loss of COSATU House. All decisions for the direction of the strike were taken at these meetings. [42]

---

41. Interview: Mike Roussos, Johannesburg, November 1997.
42. NUR, 1987, p. 19; The representatives of Rail against Apartheid were Doreen Weppler and George Revell.

In the absence of the elected officials the organisation of the strike fell to rank-and-file leaders like Nelson Ndinisa, a railway worker from the East Rand who had joined the union at the beginning of the strike.

> Virtually the whole leadership was arrested at that time. In order to maintain the strike other people moved up and new leaders emerged. We were not registered as leaders [office holders]; we were ordinary members, but whoever was a leader, like shop stewards, was arrested so people who were like us had to move up and take the leadership of the organisation. One of our jobs was to arrange things, in terms of burying people who had been shot, mobilising international committees, mobilising COSATU and so on. Also, nationally, people were starting to join us because they had seen that it has become terrible … everything was chaos and the company still didn't want to negotiate with us. [43]

Pressure was, however, being brought to bear on the SATS administration from a variety of directions. There were reports that the PWI rail track, which was the busiest in the Reef, was posing maintenance problems for SATS and that the company was finding it difficult to replace skilled and experienced workers with white scab labour. A strike publicity committee produced leaflets and issued press statements, and committees from the shop stewards council contacted township organisations and rallied support from the community. Black commuters were taking advantage of the absence of ticket examiners to travel free of charge and SATS revenue was badly affected.

In addition to the international support organised by SACTU there were gestures of solidarity from a number of other organisations. The South African Council of Churches provided temporary accommodation for the union in its own building, Khotso House (itself bombed the following year), and church leaders called for negotiations to end the strike. Despite the misgivings of some of its moderate leaders about the strike, COSATU provided publicity and support. The Paper, Wood and Allied Workers Union and the Food and Allied Workers Union refused to handle SATS goods.

Throughout the strike the channels of communication with SATS were kept open through SARHWU's legal advisers and the involvement of other third parties from industry and the church. Soon after the dismissal of the strikers on 22 April SARHWU lawyers made an application to the Johannesburg Supreme Court for the dismissals to be set aside on the grounds that an invalid law had been used. The case was due to be heard on 25 May but was postponed until 9

---

43. Interview: Nelson Ndinisa, Johannesburg, October 1997.

June. On 27 May the company issued eviction notices to 9 000 hostel dwellers, ordering those who wanted to retain their accommodation to re-apply on 16 June (the anniversary of the Soweto Uprising).

As the date for the hearing approached, however, the case revealed major differences within SATS management. On one hand the Director General, Bart Grove, took a hard line and wanted to see SARHWU destroyed. On the other the Deputy General Manager, Dr Anton Moolman, was willing to resolve the strike through negotiation. Moolman had participated in an internal enquiry into labour relations in SATS chaired by Professor Nic Wiehahn that argued for a limited right to strike and the extension of the principle of collective bargaining to the public sector.

> The lawyers at that stage started to adopt what you term a tactical approach. They identified the leadership of the company; they targeted Moolman and they said to him that he should approach other ministers. [Pressure was put on the company] so they created a structure based on a legal team from them to negotiate with the SARHWU legal team. So SARHWU wasn't involved, the company wasn't involved; it was only lawyers. [44]

Victory?

On 5 June these negotiations produced a formula that SARHWU was able to present as a victory. As from 8 June strikers were to be reinstated without loss of benefit, although they would lose their bonuses; no strikers would be victimised and those in detention would be re-employed on their release. Workers with over two years' service were given permanent terms of employment for the first time and the right to elect their own representatives. In addition, hostels at Delmore and Kaserne would be given a R10 million upgrade. The union had never been so popular and its membership had never been so high. At the same time, however, there were signs that the victory might prove a hollow one.

Although 90–95% of those dismissed were reinstated, those who had been convicted of crimes related to the dispute were excluded. Around 1 000 members had been detained during the strike and many, including many of the leadership, remained in jail. Mike Roussos was confined for two and a half months. He was released after lawyers successfully argued a test case that his Section 29 detention was illegal, but the authorities refused to release those others detained under the same section who were charged with the murder of the strike breakers. Four of

---

44. As above.

these were sentenced to hang (although the sentences were later commuted) and four given lengthy prison terms.

Racially discriminatory grading and pension schemes remained and the union was still unrecognised. The Minister for Transport claimed that the settlement had nothing to do with SARHWU and refused to recognise the union. BLATU was still viewed by SATS as the majority representative union and the company refused to hold a ballot to prove representativity. Despite the agreement that had been reached, workers were victimised. Members were transferred to lower category jobs and a number of strikers who had been replaced by white workers did not get their jobs back. At Jan Smuts Airport 78 workers were denied the right to apply for reinstatement until SARHWU lawyers intervened and on 30 June seven workers, five of them members of the strike negotiating committee, were detained.

Summary

The next few years were to prove difficult ones, throwing into question the role to be played by SARHWU in the final act of the liberation struggle. The 1987 strike has been described as both a triumph and a disaster. Looked at with hindsight it could be said that, in the short term, success on the political front was bought at the expense of success on the industrial front. This would, however, be to ignore the extent to which a political victory was necessary before progress could be made. SARHWU was outstandingly successful in capitalising on the discontent of the railway workers, in mobilising them and in motivating them to continue the strike for almost three months in the face of tremendous police harassment and violence. SACTU and the ANC had calculated that no other group of workers (apart from the mineworkers, whose leaders were opposed to 'political' strikes) could have such an impact and they were proved right. The strike was supported by the black communities and the UDF and acted as a focal point and a catalyst for opposition to the apartheid regime. It attracted international attention and helped to encourage South Africa's allies in the West to put pressure on the government, thus contributing to the beginning of the negotiations which finally put an end to apartheid.

In terms of the union's organisation and struggle for recognition there were also positive gains. Membership increased to around 22 000; rank-and-file leaders were energised and the kind of loyalty to the union was generated that is only achieved when people are tested together in the fire. Real improvements were achieved for members and, whilst it did not obtain recognition, SARHWU was no longer forced to operate underground in a clandestine manner. In other ways, however, the union was badly damaged by the strike.

SARHWU had rushed, or been pushed, into the dispute within only a few months of its re-formation. Its officers were inexperienced and its structures untried, and the arrest of so many of its top and middle-ranking leaders during the course of the strike left the union largely adrift in the hands of informal committees who, left to themselves, were unable to take matters forward. A culture of conflict and militant action had been fostered by the strike and the immediate challenge was to gain recognition and to negotiate some solid improvements in the pay and conditions of railway workers. As the following chapter shows, however, the next few years brought new challenges and few achievements.

5

The Struggle for Recognition

The end of the 1987 strike produced a formula that SARHWU was able to present as a victory. At the same time, however, there were signs that the victory might create its own problems. The arrest of most of the leadership during the strike had left the union temporarily rudderless at a time when membership records had been destroyed. There was an urgent need for structural reorganisation at both national and regional levels; it was in dire straits financially and it needed to defeat BLATU and win recognition from the company in order to put itself on an even keel. In order to do this it had to be united but instead it was split from top to bottom with disagreements and disputes.

The next five years were to be a difficult time in the union's development. It was involved in both a bitter struggle for recognition by management and an almost equally bitter internal struggle about the way forward for the union and the kind of leadership needed at that stage of development. Inevitably, the second interfered with the first and management and government exploited and magnified the disagreements between individuals, with the objective of making the union less effective as a fighting force.

Reorganisation

The reorganisation of the union was vital if the battle for recognition was to be carried forward. Membership was increasing in leaps and bounds; in the heartland of the strike, in the Southern Transvaal, 'everybody was agitating to be a member', and even in Natal, where the strike had barely got off the ground, 'people were making long queues and busy joining SARHWU'.[1] Accurate membership figures are difficult to determine but immediately following the 1987 strike membership was reported to be 25 000 (out of the 95 305 African employees of SATS nation-wide). In the following year national membership stood at around 43 000. Reported numbers in the Southern Transvaal rose to 22 000 and Natal grew to be the second largest region with 15 000 members.[2] Black railway workers were increasingly looking to SARHWU to redress their grievances and bring them some positive benefits but success brought new problems at a time in which the union was already suffering from organisational and leadership problems.

In a contemporary article in the *South African Labour Bulletin*, Renée Roux described the problems encountered by the union:

> The detention of experienced worker leadership was a severe blow. The lack of formal recognition, which enables union officials or other union members to service workers, was a particular problem. It was extremely hard to consolidate union structures. The union [was] forced to collect subscriptions by hand. This stretches resources and limits the income of the union ... [Following the 1987 strike] the union had to become a national force to address the needs of railway workers ... [It] has had to develop national structures and identify national priorities. To accomplish this the union has had to accommodate the different backgrounds, strengths and weaknesses of each region and distribute resources appropriately. Building and consolidating organisation after rapid growth is one of the most difficult tasks facing the trade union movement.[3]

Financial stability was a major problem. The union still refused to register because this would mean acceptance of being a 'blacks only' union, which it was not, and would not be. Although, as a result of the strike, shop stewards in some areas were now able to present workers' grievances to management, SATS was not prepared to grant recognition and the stopping of union subs out of salaries (stop orders). Subs were still collected by hand. Members paid their dues at the union office or to workplace representatives and as a result the union began to suffer financially. SARHWU had, at that time, about 18 offices nationally and about 55 employees whose salaries had to be paid. The contributions from workers were not coming in smoothly and the union's employees frequently went unpaid.[4]

---

1. Interviews: Robert Mashego, Johannesburg, October 1997; David Moeti, East London, October 1997.
2. *IR Data & Union Profiles* (9)6, August 1991.
3. Renée Roux, 1989, p. 75 .
4. Interview: David Moeti, East London, October 1997.

An organisational framework had been set in place by the 1986 conference but the arrest and detention of the majority of national and regional leaders had destroyed these preliminary structures. When Mike Roussos was released at the end of 1987 he found the administration of the union 'in tatters':

> It was partly from the detentions, partly from the fact that our records didn't even exist any more. They just kind of vanished when the bomb happened in COSATU House; they were ransacked. They just took whatever they wanted and got rid of it and it was a matter of trying to reconstruct from scratch ... So of course things were in chaos, and there was a little bit of difficulty in thinking about that sort of thing – the whole job of reconstructing, putting everything together again and basically consolidating structures that we didn't really have before – because we had all these new members now and a bit more access, because management was much more wary than they were before ... There was a lot of attempting to find ways of rebuilding structures, employing new organisers and ... just finding ways of really completing the process that had been started by the conference but had been completely interrupted (and, of course, magnified, enormously) through the strike. [5]

Regional Developments

SARHWU was disadvantaged by its position as an unregistered union – which the management used to justify continued refusal of recognition. The union was able to deal with minor grievances but not to participate in discussions at a higher level regarding major issues such as wages and general improvements in conditions of service. In order to succeed the union needed to gain recognition. SATS required that SARHWU must represent a majority of workers nationally in a particular racial category and register under the Labour Relations Act (LRA). The rights won by the strike in the Transvaal were not automatically extended to other regions and it was clear that SARHWU would have to fight for these rights, step by step, in each region. To this end, shop stewards and organisers worked hard to build the union's regional and branch structures and to provide a service for members. It was not an easy job.

> That was one of the toughest times. We didn't have the status to act as a [recognised] shop steward so what used to happen was I used to go to work my shift, then after my shift I had to run to Johannesburg and stay

---

5.   Interview: Mike Roussos, Johannesburg, November 1997.

in Johannesburg the rest of the day and night. Sometimes we were sleeping there at the office, discussing and putting structures in place. It was a question of sacrifice because we had to work, otherwise we would have been dismissed, but at your own earliest time you had to run away [to do union work].[6]

In 1987 SARHWU was not yet functioning properly as a national organisation in the way that it did later. The union was organised around five major bases – Southern Transvaal, Durban, East London, Cape Town and Bloemfontein – each of which had its own distinctive history and problems, as the following accounts illustrate.

Southern Transvaal

The Southern Transvaal was the largest of the existing regions. It had been the first region to organise and had gone to the 1986 launch with its own elected Secretary (Johannes Ngcobo) and a Central Shop Stewards' Co-ordinating Committee already in place. It had the majority of the membership and its role at the centre of the 1987 strike produced a hard core of members who had been tested and strengthened by the struggle.

> The Wits region was the most organised. Also you learn very fast that a strike organises workers. That '87 strike was a learning curve in the shortest time possible for the Wits region. During that strike they went out and used the infrastructure of SATS to deliver the message and core groups were formed in main centres. At the end of the strike there was a sufficient skeleton out there to build on from the action of the Wits region. For a long time to come that region had its way because they were the advanced sections of the organisation. The best shop stewards, the best that SARHWU has, came from that baptism of fire for three months.
>
> The Southern Transvaal region didn't have branches and so on. From the strike, that core of shop stewards became the source of leadership. Not the Head Office could tell them anything; not the regional structure could tell them anything. They had their own coffers and collected money. We never knew how much there was in the coffers. That was their business; they controlled the money and they decided which operations would be funded. So of course there were huge debates about workers who have got their own means, and a battle for the money to now be controlled by the organisation. Really, it raised all kinds of

---

6.   Interview: Nelson Ndinisa, Johannesburg, October 1997.

debates about workers controlling their own organisation and owning their resources to do so, versus debates about the role of leadership. And for the leadership it raised questions about whether or not this group is actually becoming now dictatorial or becoming a law unto itself.[7]

The region continued to operate through the Central Shop Stewards Co-ordinating Committee until formal structures were finally launched in 1989/90. The merit of the committee was that it was a broadly inclusive democratic structure that allowed rank and file members to participate in decision making. The disadvantage, according to Stephen Matlou, who later became the Chairperson of the region, was that there was very little discipline and direction:

> At certain points we had comrades who were sort of like an armed wing for SARHWU – an armed wing that had to defend our membership because we were fighting with the police, we were fighting with other forces, we were fighting with the army and we couldn't allow a situation whereby people would just perish without defending themselves. We had to form that. It was formed and it was operating but what happened was that these comrades became so powerful in the direction of discussing even policy issues that they were sort of a para-military structure that would come and try to give orders to the leadership as to what to do and what not to do – which then became counter-productive. You had a loose moribund structure. Everybody would then claim himself to be a leader and claim to be doing certain programmes in SARHWU's name because there were no structures. Interim structures were put in place. The interim leadership was Isaac Mnisi – an old man. We used to call him Madiba [teacher]. He was part of the leadership. But the problem was that we had two factions, the East Rand faction and the West Rand Central faction.[8]

In the eyes of some observers these disagreements were the source of later disunity within the union as a whole, as the two factions competed with each other for the leadership of the region and for the national leadership of SARHWU.

Durban

The second largest of the regions was Southern Natal (Durban) where the South African Allied Workers Union (SAAWU) and the National Federation of Workers (NFW), under Magwaza Maphalala and Mathews Oliphant, had

---

7. Interview: Martin Sebakwane, Johannesburg, November 1997.
8. Interview: Stephen Matlou, Cape Town, October 1997.

delivered their railway membership to SARHWU even before the re-launch in 1986. Organising was difficult, however, and early organisers like Sello Ntai (who was to become the first national General Secretary of SARHWU) were detained and harassed by the management of SATS. Among the earliest recruits in the region was David Moeti who took over from Ntai when he left for the new SARHWU head office in Johannesburg.

> Within a week or three we had already recruited about 200 workers into the union. Then I said to Sello, 'We are not being effective. Let me take some sick leave and I will go around and mobilise lots of workers.' Then I recruited about 400 or so. But then they trapped me, the security branch, with the Personnel Department in the railways. At the time I was in the office and I was issuing cards to workers and this guy is coming to join. He joins the union and I sign his card and I give the card to him. I was not aware that the guy was being sent by the Personnel Department and the security police. I was called to the staff office and I was told over the counter, 'You're dismissed'. There was no legal framework like we have now where I could take up the company legally. I told myself, 'I am not going to give in. I am not going to work anywhere. I will fight until liberation. After liberation I will come back and work here.' I worked in the SARHWU offices full time. It was me and Sello working and we had some guys. Transvaal was more advanced than us but Natal was coming up very strongly.
>
> Then the interim committee that we had formed out of comrade Pholotho and other comrades nationally took Sello who was working with me in Durban to Cape Town to go and start up working on SARHWU – because Cape Town was not even recruiting. Sello was there for three months. Then we had our first national congress. We elected the President; we elected the General Secretary and we elected the Assistant General Secretary. My friend Sello was elected General Secretary. So I had to go back and work in Natal alone. I knew the railway workers were many. I knew I could form a big union out of SARHWU. So I went out determined. I was not being paid. I was dismissed from work and I used my pension money. That is how I survived. I worked right through 1987 recruiting SARHWU, working hard in Natal and I was also being politically motivated. But while I was still working in Natal trying to recruit a guy from outside the country, an MK guy, came to me and he was looking for financial help, accommodation and everything. I really didn't want to be involved because at that stage we were already being warned not to work with MK guys. I

started helping the guy here and there and he was finally arrested and I was detained with him. For six months I was under detention. They finally released me when they couldn't charge me and when I went out I went to recruit SARHWU again. At the time when I was detained I was actually organising a strike in Natal because railway workers and joiners had gone on strike. We were not really thoroughly organised in Natal so it took a long time to try and organise a strike but it was not successful because they locked me up. So like the other trade union leaders of SARHWU in 1987, I was locked up during the 1987 strike. When I came out, the strike had boosted the union to a very high position and the union was forming. I could see people were making long queues and busy joining SARHWU when I came out and that is how SARHWU in Natal became a very big union. [9]

Outside Durban and the Southern Transvaal organisation was still rudimentary but efforts were made to build up formal structures to accommodate the new members who had joined the union during and immediately following the 1987 strike.

East London and Port Elizabeth

SARHWU in the Eastern Cape had its origins in the strong militant tradition built up by SAAWU in East London but its recruitment was slowed by management hostility and competition from two rival unions – the NUR (National Union of Railway Workers) and ARAHWU (The African Railway and Harbour Workers Union). In the early 1980s the organisation of railway workers in the area had been split between the General Workers Union (GWU), which had organised port workers in East London and Port Elizabeth, and the South African Allied Workers Union (SAAWU). When SAAWU agreed to the redistribution of its railway members to SARHWU this was opposed by a group of local leaders who supported the formation of the National Union of Railway Workers (NUR). Boyce Melitafa was local organiser for SAAWU at the time:

As an organiser with SAAWU I represented the workers in many cases. It was very difficult. Then at the time when COSATU was established in 1985 it became clear that we should go for one union. It was resolved that instead of a new union they should revive their old union which was a member of SACTU, which is SARHWU today. I was instrumental in convincing workers to join that union. It was difficult because workers were very in love with SAAWU. But we managed to convince

9. Interview: David Moeti, East London, October 1997.

them to revive SARHWU. Some individuals from FOSATU tried to influence the formation of another union here in East London. That was the NUR. NUR mainly came from SAAWU members. BLATU was a small union. There was no chance of it being a threat at the time. The only threat was NUR because that was formed by some of our comrades and some from FOSATU. [10]

The GWU lost support as a result of the failure of the 1982 strike in Port Elizabeth (described earlier) and in 1986 it merged with the Transport and General Workers Union but the NUR maintained a strong local presence. The regional management of the railways was exceptionally harsh and SARHWU recruitment proved difficult until the success of the 1987 strike and the reinstatement of those workers who had been dismissed (in contrast to the 1982 failure) provided it with a boost.

At the end of the 1987 strike the branch chairperson and secretary were Thembekile Majalisa and M Magadla. The agreement between SARHWU and SATS brought an increase in membership which shot up from around 500 to several thousand.

This company had never been shaken up by the workers. It used to dominate workers all the time. After that everybody was interested in SARHWU. Even from unions like BLATU. Workers resigned from those unions and came to SARHWU. But the management didn't want to be defeated and it used to do things that provoked the workers. For example, disciplining workers for minor things, so we used to have some problems. SATS was a government company and it was a stronghold of the then South African regime. Even if someone was a superintendent in a depot he was a soldier and had a high rank of major or sergeant. Even the regional managers were all in those positions in the SADF [South African Defence Force]. [11]

The management in East London was reluctant to implement the agreement and union members were victimised. Thembekile Majalisa was dismissed in 1987 together with 200 striking workers and although he was reinstated after three months he could not return to his former job at the harbour.

In June 1987 the Regional Executive Committee dismissed their previous regional organiser as being unsatisfactory and Derrick Simoko, formerly SAAWU organiser in Durban, took his place. Branches were organised throughout the

---

10. Interview: Boyce Melitafa, East London, October 1997.
11. Interviews: Vuyani Elvis Mzayifani, Thobile Christopher Jekwa, East London, October 1997.

region, including the 'homeland' of the Transkei but Port Elizabeth still proved a problem.

> We formed a branch executive. At that time the regional structure was not formed, but East London executive committee was acting as an interim regional committee. After that we organised Queenstown workers and set up a branch there. At that time the ANC was banned. The only organisation which was organising in the country was the UDF so we joined the UDF. We carried on organising the workers up to Umtata and up to PE. We started by organising the small towns and winning the workers there because the supervisors were very conservative. Then they resigned to join SARHWU. We didn't have any membership in PE because everybody was a member of BLATU or NUR. We were working hard to organise the workers in PE and Cape Midland, travelling by night. As soon as Derrick arrived here we were a real trade union. The NUR was in PE and Jo'burg. They were working to form it here, and there are still some members here. We worked very hard going to PE every weekend to organise the workers, travelling by night. We stationed Derrick in PE for three months and finally he was successful but there was no structure there until we set up an interim structure in 1989.[12]

Cape Town

In Cape Town too it was only after the 1987 strike that SARHWU was able to organise openly. Like David Moeti in Durban and several other SARHWU activists Otto Balfour joined SARHWU after becoming disillusioned with the Black Staff Association:

> I was treasurer and chairman of the Cape Town Staff Association. Then somebody told me about SARHWU and I said, 'This is what I've been looking for,' – because the staff association wasn't a proper union. Even the agendas for our discussions were from management. There was no mandate from the workers. In those days if you talked about SARHWU or the ANC you were caught by the police. The railways had their own police. It was difficult to recognise who was a member of SARHWU because everybody was afraid. I remember one day we decided to hold a meeting in a church. The pamphlets were distributed to the Western Cape and the then chairperson of the staff association found one of these pamphlets and asked me about them. I said, 'I know nothing about it.'

---

12. Interview: Thembekile Majalisa, East London, October 1997.

Then he requested me to attend that meeting so that I could give him information about what is discussed there!

As the years went by the thing that was happening was the dismissing of people unfairly. I didn't want to see that so I defended the people in the disciplinary hearings. And everybody I represented I organised to join SARHWU. When the strike of 1987 happened we were about 2 000 members but we couldn't participate in the strike because we weren't all in the same place. Most of the people were contract labourers who were staying in the dock compound and we couldn't get there without a permit. What we did the following year was to pressurise the railway with the other unions that it isn't right to keep the people in the dock compound. It's better to keep them in Langa compound. A lot of people were dying there and we said they were dying because of the gangsters who were attacking them. We knew that if they were in Langa compound we would get a chance to organise them into SARHWU. The following year, 1988, the railway moved the people to Langa and we got a chance to organise them to be SARHWU members.[13]

Bloemfontein and Kimberley

In the Orange Free State and Northern Cape the formation of COSATU in 1985 provided a major impetus to workers like Bonakele Jonas who later became President of SARHWU.

The union in Bloemfontein was first organised by SAAWU. COSATU had been formed; people were starting to go on strike and that captured the imagination of the ordinary worker. We joined in numbers and I was elected the secretary but we were persecuted and harassed by the police for joining the union. There were police who harassed us left and right. You couldn't even concentrate on what you were doing. Management also used to harass our members, send special branch to us who would take you and then try to portray you as an impimpi, a traitor. It was during that time when the necklace was rife and if you make a mistake you are dead. We joined in numbers but our progress was hampered by this police harassment.[14]

Bonnie Thekisho came to SARHWU through his involvement with the UDF.

It was through the area committee of the UDF that I was introduced to SARHWU and I was given the task of recruiting railway workers in

---

13. Interview: Otto Balfour, Johannesburg, October 1997.
14. Interview: Bonakele Jonas, Johannesburg, October 1997.

1986. There was a drive that we need to bring all of the progressive unions into the Northern Cape. Certain comrades were allocated to certain unions to focus specifically on those unions and that is how I came to SARHWU. There was a state of emergency. Everybody was in hiding except workers who didn't belong to unions. We started off by identifying strong key activists so that they could go into the workplace and recruit some of the workers. It just caught like a veld fire. We started off with a first meeting with a grouping of about six. The next meeting it was half a hall full, the next meeting it was a whole hall and we had to move from a small hall to a large hall. Even the security police did not expect it. When the railway workers surfaced it was just too fast for them. They didn't have the time to think and plan against that so that when they knew these workers were organised they started by indiscriminately detaining and harassing but they didn't want to provoke a strike. [15]

Charles Ntlangula, one of the earlier recruits, was himself responsible for recruiting Johnny Potgieter who became chairperson of the Kimberley branch before being elected to national office in 1988. Response to the 1987 strike was patchy. A number of leaders including Bonakele Jonas were arrested; workers in Bloemfontein struck but were forced back to work at gunpoint, and in Kimberley the level of organisation was insufficient to sustain strike action. During the course of the strike Kimberley acted as a base for national officials such as Themba Khuswayo who left Johannesburg to avoid arrest.

Relations with SATS

At the time of the 1987 strike SATS still clung to the attitudes of the early 1980s. As part of the public sector it was regarded as an essential service. Strikes were prohibited and the railways were excluded from the 1973 Labour Relations Act (LRA). The 1983 Conditions of Employment (SATS) Act laid down labour relations regulations in SATS and only BLATU was recognised by the Ministry under the terms of the LRA. Skilled jobs were reserved for whites, and discrimination within the grading system meant that whites in lower grades were paid on different scales from blacks in comparable jobs. SARHWU was not accepted as being representative of black staff and was accused of having obtained its support through illegal means and intimidation.

---

15. Interview: Bonnie Thekisho, Kimberley, October 1997.

No industrial relations office existed within the company and there was nobody qualified to deal with industrial relations matters. During the course of the strike SATS was given special permission by the Minister to dismiss workers without notice. Because there was nobody capable of conducting negotiations, the Regional Manager of the Kimberley region, Brian Berndt, was brought in to manage discussions but the Minister took the decisions and Berndt was a messenger rather than a negotiator.

At the end of the strike Brian Berndt was transferred to Johannesburg to set up the company's first industrial relations department. Two managers, John Smith and Jan Bredenkamp, were brought in from outside and Vic van Vuuren, then a legal adviser in the commercial department in Durban was appointed as a legal adviser. According to Van Vuuren:

> One of the major tasks we had was to establish an Industrial Council. This we did but at no stage was SARHWU involved in the establishment thereof. They had not yet been recognised. Transnet did not fall under the Labour Relations Act and we therefore had to bring in separate legislation in order to bring about the first Industrial Council. This took up a lot of time and the SARHWU issues appeared to have abated somewhat, with the security police under the impression that the matter was now under control. I have no knowledge of how the police conducted themselves and, other than having contact with a detective who would keep us informed, we never had any real dealings with them. I assume, however, that at higher levels discussions did take place. [16]

From the union point of view the strike had brought some benefits. It was agreed that workers would be allowed to choose their own representatives to negotiate with management and represent the workers in the workplace. The majority of these elected representatives were members of SARHWU so there was, at least, some means of talking to managers. Another benefit was the transfer of employees with over two years' service from the temporary register to permanent conditions of employment. For those on the temporary register benefits were extremely limited, no matter what the length of service, disciplinary procedures were draconian, and workers were liable to instant dismissal. Transfer to the permanent register gave improved security and employment rights for the first time to many long-standing employees.

These developments enabled the union to make some progress in developing its understanding of the industrial relations process and the necessary negotiating skills.

---

16. Notes by Vic van Vuuren, April, 1998.

After the '87 strike, some relationship [with the union] started and because management learned that they were not so skilled [at industrial relations], because they had never had occasion to negotiate seriously with anyone, they started employing people from the corporate sector. That's when Vic van Vuuren and Jan Bredenkamp came from the corporate world. They started to introduce them to new ideas and were fighting with them to say, 'We have to change!'

The linkage between SARHWU organisers and T and G [Transport and General Workers Union] organisers also brought some fresh contributions. We were not schooled in formal negotiations because we were not even covered by the general Labour Relations Act; we were supposed to be civil servants and there was no space to negotiate. Our T and G comrades used to take us with them. If an organiser had a negotiation session in a factory somewhere we would go with him and sit there and learn how these things are done. The basic problem was that of fighting for recognition. The union was not allowed to represent a worker. Only the shop stewards were recognised – as SATS employees. The problem was that they had no training to properly represent the workers. We had to go into intensive training of shop stewards – how to handle cases and so on – and we had to also fight for recognition of the union, even if it was at depot level. Our task as officials was to try and win over certain managers in that area. This was good for us as it was giving us some type of access into the company. Gradually we were coming into some kind of understanding. [17]

Nevertheless, harassment by supervisory staff and the police continued to make union organisation difficult, particularly in the Transvaal where activists like Stephen Matlou were victimised on their return to work.

When I went back after the strike I was asked to come and see the Personnel Officer and in the Personnel Office I was asked questions about my political affiliations, the strike SARHWU embarked upon and who engineered that. They said they knew that I had a role in that. They knew that I was a comrade in Thembisa burning people to death and so on and so forth – which was just nonsense. They closed me in the office, locked the offices and interrogated me at length – the management of SATS. The attitude and the working and operations between SARHWU in my area and the management then became apparent from that moment because I took a stand that I will never ever tolerate this. I will show

---

17.   Inteview: Derrick Simoko, Johannesburg, October 1997.

them who I am no matter what it takes – and I'll have the workers backing me up. [18]

Not surprisingly, such victimisation had an adverse effect on recruitment:

> We were starting to lose even the members that we had gained. From that big number we shrank. We were shrinking very rapidly because management was starting to hit back. There were still policemen and the system was still at work and people were being cowed right back. The carpet was being rolled up and the workers didn't believe in the organisation any more. We were phoning this one, talking to that one. We tried to go in and talk and they agreed because Vic van Vuuren has said they must talk to you. But the minute you go, they go back against everything and the queues are endless of workers holding yellow papers; they have been suspended; they have been dismissed; they are fined. Half the time they are fined more money than they earn. It was ridiculous. They were targeting strong people, the best workers who had learned something in the strike, and getting rid of them. And, of course, if you have a very strong influential shop steward being dismissed and the union is not seen to be able to bring him back, all the people he organised also disappear.
>
> The workers had to go to lawyers and they would write papers and we would wait and the workers would come to hear how far their case has got and you would look them in the eyes and you would have no answer to their problem. They blamed us for the fact that they were back where they started and things hadn't improved. We had told them to compromise but they were still being victimised. BLATU people were getting promoted while SARHWU people were getting the stick. We had to organise against that tide. [19]

It was at this stage that two groups emerged in SARHWU with fundamentally different approaches to the way in which the union should pursue its objectives.

The Struggle for the Union

One group, which wanted to build up the organisational base of the union and took a legalistic approach to recognition, was based around Mike Roussos and Sello Ntai at head office. The other consisted of a number of regional organisers who felt that further militant action was called for. Among these were Johannes

---

18. Interview: Stephen Matlou, Cape Town, October 1997.
19. Interview: Martin Sebakwane, Johannesburg, November 1997.

Ngcobo in the Southern Transvaal, David Moeti in Durban and Martin Sebak-wane, a newcomer who had arrived back in South Africa from studying at Warwick University in England.

After a spell in head office Sebakwane had moved to work first in the Southern Transvaal and then in the Northern Transvaal office which split off from the Southern Transvaal to form a separate region in 1988.

> Northern Transvaal was a sort of sister branch of the Wits region. We had to build it up and make it an independent region on its own, constitutionally, having its own branches, its own regional structure and so on. That was achieved with a lot of work, considering that the area in Pretoria was a very right-wing area, even more than the Johannesburg area. The region stretched from Pretoria, right up to the Zimbabwe border and went right into Northwest Region, up to Rustenburg and Zeerust. There was no transport or resources except those which the workers themselves were collecting and making available using their own private cars. We also used the railway company's transport! Organisers would be given free rides in trains, in all kinds of possible transport that was delivering goods to different destinations, and so that is how the work was happening.
>
> The Pretoria region was launched and that is how I first got into the NEC of SARHWU. I started to meet and act with a lot of comrades whose names I had heard about, that I hadn't met. Then we found that our concerns were the same; the employer was doing the same things in all different regions. That convinced us that there was a possibility of one national programme of action to deal with all these similar issues, not piecemeal, one by one, region by region. And that we had to combine everything that we were doing, trying both the legal way of solving the problem and other forms of action.
>
> The organisation had to start thinking how to translate the experiences, the gains, of the '87 strike – to move it to a really national organisation. That became a passionate issue between a group of us as organisers. It became very clear that the current core in the Head Office is part of the obstacles and we have to move in such a way that we remove all obstacles. This was slowly becoming an issue in the rest of the union. You need a very strong head office to get that kind of national programme in place. All regions were starting to put similar demands to the head office to say, 'Give us the following things; give us the tools to fight with; give us the necessary back up,' and, to a large extent, these were not forthcoming.

It was not only about organisational problems. There were also material issues. The head office was not paying us any more. The bulk of the money was coming from the regions that we organised. We sent it faithfully to the head office and because we were renegade organisers we didn't get paid. Once it starts to become material, you start to say, 'We need a head office that is friendly to the progress of the organisation but also friendly and sensitive to our own livelihood because, if this goes on, even the enemy will start buying us.'

We needed some central theme that could unite all railway workers so that they could rise up in one day, in the same action. That was the only way to paralyse the management of the railways. We started to shift our thinking to say, 'SARHWU is an organ of struggle, not just about wages. We have to start defining our role and thinking about when the movement is talking about these issues how do we prepare ourselves and gear this organisation to contribute in the broader struggle?' The workers were saying, 'We want MK now. We want those guns now. Never again are we going to be shot at without us shooting right back.' Who are we to say to them, 'No, you are not ready. We have to give you lectures on Marx or Lenin or the Communist Manifesto?' This *is* the Communist Manifesto, they are teaching us. Then the whole thing about how you combine trade union struggles with community struggles and the liberation movement comes together. It sort of lights up in your mind.

In fact, SARHWU became seen as the most central piece in the whole insurrectionary question of South Africa. You had the most militant workers who have demonstrated three months of the most intense strike. They also were all over the country and whenever they had some skirmish or a strike or something, somehow they were mobilising the communities to support them.

We saw that to grow the organisation you have got to have a strike. This time, we have to build towards a national strike and that strike must give us a national organisation; we can see it; it is possible; it can be done. Then it became a point of huge debate and conflict in terms of approach to working the organisation. We said, 'Our role is to instigate these things, to build up, to link workers, get them to go into other learning experiences in the townships; get them out of the hostels so that they go and mix with people in the community and broaden the whole space.' We started realising the legal way is not going to take us anywhere. We were wasting time. All the money we got from overseas ended up with the lawyers because we already owed them so much. Then we realised, 'No, there is no point. We have got to scrap the whole law. How do you scrap it? You just have to throw yourself at the whole thing. Throw yourself at Transnet.' [20]

The 1988 leadership contest

The friction eventually developed into a struggle for the leadership of the union between the incumbent officers and a rival group of regional organisers. The Head Office of the union was run by Sello Ntai and Mike Roussos, both now out of detention, and Stan Nkosi, a respected Robben Island detainee who was drafted in from the NUM to strengthen the leadership and help to build up regional structures. Much of the criticism was directed against Mike Roussos. He, on the other hand, saw regional discontent as nothing more than self-interested factionalism, orchestrated by those displaced from leadership positions in 1986.

As noted previously, Roussos had been involved with Johannes Ngcobo in the organisation of the 1986 relaunch of SARHWU and he was active as a leader during the 1987 strike before being detained by the police. Ngcobo was convinced that Roussos was ambitious to become General Secretary of the union.

> Comrade Mike Roussos, in the founding congress, wanted to be the General Secretary so we went to Ntai and said, 'You must stand.' At first he refused but then he agreed. Ntai won the election. Mike then stood for the Deputy against Comrade Themba Khuswayo. He lost the election and we asked him to work as an educator and a co-ordinator. Then, before the strike, Ntai was arrested. During the strike, Comrade Themba left the union and we were all arrested. Comrade Mike was released first and he was appointed as Acting Assistant General Secretary. There was this tension in the organisation. Comrade Mike Roussos wanted to see himself leading this organisation and he was perpetually dividing it. A Congress was called, fortunately when we were out [of prison]. When we got out we said, 'Mike is not going to be General Secretary.' We then elected Comrade Ntai as General Secretary with Comrade Moeti from Natal as Assistant General Secretary. Comrade Moeti then resigned for some reason and Comrade Mike acted as an Assistant General Secretary without a mandate. [21]

---

20. Interview: Martin Sebakwane, Johannesburg, November 1997.
21. Interview: Johannes Ngcobo, Johannesburg, October 1997.

The rebel organisers promoted the election of Martin Sebakwane as the next General Secretary. Sebakwane had not played an active part in the labour movement before he left South Africa. He had studied at the University of the North and at Wits University before being sponsored to study for an MA in Transport Policy at Warwick University. His intention was to return to take up a job in management but he became increasingly concerned with the struggle inside his home country and increasingly at odds with the point of view of the small group of ultra-left (mainly white) South African exiles based at Warwick.

His dissent was noticed and he was 'talent spotted' by the SACTU office in London, which was keen to influence developments on the industrial relations front in South Africa. Archie Sibeko was concerned to strengthen the leadership of SARHWU and thought that Sebakwane's knowledge of the transport industry would be an asset.

At the same time he wanted to ensure SARHWU's continued alignment with the SACTU policy of politically committed unions. He persuaded Sebakwane that he should return to work for the trade union movement in South Africa and this he did – with some misgivings and against the wishes of his wife, who stayed in England and later divorced him.

In the political circumstances of the late 1980s police infiltration of organisations such as the Civic Associations and the trade unions was a common government tactic. Many activists were betrayed and arrested. Feelings ran high; fear and suspicion were everywhere and those working in the liberation movement mistrusted even their closest colleagues. The trade union movement was split into factions. In such an atmosphere it was not surprising that an unknown newcomer should be treated with caution and that Martin Sebakwane did not receive the welcome he might have expected.

Mike Roussos resented what he saw as the imposition of the new man, without consultation, 'by some big chief on a hill somewhere'.[22] (And possibly he felt that a university-educated African posed a threat to his own influence in the union.) According to Derrick Simoko:

> When Martin came there was immediately a problem. Martin started in Warwick University and then was very much involved in SACTU in London. And then SACTU in London advised us that there was this guy who had studied transport and that we need to make use of him as a trade union. In fact he was not imposed but it was said that we needed to make use of him. He was accepted by the leadership at first. But

---

22. Interview: Mike Roussos, Johannesburg, November 1997.

during the course of working I think there were problems at head office. I remember we had an NEC where it was said by one of the leaders that he [Martin] was a sell-out and that I personally must do something. I refused. I said that first of all I needed to establish whether or not Martin is a sell-out. I can't just stand up and say that. After that the guy said, 'Okay, maybe he's not a sell-out, but he is an opportunist.' There was that type of fighting. [23]

Observing SARHWU on his arrival, Martin Sebakwane recognised Roussos's organising abilities, his commitment and the strong position that he occupied in the union.

Mike was very strong, a very strong personality. He was somebody who would take over and also he was skilled. He had knowledge; he had access to all kinds of resources and things and he was also a movement person, you see. He had been detained and he had paid heavily for believing in what he believed in. He wasn't just an intellectual from Wits. At that time, inside the country, white people who were popularly accepted in the popular movement or who had made it to the very inner circle were very few and Mike was one of those few people. He had absolute power and you had to be careful how you approached him. You didn't want to mess around with him that easily. From the early days there were people who knew Mike, have done things with Mike, have worked with him – and once you have got that relationship based on struggle, on certain things that you were baptised with, you bond. You don't question the person that you have worked with in that kind of way.[24]

Roussos had some strong supporters but others found him authoritarian by temperament and he had alienated many of the younger organisers. The fact that he was white was also undeniably an issue. Johannes Ngcobo argued strongly that, although SARHWU was non-racial, the vast majority of its membership was black and it was inappropriate at that point in its development for a white person to occupy a leadership position.

We belonged to a non-racial organisation. I must stress that. We didn't have any personal problem with Comrade Mike Roussos but amongst ourselves we said the labour movement should not be led at the moment by a white comrade ... We were drawing our experiences from FOSATU. The majority of General Secretaries in that federation were

23. Interview: Derrick Simoko, Johannesburg, October 1997.
24. Interview: Martin Sebakwane, Johannesburg, November 1997.

white but there were no white workers. So we said that if we want to see workers identifying themselves with the trade union they must be led by people who stay [live] with them, where they sit and eat porridge together. That was that – not that we hated him because he was white. We wanted to be led by black leaders.

We understood that Comrade Mike was an underground worker in the Party. He was respected by comrades in the movement outside the country and he had access to funds, but in practice he thought that we [black organisers] didn't have the ability to lead. We said, 'No; we can lead; we have proved that.' What made the 1987 strike successful was that black workers could come to us. We were accessible. That intimate relationship counts for a lot. The key thing was to elect a General Secretary that workers can identify themselves with, a black person. We were not advocating racism or anything. [25]

Roussos denied this, accusing his opponents of being either corrupt, racist or police informers:

I had been thinking a lot about my involvement in the union while I was in detention. At the [launching] Conference I had said I wanted to pull out but the guys had said, 'Stay in Education'. I ended up being much more central than just an education person because the guys were inexperienced. But while I was in detention there was a lot of racial stuff that was going on with what were essentially opportunistic attacks on me that had been taking place within the union ranks. It made me think that it didn't really make any sense. I should actually try to find a way of, as quickly as possible, of moving out of the union. So I came out of detention feeling that I had to try and help rebuild things but as soon as reasonably possible I wanted to get out.

I thought it was too easy for both the security police and opportunists in the ranks of the union to use the racial thing to actually undermine really important initiatives, solid direction. People like Justice and Sello and Stan and myself were obviously putting a hell of a lot of effort into trying to rebuild the structures, but there were always rumbling and personal attacks and it built up to a point where there was a lot of problems in terms of police informers and infiltration into the union. [26]

Roussos attributed the criticisms of the direction taken by the leadership that came from regional organisers to their deliberate fomentation of factionalism

---

25. Interview: Johannes Ngcobo, Johannesburg, October 1997.
26. Interview: Mike Roussos, Johannesburg, November 1997.

and disruption, and accused his critics of being police spies. Sebakwane found that at least some of the mud thrown had stuck and he had considerable difficulty in becoming accepted within sections of the union.

> The foremost of people who really believed this was the General Secretary of SARHWU at the time, Sello Ntai. When I came into the union he was still in detention and Mike Roussos had just been released. Mike was the Education Secretary but he was the *de facto* General Secretary. He completely overshadowed Sello, and as a result my relationship with Sello was strained because of the misperceptions that he got, principally from Mike. There was really a zeal on his part to make sure that I am not in conversations that might compromise the organisation. It made the work difficult.
>
> There was this thing about, 'Where do you come from? You haven't been around here. We have not brought you up. We don't have our own stamp on you to say, "Now you are ready to say certain things about the organisation which must be listened to or taken seriously".' I knew I wasn't an impimpi [spy] but it was very convincing and sometimes even I wondered if I really was and I just didn't know it! At that time, a lot of people had bonded. People shared cells together in prison or wherever, and they shared tear gas together; they shared all kinds of things together and to try and break in into that circle is foolhardy. You have to wait for new situations that you will also take part in. If those events don't come immediately, it means you can't create them; you have to wait. In the meantime, of course, you must give your back to be flogged and to be named all kinds of things but it makes you grow. [27]

The conflict came into the open at the annual congress, held in October 1988. Sello Ntai, weary of the faction fighting, stood down from the leadership. The conference delegates signalled their desire for a reconciliation of differences by electing Martin Sebakwane as General Secretary and Stan Nkosi as Assistant General Secretary but Mike Roussos walked out, vowing never to return. The result of the election was challenged and the ballot was repeated a few weeks later with the same result.

As with all faction fighting, there is a certain amount of confusion as to the objectives of the rival groups and who supported whom. From the point of view of Mike Roussos, the 'anti-faction' was destroying the union:

---

27. Interview: Martin Sebakwane, Johannesburg, November 1997.

The anti-faction put up Martin as the opposition and they won the election. At that point, I just said, 'Well if the workers want to support a faction that is basically destroying the union from within through all this factionalism and is actually promoting some of the things that we worked for years to overcome in terms of organisation, discipline, direction and is in fact quite racist, then I don't want to be part of this union.' Then Martin and his crew came and took over. [28]

According to Martin Sebakwane, it was Mike Roussos who wanted to maintain control of the union and he, Sebakwane, who tried to avoid a split by proposing the election of Stan Nkosi before finding that he was himself drafted by the membership.

Somehow by default or by design, I don't know, I started to represent an alternative or articulated view of a side which is existing in the organisation, a side that hasn't got resources, that hasn't got legitimacy, that hasn't got anything else and of course, that led to the sort of perspective that, 'Yes, you see now the system has planted somebody and they are beginning to organise and are splitting the organisation.' Stanley Nkosi made a big contribution to slowing down what had become rabid confrontations and issues that really had nothing to do with the movement's politics but were really personality issues. Clearly, Mike wanted to become the General Secretary and all of us were convinced that he cannot. He is a useful national official, very strong, very resourceful but he cannot unite this organisation or take it forward the way we think it should really go. We thought the coming of Stanley Nkosi gave a very good alternative, because, next to Mike, he had the right stature. It became a race thing, black racism against a very good white comrade and it was difficult at the time to separate these things.

Now we all converged on Jo'burg for the Congress. Traditionally the night before is workers' night. They meet on their own and they sort themselves out; they talk about themselves. We, the full-time officers, don't get into their meetings. They had their own assessment of the organisation; they had their own idea about what type and which direction of leadership they would like to have and, as fate might have it, they then informed me that they are going to put me up for General Secretary. In the morning there were nominations and they put my name right in there and the election went on and the process became

---

28.   Interview: Mike Roussos, Johannesburg, November 1997.

irreversible. As soon as the results were announced, Mike Roussos stood up and walked out of the hall never to come back to SARWHU. [29]

Rather than healing the rift in the union these elections simply widened it further.

In fact, the union was splitting. There were embargoes from the regions – they are not sending in their money to that office; they don't trust those people with their money and so on. Now the head office can't function because there is no money coming in! Then we said, 'No, no, we step down and they go in because the organisation has to go on,' and I went back to Pretoria, the region. Then, there was a congress organised by COSATU. Accusations were put forward and everybody must put their story to say exactly what is happening. At the end, the judges were the workers and they say, 'This is our organisation and what we have decided in that congress holds and stands. You, Mike Roussos, are still the Education Secretary. Go to the office and work with everyone else and build the organisation.' We went back and Congress was over but he didn't come back any more. Stanley Nkosi also finally took his jacket and left. Sello Ntai also refused to work in the head office. He went to work in the Southern Transvaal region. [30]

Different regions continued to take sides so yet another attempt was made at reconciliation with the assistance of the SACTU office in London. What followed took on the flavour of a farce as Sebakwane became entangled in what appeared to be internal SACP/ANC/SACTU politics. At that time 'Third Force' activity was rife, setting people against one another. It is not surprising that there was a high level of suspicion, sometimes amounting to paranoia, in the liberation movement. As a result the internal security structure of the ANC was barely under control and many blameless activists were arrested as well as those who were genuinely suspect. On their way to a meeting in Lusaka, Sebakwane and his supporters were stranded in Zimbabwe for a week, in the transit lounge of Harare Airport, unable to fly to Zambia because the old accusations of treachery had been resurrected and doubt had been cast on their credentials.

The delegation was eventually allowed to continue its journey after the intervention of Chris Hani (the popular Chief of Staff of MK) but it was detained once more on arrival in Lusaka and was only released after a second intervention by Archie Sibeko in the London office of SACTU. There they waited for the arrival of Mike Roussos and his supporters but they failed to put in an appearance and it was not until several weeks later that Sebakwane was finally able to return

29. Interview: Martin Sebakwane, Johannesburg, November 1997.
30. As above.

to South Africa. Little had been achieved but it did seem that, for the time being at least, he was no longer considered to be a traitor.

The 1988 wage campaign

To what extent these internal disputes were a result of genuine differences, what part Third Force interventions played and to what extent personality clashes were deliberately manipulated by management and government may never be known. Factionalism is a common feature of labour and political movements. Nevertheless, the disruption of the union came at a particularly difficult time in terms of the struggle for recognition by SATS. The political and economic circumstances of the time were such that a decision had been made to commercialise state enterprises. This entailed retrenchment, a freeze on new employment, reluctance to recognise progressive unions and attempts to reduce real wages in preparation for the eventual privatisation of much of the state sector.[31] The government was in the process of splitting up SATS and replacing it by a new company, Transnet, which was divided into a number of commercial divisions.

If SARHWU was to have any impact on the results of this process it was vital for it to gain recognition as soon as possible but it was in a 'Catch 22' situation. In order to win recognition and the right to negotiate on workers' behalf it needed to demonstrate that it represented the majority of the African employees of SATS; but in order to attract members it had to win some significant improvement in railway employees' terms and conditions of service. A recruitment campaign was introduced, aimed at attracting members of BLATU, but this was blocked by the management, which refused to process resignations and continued to deduct BLATU subscriptions from all workers' salaries. At the same time it was announced that there would be a wage freeze with no increase at all to compensate for the workers' losses during the 1987 strike and the increased cost of living.

Although the Natal region of SARHWU instituted a legal test case and won an order prohibiting SATS from continuing to deduct BLATU subscriptions, the union needed a major victory to win over BLATU members nationally. It was against this background that in September 1988, just before the 1988 National Congress, the National Executive Committee meeting in Bloemfontein resolved to launch a Living Wage Campaign centred on the demand for a minimum of R1 500 per month for all African railway workers. Unfortunately, however, disagreements within the union meant that the campaign was insufficiently co-ordinated and strikes broke out prematurely in East London and Durban.

---

31. *South African Labour Bulletin* 14(8), May 1990: p. 11.

In East London workers were already angry as a result of the dismissal of ten workers at Ben Schoeman Airport for refusing to work overtime and of three employees of RTS (now Autonet) for participating in the stayaway on 22 April 1988 in memory of the SARHWU members killed in the Germiston massacre. SARHWU was not recognised, but the terms of the 1988 SATS Act (Clause 19.4) allowed any non-union group of workers to put proposals to the management. Accordingly a group of workers (who were in fact SARHWU members) approached the Regional Manager of the Eastern Cape Region of SATS with their demand for an increase in the R437,50 per month paid to general workers. Management refused to negotiate and as a result the workers decided to embark on industrial action.

> One could see a situation in the railways where workers had the opportunity now to voice out their grievances. They were very much more militant. They wanted in fact to crush the Boers. Part of their struggle was to liberate the country but also it was the idea of getting money that was influencing them. Then they were earning something like R437 a month. We agreed in an NEC we should go for wages and the demand would be R1 500. We resolved at a national level that we were going to strike demanding R1 500. When the report back was made to the workers, they quickly said that we should get them back in action and then everybody was mobilised quickly. Initially a group of workers in East London went to negotiate. I think it was about 40 shop stewards went to a meeting and then there was a deadlock immediately. The management said that it was ridiculous and we couldn't get that money and that it was unreasonable. We knew that maybe it was unreasonable but we needed that money. Then we decided to go on strike … It was difficult for one to say, 'No, don't strike,' once we'd talked about money. Nobody would listen because they would like to get that money. Our mobilising was very quick then. [32]

David Moeti, at that time an organiser in Durban, pulled out his members at the same time but other regions failed to follow suit, leaving the two regions high and dry. The strike in Durban was short lived and Moeti was able to negotiate a settlement with Vic van Vuuren that led to the reinstatement of workers and the limited recognition of SARHWU in the Natal Region. The workers in East London were left to suffer for their precipitate action and for the lack of support by other regions. The strike was just the opportunity that managers in the inefficient and over-manned Eastern Cape had been looking for.

---

32. Interviews: Derrick Simoko, Johannesburg, October 1997; Thembekile Majalisa, East London, October 1997.

The strike took from December 1988 to February 1989. The management dismissed all of us. All of the workers were on strike but unfortunately as a result we were dismissed – 1 700 of us, 436 workers were
not re-employed. All of those over 45 were not taken back. [There was]
an agreement that no workers would be victimised or dismissed for
taking part in this action. But here in our region, our regional manager,
Mr du Toit, decided to do his own thing. He said, No, he's the boss in
this region, he's going to do what he wants to do. He decided to dismiss
the workers who were in that action. In short we can say we lost the
strike because other regions didn't assist us. It was a setback. And
although my service in this company is nearly 20 years I have only eight
years because I was re-employed in 1989 and I lost my benefit. [33]

Derrick Simoko and David Moeti, the organisers concerned in East London and
Durban, are both clear that the fault lay with the national leadership which was
too preoccupied with the struggles for control which were taking place to ensure
that the Living Wage campaign was properly planned and co-ordinated.

The leadership advised that it was wrong to pre-empt a decision to strike.
The other areas started mobilising but the leadership tried to stop them
from striking. There was no programme to say, 'On such and such a date
ABCD is going to happen.' We agreed that we needed to go on strike
with these demands because the union then was not recognised and we
wanted recognition. We consciously said that we need to demand money
because it is a mobilising factor and we will achieve money and also
recognition. But unfortunately, the leadership didn't realise that there
was a need to quickly mobilise other areas, then to push for recognition
instead of stopping the area or the two areas [i.e. Durban and East
London].

It was not a success because we didn't achieve anything and because
workers were dismissed in East London. The mistake that we made, in
particular national leadership, was that of concluding an agreement for
Durban area. Then that was it for East London. Management then was
very much interested in solving the problem in Durban but not very
much interested in what was happening in East London. (Because, in
terms of clients and business, there is no business there.) That resulted
in our workers in East London being dismissed and then some being
re-employed. Some of them even today are still out of work. [34]

---

33.   Interview: Vuyani Elvis Mzayifani, East London, October 1997.
34.   Interviews: Derrick Simoko, Johannesburg, October 1997; David Moeti, East London, October 1997.

Recognition

The action in East London coincided with the leadership disputes taking place at national level and these can be blamed, to a large extent, for the union's failure to negotiate reinstatement and for the subsequent bitterness enduring in that region to this day. At the time of Martin Sebakwane's election negotiations were already taking place with management. These too were severely disrupted.

> There were pamphlets all over explaining why certain comrades are disgruntled with the outcome of the elections. They were all over Johannesburg and the regions. They were citing all these things about the CIA and this and that. After Congress, the next week was supposed to be the first formal negotiations with Transnet towards recognition and the pamphlets were saying, 'Yes, at this critical time, just when Transnet is about to discuss with us formally, they have manipulated the elections so that their own person that they planted must be the one to discuss with them'.
>
> The head office was working on those very complex fragile processes and you can't just walk in and say, 'I will take over and I will do those things.' It wouldn't help the work itself, because the other side would really love it. So we, the new executive, we called them in and said, 'You continue those negotiations and do the best you can. Let us not link these negotiations with the issues of these elections because you have to go and continue that process, we can't come in cold. It wouldn't be in the interests of the organisation.' Then there was a group who said, 'No, you all go, because if you don't go, the enemy will say, "The leadership of SARWHU is not here. Who are you? On whose behalf are you talking now?" '
>
> Then there was a compromise. We brought people in to bring us together to say, 'We have to rise up above these things. This has to be in the interest of SARWHU first.' So it was that we went there and of course, management knew about these things. Management always knows. The first question was, 'Well, who should we speak to? Who is the real representative for SARWHU workers here? We don't want to talk to one person and sign agreements and those agreements don't work because people are not really the true representatives.' And so it went on. I think we didn't really get much out of those negotiations. [35]

---

35. Interview: Martin Sebakwane, Johannesburg, November 1997.

Before discussions on recognition could go any further, SARHWU was forced to overcome its long-standing opposition to registration. David Moeti had by that time been elected Assistant General Secretary to Martin Sebakwane.

> Something which we had to work on was the recognition of the union, because we needed to try and get stop-order facilities so that we can maintain the union. We did have some support from the National Union of Railway Workers in Britain but we could sometimes go without salaries because there was no money. We didn't have even money to pay rent. We couldn't pay our telephone sometimes but we survived. Something magic had to be done because we had recruited about 45 000 people, which was much bigger than any union that was existing at the time, but still they refused to recognise us. [36]

In order to force the hand of the management and to make up ground lost by the failure in the Eastern Cape the union resorted to the desperate measure of another strike.

In November 1989 about 40 000 workers struck in all main centres demanding recognition of the union, reinstatement of the 400 sacked members in East London, amendment of the new Disciplinary Code (introduced in September 1988), and a minimum wage of R1 500. The strike was a violent one during the course of which a number of people lost their lives and over 5 000 workers, mainly hostel dwellers, were dismissed. It was eventually resolved in January 1990, following mediation by COSATU. As a result SARHWU finally achieved the breakthrough it had been fighting for. Transnet agreed to derecognise BLATU in Natal immediately, to negotiate a master recognition agreement with SARHWU within two months, and to negotiate on wages in areas where the union was registered.

The 1989/1990 Recognition Strike

In order to avoid the mistakes of 1988 the NEC made careful plans for the strike to be simultaneous in all regions. Regions were divided up among the six members of the National Management Committee, each of whom was deputed to go and prepare for a strike. Once again, however, the strike was sparked prematurely by workers seizing the initiative. On 1 November in a rerun of 1987, 800 workers at Kaserne Depot downed tools over the dismissal of a fellow worker.[37] Both the management and union organisers were taken by surprise. Vic

---

36. Interview: David Moeti, East London, November 1997.
37. The protest was against the dismissal of Ismael Mbira and was led by Kaserne Shop Steward David Mnisi.

van Vuuren and his colleagues in the Labour Relations Department were preoccupied with setting up the SATS Labour Council:

> Much of my time was spent in negotiating the SATS Labour Council.
> SARHWU was not party to this because it was not officially recognised.
> The structuring of the Labour Council, albeit without SARHWU, was
> the first step towards bringing about an era of collective bargaining
> within Transnet. It was during this time that we at the Labour Relations
> Department realised that we needed to establish a relationship with
> SARHWU, but before anything constructive could be done we walked
> right into a major strike – my initiation into the realms of the political
> struggle for human rights through the trade union movement.[38]

David Moeti was deployed to work in the Eastern Cape and Natal. As Assistant
General Secretary he was closely involved in planning the strike tactics but he
too was taken by surprise.

> I was deployed to the Eastern Cape and to Natal, that has always been
> my region. I went to Natal where I stayed for a month organising a strike.
> Then I had to go back to head office. The day that I was leaving Natal,
> my wife had given me some provisions, some chicken, some food to
> carry with me, ironed my clothes. I had them in the boot. I had to go via
> the regional office in Natal but as I got to the office, a message came
> up. To my surprise, there was already a strike in Johannesburg. I was
> actually moving to Johannesburg to spark a strike but the strike had
> already gone boomf.[39]

Unlike in Natal, where a relationship of sorts had begun to develop between
SARHWU and the Labour Relations Department of SATS, relations with management in the Transvaal were still extremely poor. Under the new Disciplinary
Code introduced in September 1988 depot managers had the power to charge
and dismiss workers at plant level without reference to higher management, and
there was a tense situation due to the resulting number of dismissals. Workers
were reaching boiling point over a number of grievances including the refusal
of management to discuss issues with workers representatives as allowed for by
clause 19.4 of the SATS Act and confirmed by the agreement ending the 1987
strike.[40] Although the 1987 strike had brought in many new members, the union
was still unrecognised; racial abuse was increasing with the current political
tensions and 90% of members received below the August 1989 Supplemented

---

38. Notes from Vic van Vuuren, April 1998.
39. Interview: David Moeti, East London, October 1997.
40. See *South African Labour Bulletin* 14(1), 1989.

Living Level of R691.[41] By 1989 the situation was back more or less to what it had been. The union was in a mess financially and the leadership was still weakened by the internal disputes over the election of Martin Sebakwane as General Secretary.

> Nearly all of us got our work back besides those who were jailed. But while time goes on and on there were still scars of the after effects of the 22 April 1987 between ourselves and BLATU because BLATU people died, SARHWU people died, and you could not just go back and forget about everything, so there were every now and then hiccups – one member of SARHWU dying, three members of BLATU dying, members of SARHWU demanding that certain persons should be suspended because they didn't strike, all those things.
>
> Then the membership of SARHWU faded. We had, as I've said, 99% of blacks having joined SARHWU during the strike. SARHWU was aligned to both the ANC and to COSATU, of course, that was launched in 1985. So there were always strikes, marches and the likes which were called, which we have to be part of. But there were members, white collar workers, who didn't want to be seen to be striking, staying away and the likes so they were always demotivating other people not to. The squabbling became more aggressive with workers fighting among themselves.
>
> Everybody started to lose face. After two years nothing had happened and the workers were saying the union is not delivering. Then we sat around and came up with strategies. One of the organising approaches we came up with was to start to create an atmosphere where there would be an action again. And that's how we started to build up to the strike in 1989. That strike was not necessary, but it *was* necessary in terms of reviving the organisation and the membership. We had to find a new mechanism to start to reinvent and start to rebuild the union. Then we had a war of recognition which was very critical because if we didn't win that one it meant the fading away of SARHWU.[42]

A National Workers Committee was elected and met with SATS on 9 November but management refused to negotiate on the grounds that SARHWU was an unrecognised union and that a 10% wage increase had already been agreed with BLATU and the other trade unions represented on the SATS Labour Council.

---

41. As above, p. 9.
42. Interview: Robert Mashego, Johannesburg, October 1997.

There were still unsettled scores from the 1987 strike waiting to be settled between those who had struck and those who had not. These disagreements among the membership meant that when the strike was called the response in the Southern Transvaal was as bloody and violent as that of 1987. The worst incident was a replay of the massacre at Germiston Station that had taken place in the 1987 strike. Mandla Nzama was a shop steward in Braamfontein:

> I was the secretary of the Central Shop Steward Council. That organised different departments within a larger department. Of course we agreed to the strike; we did the preparations but a major mistake we made, unlike in 1987, was we called for a calm at the initial stage of the strike, hence most of the people didn't go out on strike, even those who were involved in 1987. That led to confrontations and the death of our comrades. Many violent incidents happened on the trains and there was a disaster for us at Germiston that was organised by the police and those who were at work.[43]

Robert Mashego was present at the second Germiston massacre, as he had been at the first:

Funeral in Venda of SARHWU member shot in Germiston Station, January 1990.

43. Interview: Mandla Nzama, Johannesburg, October 1997.

How the arrangements were made was nearly the same as 1987 and exactly the same thing happened at Germiston. We held a meeting at Springs Hall; when we moved into a train, exactly very same thing as in 1987. The trains again stopping at the very same time at the very same place as arranged in 1987, but this time we were more ready. You will understand that in 1989 guns were then starting to flow in. We had our own, soldiers had their own and, realising what was taking place in this station, when the train stopped we started firing at them and also they were starting firing at us. *Bang! Bang! Bang!* SARHWU people who died there were only three but there were a lot of other people died.[44]

Although Durban had not played a major part in the 1987 strike it came to the forefront in 1989.

Durban is a major port. It is very strategic in as far as our power is concerned as workers because that is where most exports and imports go through. So I stayed in Durban right through the strike to make sure that the strike was successful. And it was successful. It was successful as well in Johannesburg, in Cape Town, in Bloemfontein, everywhere except the Eastern Cape, which was understandable because workers had been dismissed there and they really didn't want to strike again.

My God, it was the strike of my life. I have never seen such a strike before. There was never such a strike in this company. Well, of course, the workers intimidated each other here and there; they attacked each other here and there. It turned out ugly. It was a bloody strike in some places but it was the most united strike that I have ever seen. We were united with the workers. Even though they were dismissed, we kept them together. We kept them united and at one stage I almost cried tears. We had a stadium that we were using in Durban. That is where we used to assemble. Two or three workers actually fell to the ground because of hunger. They were actually taken to the hospital and when they got to the hospital they discovered that they were hungry, that was the main reason but – we survived.

We went to ask for help from Operation Hunger. We went to see some organisations for financial help just to try and feed those people who were being hungry in the strike. Now if the men who were on strike are falling because of hunger and they have to be taken to hospital, what about their children? They could be worse off.

---

44. Interview: Johannes Ngcobo, Johannesburg, October 1997.

We used our workers' power. We used our technical expertise, too, because the strike didn't only involve withdrawing from work. It became something like war. We used sabotage methods too. We had groups here and there who were meeting but we could never discuss in large meetings that we were going to do something which was illegal. From the union point of view, from the union official point of view, I knew nothing about those groups. Nevertheless I knew those groups existed. What they were discussing, where and how, I didn't want to know. The strategy was that I mustn't know anything because if I get detained then I will have to reveal what is going on. So, I didn't even want to know who did what.

But we consisted of workers that were working on the line. We consisted of workers that worked in buses. We consisted of workers that worked everywhere in the trains. We had the technical expertise of the people that worked on the line and they could break up the line in such a way that the signal-cable wouldn't release. They would connect wires from there to there and they would break up a line and face it towards the sea and the signal cables would not even be aware because the wires are still connected and they would give the train a green light. Meanwhile, the train was going into the sea. This is how it used to happen and they lost billions and billions of money on the goods trains, especially on the goods trains on the coal lines from Newcastle to Richards Bay, the coal terminal. I think they lost about two million.

That's how we swept the port of Durban clean. There was no imports, no exports, nothing. We stopped the whole process. Our tactics were to use sabotage and not to attack people. That's where I had to stand up and say to the workers, 'Look, there is no need to go and attack a fellow worker who happens not to be on strike with us. You don't have to do that. You don't have to kill each other in this process. We have to convince those people who are not on strike to join us.' That was my main job, to keep them together, to say, 'United we will go through.'

The company refused to negotiate with us and declared a deadlock because this was happening. But once they declared a deadlock at negotiations then we would go back and hit them and hit the company very hard. These were groups of people unknown to them, never discovered even today, and most probably it will never be discovered who was doing what, where and how. Nobody was even arrested for that; they were so secret. So we were hitting them with workers' power and we were hitting the equipment and we were saying, 'This country belongs to black people and this railway belongs to black people and there is no way we can be dismissed. This is our company. It belongs to us. We will fight till the last drop of our blood on this issue!'

That's when I learned to talk! I used to talk a lot because that's how I got my motivation. I was not originally a good singer but I became a good singer because singing motivated the spirit of workers. That is how I got through to the workers and that is how I united them despite the difficulties. Through my singing, through my talking to them, through my making them aware that the struggle that they were fighting was not an ordinary workers' struggle; it was a struggle against apartheid. Our struggle was mass based. The songs that we sang were the songs of struggle, songs that said, 'We are not just fighting for our rights in the company. We are fighting for our country.'

When we had gone on strike before some of our little strikes had been broken, because they would arrest us as we were walking along the street – because the state of emergency did not allow crowds to walk alongside the road. You would be arrested for that whenever we went on strike. So before we went on strike we prepared for the strike. We couldn't gather in an open space because we would be arrested under the state of emergency. So we worked through the Council of Churches. We would talk to certain ministers and we would book churches inside Durban. That is how we worked in Durban. We would book churches so that on such a day we will have a strike and we will house our people in certain churches so that they are not arrested and so that they don't break our strike because of the state of emergency. We were dismissed at one stage, 42 000 of us, but we were very, very strong, very, very, very confident. We had power. We had workers' power. We didn't have power from the law; we didn't have any economic power, but we had workers' power. We did have that and we were certain that there was no way the company can dismiss so many of us and be able to survive.[45]

SATS's refusal to make any concrete offers aggravated the strike and created obstacles to settlement but, in contrast to 1987, there were informal meetings between the management and union representatives that kept the channels of communication open.

---

45.   Interview: David Moeti, East London, November 1997.

Negotiations

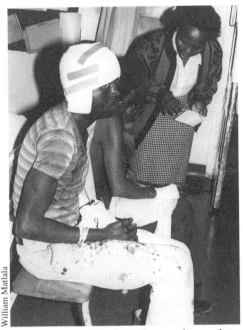

William Matlala

Catherine Mavi (Southern Transvaal) attends to members of SARHWU shot by management security at City Deep, June 1990.

On 23 November SATS accepted that SARHWU had proved overwhelming support in Natal, and the company agreed to derecognise BLATU and provisionally recognise SARHWU in Natal with immediate effect. It would begin negotiating a master agreement in Natal one week after return to work and support SARHWU's application for registration in that province. Full recognition in Natal would follow within two months and this would be extended to other regions as and when they proved that they represented a majority of African employees.

Nevertheless, there was still no agreement on substantive issues such as the wage demand, disciplinary procedures, privatisation and the reinstatement of dismissed workers. It was noted at the time that:

> Many details of the strike resemble the political situation in the country as a whole. Like the state, SATS is forced to recognise the majority. It combines a strategy of reform and repression and uses devious means to undermine the resistance of the workers. One of these is to pretend it has made substantial moves and to try to portray the workers as being unreasonable … Like the state, SATS doesn't really listen and doesn't really hear how fundamental and deep-seated workers' grievances are and how their workers are no longer prepared to wait or listen to promises. Decades of poverty wages and abhorrent living conditions have created an enormous barrier of suspicion and anger. Only when 'good faith' becomes concrete and when conditions start improving visibly will there be any hope of fruitful negotiations.[46]

The 'concession' made on recognition had in fact already been made following the 1988 strike in Durban but had not been acted upon. The wage demand was refused on the grounds that a wage increase of 10-20% had already been

---

46. R. Roux, 1989, pp. 119-122.

negotiated with the SATS Labour Council (of which BLATU was a member but SARHWU was not). At the same time the management tried to use the strike as an excuse to weed out thousands of workers in preparation for the privatisation of SATS and formation of Transnet. A trade-off of independent arbitration on this was offered against the dropping of SARHWU's wage demand but the union rejected it.

It was only in January 1990, after three months strike, that the company agreed to negotiate with SARHWU on substantive issues. The reasons for this, as seen by Derrick Simoko were threefold:

> One, there was this monster destabilising the Company and they wanted to resolve, how they could manage to control it. Because it was very difficult for them to operate. They couldn't afford to lose a lot of clients. Two, in that period, we were moving towards being changed into Transnet. Three, they were not used to strikes on the railways. Then there was this SARHWU and there was a strike in '87, there was a strike in 1988 and there was a strike again in 1989. They couldn't control it so I think in their debates they decided instead of being intransigent and refusing to recognise this thing they needed to recognise it.[47]

Simoko welcomed the fact that the company now contained managers like Vic van Vuuren who were prepared to recognise SARHWU's grievances and negotiate a settlement during the 1989 strike:

> The person heading Human Resources was Vic van Vuuren. Vic van Vuuren was a little bit flexible. I think he helped SARHWU and I will commend him for that. Although the strike helped us it was also the fact that there was a liberal guy heading the Human Resources Department in Transnet.[48]

Other leaders, such as Nelson Ndinisa, were more hard-line and suspected a trick.

> In the '89 strike the government had finally accepted that the ANC is coming and they will have to give up power. In '87 the government was holding on in power: they only had one plan for dealing with us – that they will catch us. In '89, they started to say, 'Now things will be changing; we need a second plan.' And that second plan was very successful in their terms because for the first time they were able to create confusion and conflict within the union and put one against another, which didn't happen in '87.[49]

---

47. Interview: Derrick Simoko, Johannesburg, October 1997.
48. As above.
49. Interview: Nelson Ndinisa, Johannesburg, October 1997.

Negotiations were influenced by attempts by the company not to reinstate certain individuals and by developments on the political front. The process of releasing ANC leaders imprisoned on Robben Island had begun and COSATU was concerned that the strike could jeopardise the progress that was taking place in setting in train a negotiated end to apartheid.

> That strike came at a time when the national leadership was being released from Robben Island. Comrade Sisulu who was arrested with Comrade Nelson Mandela called us into a meeting to discuss the suspension of the strike. Our members were prepared to suspend the strike but what was happening at the time was that the management had organised criminals or people who did not want to go on a strike to beat up those on strike. So the question was that if they go back they get assaulted but we managed to resolve things. [50]

David Moeti also opposed any concessions.

> Whilst we were on strike, I remember at one stage officials from COSATU, Cyril Ramaphosa, General Secretary of the NUM, they sat together with us, the national leadership, trying to convince us to go back to work because workers had been dismissed and now we had not only to negotiate for recognition but also for reinstatement. We said, 'No, we are not going to do that.' And they said, 'Gentlemen, the workers are going to lose their jobs. That will happen.' And we said to them, 'No, no. Comrades we respect you as our national leaders but this company is known by us. We know what's going on inside the company. We know how far our power goes. At the moment, we are hitting the company.'[51]

As a result a deal was reached for a return to work and all strikers were reinstated, even the five leaders (including Robert Mashego) whom the company had tried to debar. Following the reinstatement of strikers in January 1990, SARHWU began national recognition negotiations. Temporary recognition was agreed for the period of the negotiations – first until June and then until September, when agreement was finally reached, though only after a further demonstration of strength by the union. David Moeti, the Assistant General Secretary, was one of the chief negotiators.

Recognition depended on registration. Before granting recognition the Company insisted that the union should be registered under the LRA but this was a difficult issue for the union which had long held out against accepting this form

---

50. Interview: Johannes Ngcobo, Johannesburg, October 1997.
51. Interview: David Moeti, East London, November 1997.

of government control. The 1988 strike in Durban had resulted in an agreement on recognition in Natal provided the union registered but the Company still dragged its feet.

> Their refusal was based on registration. We didn't really want to register under the government that we were fighting with. We didn't really want to do that but we finally registered the union for Natal. Then there was an objection. The union BLATU objected to us. In South Africa, you cannot register a union if another union objects and represents the same people. The Company tried to say that we didn't have fifty plus one per cent of the workforce but we were more popular than BLATU in terms of the number of members that we had.
>
> The union was registered immediately after the strike and Vic van Vuuren, who was the labour relations manager at the time, still refused to recognise the union. Even though I put about 45 000 stop orders in his office he still refused. Then I said to him, 'You want us to go back to strike?' He said, 'No.' I said, 'What do you want?' 'I want your registration certificate.' 'We have registered.' But he says, 'No, you have registered for Natal only and I will give you recognition for Natal.' I said, 'Okay. Give us recognition for Natal.' Then we negotiated the first recognition agreement and it was signed. It said that we could have stop orders nationally but we were only recognised for Natal. I still went back to him and said, 'Recognise us,' and he said, 'No.' Then I went there in the absence of Martin and I told him, 'Look, Vic, you don't want to count the stop orders, the 45 000 stop orders that I have given you. So it looks like you want to count their feet. They will walk here to this office.' We organised a large march in Johannesburg. It was a huge march. People came in buses to Johannesburg and it also included other unions who marched. This is how he recognised SARHWU for the last time. He had to stand outside and say, 'I have already recognised SARHWU in Natal. Now I recognise SARHWU nationally.'[52]

Implementation of the strike settlements did not go smoothly and there were a number of confrontations around the country including strikes at Pietersburg in April, violence at Braamfontein in May, and strikes at Roodepoort, Harmonie, and Port Elizabeth in June, July and August 1990. Eventually, however, on 1 November, an agreement was signed covering

- Recognition
- Freedom of association

---

52. As above.

- Negotiating procedures
- Dispute procedures
- Disciplinary hearings and appeals
- Grievance procedures
- Retrenchment procedures, stop orders
- Shop stewards rights and obligations.

Although the issue of wages was still not settled, the agreement ushered in a new era in the relationship between SARHWU and the newly formed Transnet (incorporated on 1 April 1990) which would force both sides to put away their methods of bulldozing confrontation and to learn the art of negotiating.

Summary

As a public service union SARHWU was confronted by successive racist governments that refused to recognise it or to negotiate with it, and did their best to destroy the union. The choice was stark – either fight or go under, either support the ANC or co-operate in their own oppression. The union and its members chose to fight – both ideologically and physically. As an affiliate of SACTU, SARHWU was centrally involved in organising labour support for the anti-government campaigns of the Congress Alliance in the 1950s. SARHWU activists were among the first to join MK and to go abroad for military and political training in the 1960s. This tradition continued in the 1980s. The re-launch of SARHWU in 1986 was planned by these activists working from exile or underground to organise public service workers, first into general unions and then into industrial sectors. They found willing followers among the many ordinary railway workers who were already rejecting the non-political, company unionism of BLATU.

The militancy of the railway workers was largely fuelled by the economic and social conditions that they were forced to endure, but it was also reinforced on the one hand by the political activity of the UDF and on the other hand by government oppression which was especially fierce during the state of emergency. The new SARHWU leadership saw part of its role as being to educate the membership about the link between their struggle in the workplace and the broader struggle against apartheid. It was not hard to make that connection, as railway employees were in the front line of those affected by apartheid policies. They were spoiling for a fight.

The fight was not long in coming. It was a bloody one, characterised by violence and intransigence on both sides in a series of strikes. SARHWU's campaign was not an ordinary industrial relations struggle. It faced not just the management of the railway but also the government, the army and the police force that the government directed. It is not surprising, therefore, that time and again the language used by SARHWU members and outside observers to describe SARHWU's aims and methods was that of war, revolution, struggle, traitors and spies.

The union was closely identified with the UDF, and some of the new young leadership at that time were directly involved with MK. But SARHWU's policy was to steer clear of the kind of overtly political campaigns and activity that had led to the arrest of so many of its leaders in the 1950s and 1960s. Instead it concentrated on mobilising workers around the labour issues that directly affected them, and used mass strikes, both to recruit more members and to put pressure directly on the government.

The first of these strikes was the major strike of 1987. Although SARHWU was not yet properly reorganised, leaders were able to take advantage of, and to articulate, existing rank and file grievances and demands. These were rapidly escalated into confrontation with the state. Pitched battles erupted between strikers and security forces, not just within the confines of the compounds or townships as had happened before, but also on the streets of central Johannesburg.

A revolutionary situation was created. Along with that there was a revolution in the expectations of SARHWU's supporters and an intolerance towards any opposition – whether from the government, from the railway management, from members of other unions or from within their own ranks. The situation on the ground was difficult to control. The action of the army and police inflamed the workers' anger, and lethal violence between supporters of SARHWU and BLATU was stoked and manipulated by the security forces in order to undermine the solidarity of railway workers. Many leaders were arrested and the day-to-day direction of the strike was in the hands of militant shop stewards and rank and file activists who developed an uncompromising and single-minded culture of their own.

According to a number of interviewees, SARHWU's strategy was to channel this revolutionary violence in order to build up the strength of the union until it was in a position to force recognition by the railway management. Strikes were also seen as a means of mobilising community support for SARHWU and for the liberation movement.

> There was a growth of the organisation from the '87 strike to the one in 1989-90. That had greater depth and it created new layers of workers who got baptised in the fire of a strike. And not just any strike. Usually, SARHWU strikes are political interventions of a sort. You have the

strike support committees in the community; the whole community starts to raise its own issues around the SARHWU strike and then the communities start to go on fire themselves. If it is national, the sum total is you are actually starting to galvanise and shape communities all over the country, bringing them into experiences that had not reached them before. As a result SARHWU workers enjoyed great popularity and respect so when you wore the red T-shirt with that emblem you wore it with pride. You had earned it.[53]

The strike of 1989-90 was in some ways even more like a war than that of 1987 because by this time it was not only the soldiers who had guns. MK units had been infiltrated into key areas and firearms were now more widespread and available to workers who before had had access only to pangas and knives. At the same time the tensions between strikers and non-strikers increased. Transnet management accused union officials of being involved in violence and intimidation of non-strikers.

At all times the most volatile and dangerous place was the City Deep and Kaserne Depots ... The workers at these depots seemed to pride themselves on being more radical and ungovernable than anywhere else. This tendency persisted even after some normalisation was brought about and in my own opinion was an area that the later union officials battled to keep under control ... The strike was very violent and employees were killed for not participating. Some of the trade union leaders would drive around armed and threaten workers who did not stay away ... Union officials would climb on to goods trains and physically remove people who were working. The next day one would inevitably find that a worker had been thrown off a moving train.[54]

Official SARHWU policy was against the use of intimidation, which was seen as giving management a weapon to beat the union with. It is likely that many of these incidents were planned and executed by 'Third Force' operatives working for the security forces. Nevertheless, interviews with a number of people who took part in the strike show that many knew that intimidation was happening and some, at least, took part in pressurising non-strikers.

The militancy of the rank and file was one of SARHWU's key weapons against management and the state but there were disagreements within SARHWU about how far the strike weapon should be used. These disagreements were one of the causes of factionalism and mistrust between sections of the membership and the

---

53. Interview: Martin Sebakwane, Johannesburg, November 1997.
54. Notes by Vic van Vuuren, April 1998.

union leadership at head office. It was an element in both the leadership struggle of 1988, which led to the resignation of Mike Roussos and Stanley Nkosi, and the weakening abortive strike in East London in 1988. It also precipitated a major crisis in 1991/92 when, as we shall see, workers rejected the wage agreement negotiated by the union leadership and Southern Transvaal shop stewards occupied the head office and kidnapped Martin Sebakwane.

6

Turbulent Times

Introduction

SARHWU had won a significant victory. The signing of the recognition agreement with Transnet on 1 November 1990 should have heralded the dawn of a new era of prosperity and success for the union. Recognition gave relative financial security. Workers who joined the union would be asked to sign stop orders so that subscriptions would be automatically deducted from their pay and it would no longer be necessary to collect them by hand. The union could rely on a regular income for the first time; organisers could be paid and debts settled; and the change in the political atmosphere signalled by the un-banning of the ANC and SACP in February 1990 suggested to some that industrial relations in the railway industry would also take a turn for the better.

The union was now able to take part in wages negotiations in a way that might bring results, and workers were no longer afraid to join SARHWU as had previously been the case.

> After that there were disagreements but most of the workers joined hands with SARHWU because what we did get was recognition and we were able now to organise openly within the plant. Before the recognition people were actually afraid of joining hands with SARHWU, because the organisation was termed by the then government as an organisation of communists, an anti-government organisation. The workers were afraid, and also the staff associations were helped by management to organise.[1]

---

1. Interview: Mandla Nzama, Johannesburg, October 1997.

173

As a result SARHWU regained a large part of the membership that had begun to drift away after the failures of 1988, and BLATU lost about half of its membership, which fell from 60 000 to around 30 000 by 1990.[2]

To a large extent it seemed that militancy had paid off, but there were some ominous signs of trouble ahead. Conditions were nowhere near as favourable as they might appear, and it was to prove difficult for SARHWU to break away from the influences of recent history – in particular, the continued mutual hostility and suspicion between SARHWU and Transnet and the factionalism and internal tensions that continued to dog the union. Although the militancy of the workers and the changing political environment in South Africa had forced Transnet to recognise SARHWU, the attitude of the management was still inflexible. Despite the strike, the union had failed to win either reinstatement of the 400 sacked East London workers or the R1 500 minimum wage which had been the main motivation for its members. In fact it had failed to win any increase at all. Workers were dissatisfied:

> Not everybody was satisfied with the agreement that was signed. As shop steward leadership we were aware that R1 500 was the main demand to organise workers. It was impossible for one to get R1 500, but we knew we would get the political gain, the recognition of SARHWU. But when it came to the signing of the agreement, it was clear that most of the general workers were not actually in agreement, as it didn't reach their expectation which was R1 500. [3]

Nor, as Mandla Nzama explains, did the recognition agreement put an end to poor relations with management or the violent rivalry with BLATU.

> Immediately after the strike, around May, there was tension between ourselves who were on strike and those who were not on strike: the members of the staff associations. There was a calculated campaign by management, especially in Braamfontein, whereby we on strike were not welcome to come back. I was working in the trains then, as a guard. One week when we were in a protest we went off for a stayaway, several members. When we came back on a Tuesday we found white workers were working as barrier attendants in the place of our core workers. We sat down and strategised and decided to fight with them. The following morning at about 7 a.m. we decided that we needed to leave everything and fight those guys. We fought them and we beat them. As a result one

---

2.   *IR Data and Union Profiles*, August 1991 puts SARHWU's paid-up membership as 36 243, compared with 16 400 in 1989.
3.   Interview: Mandla Nzama, Johannesburg, October 1997.

was seriously injured and taken to hospital. I was dismissed. SARHWU took the case for arbitration after my dismissal and I stayed out of a job for 3 or 4 months and then we won the arbitration case and I went back to my position as a guard.[4]

The agreement reached between SARHWU and Transnet stated that the union's representation should be determined by the number of stop orders in operation at any given time. However, it is important to note that this clause had the capacity to pinion SARHWU because it was the employer who computerised the workers' stop orders.

> Where SARHWU could not prove that they had 40% + 1 members of a particular grade, Transnet would not recognise SARHWU for the purposes of collective bargaining. This loophole was exploited by Transnet which was hell-bent on reducing SARHWU membership by not effecting its stop orders. One episode was when we confronted them with copies of joining forms whose original copies were submitted to them by one of SARHWU organisers, Comrade Sekete. Their excuse was that they had computer problems. This was reflective of the fact that Transnet had not yet outgrown the adversarial approach to labour relations. Equally true is that SARHWU had very rigid positions which could be counter-productive at times. One such example is the suspicion that nearly paralysed the training programme that Transnet offered to its employees gratis.[5]

At the same time a very different industrial relations structure was about to be instituted, which was to present new challenges to the union. In 1988 the SATS Labour Council had been set up under the chairmanship of Professor Nic Wiehahn, with equal representation of management and the internal SATS-registered unions, including BLATU. Plans were also in hand which would transform SATS into a new statutory corporation – Transnet – which would operate as five separate business units with industrial relations conducted by a new bargaining forum operating under regulations laid down by the LRA, from which the railways had previously been excluded.

The release of ANC leaders from jail was a signal that the government was in retreat from the confrontational position which it had previously adopted and was prepared to allow the railways to come under the normal industrial relations system rather than under direct government control.

---

4.   As above.
5.   Vanguard Mkosana, p. 5. 'Bantu Education' had for so long been geared to preventing Africans from gaining advanced knowledge and skills that it is not surprising that workers were suspicious of Transnet's offer.

These changes, which came into effect in October 1991, were to have an effect upon the railway industry, which SARHWU perhaps failed to appreciate sufficiently at the time. Once the industry was released from direct government control, commercial criteria assumed a prominence that they had not previously held, although the attitudes of managers did not change overnight. In future the issues to be confronted would be less the political ones of government racism and oppression and more those of unemployment and low wages.

The State of the Organisation

> The recognition agreement brought to the fore new challenges. The union had to prepare and strategise for wage negotiations. There were clearly defined procedures to follow regarding disputes, grievances and retrenchment. Shop stewards had to know what was expected of them. All these implied that the organisation had to reshape itself to meet these challenges.[6]

It was only after recognition of SARHWU, that attention could be given to matters of strategic organising. Knowing the location, number and conditions of the membership was central to developing an organising strategy. The exact number of SARHWU members was not known. Membership was estimated at 50 000 signed-up, but of these only 34 000 were verified by SATS. The verification process could make or break SARHWU because, according to the recognition agreement, 'the company agrees to deduct subscriptions in favour of the union from the wages of those employees whose stop order forms have been submitted to the company, provided that an employee shall not have more than one trade union stop order in operation with the company at any given time'.

> This was a powder keg. This clause allowed Transnet to play SARHWU against BLATU over the question of dual membership. Some workers joined BLATU before SARHWU was relaunched in 1986. When they wanted to cross over to SARHWU their stop orders reflected BLATU and therefore, as long as Transnet did not remove their BLATU stop orders, there was no way they could contribute subscriptions to SARHWU. Nor could they be recognised as members of SARHWU. This kept SARHWU membership figures open to Transnet manipulation. Using their monopoly over computerisation of stop orders, Transnet conducted selective implementation. Stop orders of SARHWU were effected for the general workers' grade. This meant that SARHWU

---

6.   As above, p. 6.

would represent only the grade of general workers for collective bargaining purposes. At the end this could save Transnet huge sums of money during wage negotiations. At the same time it had the potential of dividing the union between would-be neglected members and favoured members. SARHWU leadership and the entire membership had to work hard to reverse this and the union lawyers were also involved.

An interesting phenomenon with SARHWU was that the growing membership was all organised into SARHWU by the very workers themselves, not by union-employed organisers. This remained the case until some of the former employees who were expelled by Transnet were engaged by SARHWU as organisers. This worker participation in organising work made workers highly sensitive to their organisation. Anything that threatened SARHWU was regard as a direct threat to them. In times of crisis they were fast to express those sentiments. One of SARHWU's most committed members – known as Comrade Manoeuvre – would say '*Comrades sinibhekile, if niya manoeuvr(a) lapha anizokuphumelela*. [Comrades we are watching you, if you manoeuvre against this organisation you are not going to succeed.] We built SARHWU from scratch on our own. We are still capable of doing that.' This was a stern word of encouragement to the organisers who were sometimes seen as being extravagant in the use of resources.[7]

SARHWU had nine regional offices throughout the country: Northern Transvaal in Pretoria, Southern Transvaal in Johannesburg, Northern Natal in Empangeni, Southern Natal in Durban, Eastern Cape in East London, Cape Midlands in Port Elizabeth, Orange Free State in Bloemfontein, Northern Cape in Kimberley and Western Cape in Cape Town. There were also supporting offices in Pietersburg, Nelspruit, Witbank, Springs, Germiston, Vereeniging, Ladysmith, Pietermaritzburg, Kokstad, Umtata, Queenstown, Uitenhage, Kroonstad and Klerksdorp.

The SARHWU organisational set-up took into consideration the fact that Transnet was used as a fighting arm of the apartheid government. Past strikes had taught SARHWU that if the coastline Transnet workers were left unschooled in SARHWU's politics there was a possibility that Transnet could undermine international sanctions against apartheid. Southern Natal was strong in membership but highly divided in terms of how to tackle the challenges facing SARHWU. Northern Natal, where the Richard's Bay 'Coal line' was a threat to sanctions, was very weak at this stage. There was clearly a need for people whose

---

7.   As above, pp. 10-11.

sole responsibility it was to deal with organisational work on a full-time basis. Where they were already in place they needed training. Such changes were effected with the help of SACTU.

The role of SACTU

SACTU in exile had played an important role in encouraging the revival and development of progressive unionism in South Africa, in building international solidarity and in encouraging the unity talks which led to the setting up of COSATU.[8] The unbanning of the ANC and SACP raised questions about the future role of the labour movement and its relationship with the political parties. SACTU's position was one of continuing support for the ANC whilst maintaining the importance of an independent role for trade unions. Avoiding attempts to create a split with COSATU it began discussions with the labour movement inside South Africa. In March 1990 representatives of SACTU and COSATU met in Kafue, Zambia, and a SACTU NEC proposal that SACTU should phase itself out in favour of COSATU was endorsed and adopted. Following from this a Joint Facilitating Committee was elected. On SACTU's side it had Archie Sibeko (known by his MK name, Zola Zembe, or Comrade ZZ) as the convenor of the Committee. Other SACTU members were Thobile Mhlahlo, Ilva Mackay-Langa, Martin Sire and Vanguard Mkosana, and COSATU had a corresponding number of committee members. The main task of the Facilitating Committee was to ensure the smooth fusion of SACTU resources into COSATU. In this regard the first thing was to deploy SACTU cadres into COSATU affiliates.

Vanguard Mkosana was one of the first exiles to return.

> This original arrangement was that I would be deployed in the National Union of Mine Workers (NUM). NUM was my natural home because of my background as a former miner and the role I played towards the formation of NUM. This did not materialise. I was asked by Comrade ZZ to go to SARHWU. To motivate me for this move he cited reasons which I, together with my other colleagues in SACTU leadership, agreed with. Among these was the fact that SARHWU had just emerged from the devastating strikes of 1987 and 1989. It was faced with a gigantic task of consolidating the gains of those strikes and rebuilding the union in a changing environment. It needed strengthening at leadership level. I knew the leadership of SARHWU from the interaction we had with them trying to resolve some of the problems they from time

---

8.   Interview: A. Sibeko, May 1998; R. Roux, 1990, p. 48.

to time sent to SACTU in Zambia for discussion and resolution so it was finally agreed that I should go to SARHWU.

I landed at Johannesburg International Airport from exile in Lusaka on Monday 10 December 1990. My first day at SARHWU was on Tuesday 11 December 1990 when the leadership of SARHWU welcomed me. I was asked to establish the Communication Department of SARHWU. This was important for effective internal communication among the members within the organisation and for outside publicity and marketing of our union. In April 1991 the first issue of a fortnightly *SARHWU Information Sheet* [SIS] came out and *SARHWU Voice,* the official organ of SARHWU, was published in July 1991. *SARHWU Voice* put more emphasis on education of membership and organising workers into the ranks of SARHWU. It was published once in two months. *SIS* and *SARHWU Voice* complemented each other.

The 1990s ushered in a new era in SARHWU whereby worker leadership and union employees had to have certain skills to ensure that the union survives and remains the worthy defender of workers' rights. Education became central in this regard. The first wage agreement with Transnet did not cover all membership but mainly track and general workers. In preparation for the 1991 wage negotiations, leadership called for expansion of their mandate to negotiate for all grades.

For this a collective bargaining workshop for the SARHWU National Negotiating Team was organised in February 1991. Coupled with wage increments SARHWU introduced to its membership the importance of including other benefits like maternity and paternity leave, medical aid, health and safety considerations at the workplaces, decent housing subsidy, etc. On the other hand, SARHWU organised group funeral insurance schemes for its members and employees. All these put pressure on SARHWU to be fast in developing a new brand of cadres capable of engaging Transnet at a sophisticated level. Among other things the organisation had to restructure itself. In this regard, besides my Media department, it was decided to establish Education, Legal and Bargaining and Research departments. For these departments to be established SARHWU relied on the returning SACTU exiles. I was in charge of the process of facilitating their return. Apartheid government did not make things easy for them to return. I worked closely with SARHWU lawyers – Cheadle, Thomson and Haysom – until they were allowed in.

179

In preparation for the forthcoming national congress discussions were held between the Transport and General Workers Union (T&GWU) and SARHWU leadership on 16 February 1991. Among other things they agreed to accept the COSATU policy of 'One industry one union' and to support each other in a process of 'Unity through Action' which would lead eventually to merger. COSATU was to be asked to support these efforts materially.

The Third SARHWU Congress

The Third Congress of SARHWU started on 27 February and ended on 2 March 1991. Its opening session was addressed by Ahmed Kathrada of the ANC, Dr Mkhari of SACP, Sydney Mufamadi the Assistant General Secretary of COSATU, Willie Matsi of the Namibian Transport and Allied Union (NATAU), the Assistant General Secretary of the Transport and General Workers Union and Zola Zembe (Archie Sibeko), who was also elected Honorary President of SARHWU. Among the international guests were the FNV (Holland), CGT-Railway (France), and the British National Union of Railwaymen (now the Rail, Maritime and Transport Workers). Also, for the first time ever, the coloured and Indian unions in Transnet were invited guests, and the National Council of Trade Unions (NACTU) and its transport affiliates were also invited.

Among the key issues discussed by the Congress were:

- The release of the four SARHWU members on death row for their role in the SARHWU strike of 1987: George Maungedzo, David Mamphanga, Wilson Matshile and Patrick Molefe
- Support for the COSATU policy of one union in one industry
- Support for COSATU's campaign against retrenchments and ways of building up the union's organisational structure.

In all, 25 resolutions were passed including one on education, one resolving to maintain the policy of non-alignment internationally and one regarding the decentralisation of funds and their distribution to the regions.

The entire leadership was returned with the exception of one change. Bafana Sithole was replaced by Johnny Potgieter as Assistant General Secretary, Justice Langa remained the President, TE Moshoeshoe the 1st Vice-President, Thembekile Majalisa, the 2nd Vice-President, Jonas Makhavhu the National Treasurer and Martin Sebakwane the General Secretary. Sebakwane was not the unanimous choice of delegates and many, including Zola Zembe, attempted unsuccessfully to persuade Vanguard Mkosana to stand for election. At the same time there was some resentment at the role played by the newly returned SACTU cadres.

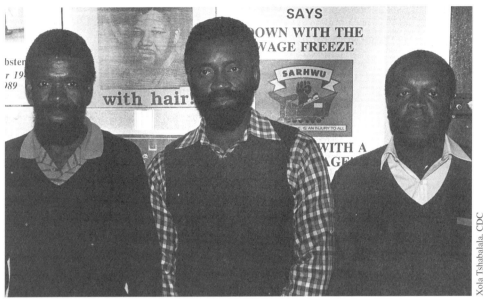

From left to right: Justice Langa, Martin Sebakwane and Bafana Sithole.

Also, around that time, there was the issue of the role of the SACTU comrades who had just joined the organisation. It hasn't been a very long time since our SACTU comrades came in. Now what happened around that area? I think for a very long time the Southern Transvaal needed a credible person, a credible leader of standing which they could use to vent their frustrations. Such a personality was provided for the Southern Transvaal by Vanguard [Mkosana]. I think we never had a real one-to-one relationship between the leadership and him and people from SACTU. In fact, there were people beginning to say, 'SARHWU is the first union where SACTU wants to take over and come re-casting itself into the life and bodies of current trade unions. It is a SACTU caucus.' Events had moved so far politically that that wasn't possible, but the perceptions were there and I always believe if perceptions are there they are sustained by some activities. There was definitely a power thing happening there but those are things that happen in organisations.[9]

Immediately after the Congress the union began the process of implementation of Congress resolutions. A National Finance Workshop was held on 22/23 March. A National Staff Meeting was convened in Bloemfontein on 2/3 May 1991 to discuss a number of organisational matters including the structural framework of SARHWU in the context of the changing environment, job

---

9.   Interview: Martin Sebakwane, Johannesburg, November 1997.

descriptions and staff training and upgrading. Vanguard Mkosana was tasked to head both the Education and Publicity Departments of SARHWU and worked with Bafana Sithole to create an education structure. Of the seven other SACTU exiles expected to join in the educational work only Eric Mtshagi, who was to be the regional education officer in Southern Natal, and Xolani Gogwana, who was sent to Northern Cape to be the regional education officer, had arrived at that point. Mkosana began immediately.

> We developed training material for shop stewards who were our main target. This material was also published in our journal *SARHWU Voice*. When these comrades from exile finally returned our team was strengthened. We called them to head office to work from there for a start and embark on a vigorous education campaign. Actively involved in that campaign were myself, Albert Mashoai, Sikhumbuzov Majeke, Sanku Gwala.
>
> In our strategy we planned to train trainers first in order to ensure continuity and target shop stewards for mass education of our members. At the same time the employer's role in training was identified. We encountered problems of mutual mistrust between Transnet and SARHWU members. The employer developed ideas on what type of training scheme they would give to employees. SARHWU workers rejected this.
>
> They had adult basic education and Management 2000 among their education projects. After going through these we found positive elements which help in development of skills of our members. I had a number of meetings with Dr Wolmarans of Management 2000 who was panicking that this programme was destined to collapse. I had sessions with shop stewards trying to show them that we need not be over-suspicious of Transnet regarding training. This is our right. The white workers have been enjoying this right. Moreover if we feel we are taught wrong stuff we should detect that in the course of learning and demand change. At the same time we put pressure on Transnet to consult with us on matters relating to education and training of our members.[10]

Wage negotiations

With the transformation of SATS into Transnet, the Labour Relations Act was to become applicable to both SARHWU and Transnet on 6 October 1991. *Inter*

---

10. Vanguard Mkosana, 1998, p. 17.

alia this meant participation by SARHWU in the new Transnet Industrial Council on the same terms as the other 12 Transnet unions who before then were party to the undemocratic Labour Council (which had been challenged by SARHWU). The Industrial Council was formed on 13 September 1991 and Nic Wiehan was elected chairperson. This was an important forum because some important collective bargaining matters were handled there but as a forum for determining SARHWU's immediate wage demands it was totally ineffective.

All SARHWU membership had been given the opportunity to discuss the wage demand through a series of regional wage conferences culminating in a national wage conference held in Bloemfontein on 7/9 June 1991. It was agreed by the conference that SARHWU should negotiate on behalf of all its members, not only those for which Transnet had recognised the union.

It was noted that there were racially-based categories in the employment structure of Transnet. For example, Group C (graded employees with no training) consisted of blacks only and Group D (non-graded employees with no training, no compensation and no allowances) was also blacks only. The conference resolved to demand:

- The elimination of wage disparities based on race
- A 40% increase for Group A employees of all races
- A 40% increase for Group B employees plus reduction of unnecessary grades in similar work
- Upgrading training, promotion and corresponding pay for acting up in a job
- For Group C and D employees a R1 500 minimum wage
- Training, health and safety measures, upgrading and promotion.

In addition, the conference demanded a 40-hour working week. Unemployment Insurance Fund payments should be made with no delay in the issuing of the unemployment card. Death through injury on duty should entitle the wife to get the husband's current wages immediately and Transnet should help with transport to the funeral. Transferred workers should be properly accommodated.

In mid-June Transnet had reached an agreement with BLATU and the other eleven unions in the SATS Labour Council for an 11,5 % increase and a R900 minimum wage, and BLATU had issued a pamphlet challenging SARHWU to do better. The increase was rejected by SARHWU, which insisted on a renegotiation, but no agreement could be reached. In all some fifteen meetings were held, after each of which the SARHWU negotiating team was expected to report back in every region and renew its mandate for the following round of talks. Transnet refused to increase the 11,5% and would only offer a one-off bonus of

R60. SARHWU refused this and on 23 September a special National Executive Committee was convened at which the General Secretary reported the situation.

> After this presentation anger and frustration were evident. Orange Free State was tasked to further develop the Transnet bonus offer to our members' benefit. Southern Transvaal was first to propose industrial action before 1 October 1991. All regions supported action against Transnet save OFS. It was agreed that on 30 September 1991 the strike begins. The group to strike should be the Sunday night shift workers. They were to stage a sit-in within Transnet premises. The meeting concentrated on preparations for the strike. The NEC meeting scheduled for 9 October was postponed indefinitely.
>
> Delegates were welcomed by the Honorary President, Comrade ZZ. Among other things he said, 'Our country is at a crossroads and that is the time to choose whether we go North or South, West or East. It is necessary to sit and think which way forward. Our enemy is out to destroy SARHWU. Unity is the key to our survival. Leaders must articulate our views and lead.' Comrade ZZ pointed to important matters to be considered if our strike is to be a success. These were:
>
> 1. We should canvass the support of our sister organisations. Unity was the imperative of the time.
>
> 2. We should learn from our past experiences that we need thorough planning for this strike.
>
> 3. The most important thing is that we are one family. From this moment all trivial differences should perish. The main enemy is Transnet … We must be smarter than we were before.

Strike Co-ordinating Committees were set up in such a way as to enable the democratic participation of the whole of the membership. At the centre was the National Management Committee (NMC), headed by the President of SARHWU, Justice Langa, to direct the strike nationally. In the regions the Regional Secretaries were to be the co-ordinators in a committee that included branch secretaries. The Branch Co-ordinating Committees were put under branch Chairpersons and these committees were to involve secretaries of the Central Shop Stewards Councils. It was announced that,' This special NEC has declared war on Transnet,' and all left ready to galvanise their members into action.[11]

---

11. Interview: Thobile Jekwa, East London, October 1997.

Disunity

Already, however, there were signs that the call for unity had fallen on deaf ears. At the opening of the NEC it was noted that the delegation from Southern Transvaal was not there. Information was received that they had gone to a meeting with Transnet. The NEC meeting was adjourned to get them to join the other regional representatives because it was said the decisions of that meeting were going to be too vital to have a region absent. After discussion, Eastern Cape moved that the Southern Transvaal leadership should be suspended for undermining the national leadership of the union. Eventually, however, the meeting agreed to send a delegation to Transnet to recall the Southern Transvaal members and they finally joined the rest of the NEC after lunch.

The relationship of the Southern Transvaal with the other regions had become progressively worse since the end of the 1989 strike.

> Since after the strike, up until this period Southern Transvaal became most militant and most vocal. One thing which is positive about Southern Transvaal is that, when going to Congress, when going to NEC, you come prepared on all kind of issues that the union has to take positions on in terms of resolutions … But one problem with that was that a specific culture and attitude developed. People, other SARHWU regions, started to see Southern Transvaal as a region which claims and wants to be the leader of all SARHWU structures. Then people started to form certain negative attitudes. Meetings in NECs became totally destructive because whenever any person from Southern Transvaal speaks that person will be shouted at and won't be listened to. At certain points people will just disagree because Southern Transvaal is coming with a particular position. There were clear fights and divisions in the union.

> Also it is true that Southern Transvaal leadership was arrogant because they had a belief that they were the only ones who could advance SARHWU, the only ones who knew better in terms of resolutions and whatever political issues SARHWU faced. That went on and on, up until there was a breakdown in communications between Southern Transvaal and SARHWU Head Office to such an extent that the Head Office would not allocate funds to Southern Transvaal for the running of the office, for transport to NEC meetings and all that kind of thing. That resulted in creating corrupting tendencies within SARHWU

185

because people started to backbite each other, to speak behind each other's backs, to bring all kinds of accusations against each other. [12]

At a special Southern Transvaal regional executive committee meeting on 7 September it was complained that the National Management Committee (NMC) was unresponsive to regional views, and there was a crisis in the union's finances, meaning that SARHWU could not meet its obligations including the payment of salaries. A proposal that the region should withdraw all payments to Head Office was only narrowly defeated and the region reserved the right to inform other regions if its complaints were not dealt with. [13]

At the same time there were external influences being brought to bear on the SARHWU negotiating team which were causing Martin Sebakwane to doubt the wisdom of a strike strategy. Negotiations between the ANC and the National Party were on a knife-edge. The security establishment and those on the right wing of the government were determined to derail the talks. To achieve this they engaged in the illicit funding of the Zulu Inkatha Freedom Party (IFP), which was opposed to the ANC, and of a mysterious 'Third Force' which was responsible for destabilisation and the encouragement of 'black on black' violence throughout the country.

> These negotiations were happening in a very peculiar time and environment ... The [political] parties had already signed the agreements around de-escalating hostilities, peace agreements, peace accords. A climate had been defined which, in terms of classical SARHWU strategy of taking on management head-on, was completely contrary to what we were used to – because, if SARHWU goes on strike, it is a revolutionary situation but if you are part of an alliance, if the main body of the revolution has set a certain agenda and you are an ally in that, do you take your own route, bring the alliance partners into situations that will be embarrassing? You have to strengthen the side that you belong to.
>
> The dynamics of wage negotiations is that you have a series of negotiations [during which] you report back, get a mandate, go back and negotiate again. We had the national negotiating team which had become quite proficient over a number of years. They were solid, tested worker comrades who understood the processes of negotiation. They also understood the need to give guidance to constituencies – to lead and persuade and facilitate agreements on very difficult issues,

---

12. Interview: Stephen Matlou, Cape Town, October 1997.
13. Minutes of Special Regional Executive Committee, Johannesburg, 7 September 1991.

sometimes, where we had to sign agreements with management. In this particular instance, the negotiating team exhausted its discussions with management. It was very clear that management did not want to move any further. Management hadn't met the demands which members had wanted.

Under such circumstances, we would call an NEC which then decides the way forward. The negotiating team reports that, 'We have tried this, we have tried that, we have tried that; it is not working; we have proposed the following,' – that kind of analysis. The Southern Transvaal members on the negotiating team were arguing that on two occasions, when they had big report-back meetings, the Inkatha people were killing our members. We were having funerals all the time to go and bury people. They very succinctly argued that, politically, it would be correct to avoid any situations where we would have to further bury our members and there is no way that the workers will follow us when we call out the strike.

Then we said, 'Well, if the rest of the regions are saying no, we have to be seen through our efforts to have gained something slightly more than what BLATU has signed to. We have to find other means which will not expose our members to being killed by Inkatha and so forth.' Because if we go on a full scale strike, of course, Inkatha and the Third Force at that time was really coming out very strongly. The debate was swinging this way and that way, this way and that way. Of course, there was merit in the argument of the Southern Transvaal but the rest of the regions were not buying it. Also the Southern Transvaal were getting the brunt of Third Force activities in the stations, in the hostels and so on which was not the case with a lot of the other regions. So as leadership, we have to find some middle path because, at the political level, we would look like we don't understand congress politics; we would look like extreme leftists if we really said officially, 'There is a strike of SARHWU,' – knowing what a SARHWU strike would do to the climate of peace talks.

The evaluation of regional reports was clearly that the workers are not prepared to go to a large full-scale strike. It will not happen. It is out of the question. Number two, we don't even have the funds to sustain a big strike, let alone the political will. Nobody would finance a strike of SARHWU so that there is a conflagration. Even overseas they would switch off their taps, you know. Never mind that we would become a political embarrassment, just the logistic of carrying on a strike of the sort would be impossible. We hadn't recovered financially from the previous big one. So, we said, 'We can't leave a meeting like this one with the employer knowing that we are not contemplating anything. That also would not work. We have to combine approaches. We are well known for strikes, and big strikes. Perhaps for the first time now we should use the threat of a strike to get some things that we want and not go full scale.'

The symbolism of a strike was tied up with a national strike to be led by COSATU around some consumer issues. It had come to a point where if we don't go out with the whole nation on strike, when they retreat and our head is still out there, we will get chopped, even our own side will distance itself from us. So we then said, 'We will send out a signal that our going on that strike on Monday will be our starting to engage management. We will use this national thing to go in and out and when everybody retreats we all retreat and use the threat that we can actually go out again for real.' That way we are covered and protected by the national situation because we don't want to sacrifice people any more. That was the understanding from the NEC.

Then we sent word to them [the management]. Generally the action is building up; there are lunchtime demonstrations and so on. You rev the engine a bit and let it warm up. Once they get reports from Head Office of Transnet, 'This is happening in Eastern Cape; there is this in Western Cape; it is all over the place', it confuses them and it makes them think, 'Oh, they are revving the engine. They are about to take us up again'. But we knew that our own tactic is to just link with the national strike; go out, come back and use the popularity that you can actually do it, you have demonstrated you could do it.[14]

Sebakwane sought the advice of COSATU but received mixed messages. The ~heration movement was split between those who pinned their hopes on the ~tream negotiations taking place with the apartheid regime and those who ~ass action would be needed to bring about a genuine political change. ~her side was prepared to take the SARHWU leadership into its ~vane was still treated with suspicion as a newcomer who, even ~ed to be a spy, had no track record in the anti-apartheid ~vril Ramaphosa, the leader of the ANC side in the ~th the apartheid regime, went unanswered, and ~e 'too busy' to discuss the SARHWU situation.

~esburg, November 1997.

Instead Sebakwane received hints through a third party, the lawyer, Halton Cheadle, who acted for both SARHWU and the ANC:

> As the week was going on, instead of talking to us directly, our own side was talking to us through Cheadle, Thompson, who were our lawyers. The signals were coming from Cheadle, Thompson to say, 'Well, it has been heard from different quarters that you guys are planning a big strike and there is the peace accord, there are these difficulties; is it possible that we can intervene to divert and avoid what might be coming a very nasty embarrassing situation?' The lawyers were saying, 'Well, Sydney [Mufamadi] says this, Cyril [Ramaphosa] says this.' Also management has phoned them to say they might consider something, having had discussions with some of the movement people themselves. We then had discussions amongst ourselves. Clearly we are being isolated here. Nobody wants to talk to us but also nobody wants to be heard saying to a fraternal organisation, 'Don't go to strike.'
>
> The balance of arguments is, we are not a liberation movement; we are just a trade union. If the main liberation movement has itself suspended armed action, is in negotiations with the enemy, why should we want to take on the responsibility of turning the revolution? What is there to be benefited when we actually physically allow the workers to go out on strike and stay on strike? Inkatha violence, Third Force violence. Can we start something we can't have a hold on?[15]

Sebakwane's mind was made up but there was strong opposition to a settlement from other members of the National Management Committee and from Southern Transvaal representatives who, from having advised against provoking Inkatha violence, were now vigorously in favour of a full-blown strike.

On Friday 27 September the union head office received a fax from Transnet urging SARHWU to resume negotiations in order to avert a strike. A copy of the letter was faxed to all regions and a meeting was convened at Head Office, but the full negotiating team (the NMC plus one delegate from each of the nine regions) was not present. Jonas Makhavhu was called to a meeting between some of the NMC and Halton Cheadle, the union's lawyer.

> The Friday before the Monday of that strike, I was called out from City Deep. Martin phoned me and said you must come, there is a meeting. Then I came over to the office and I found out they were not in the office, they were in the meeting, in Braamfontein, with those lawyers. I found

---

15. As above.

all the leadership there except Majalisa and Moshoeshoe ... They said, there is this problem which we have to discuss. Thompson and Cheadle have arranged a meeting with management, we have to sit and discuss and try to stop the strike. Then I said, 'Now what is the idea of us stopping the strike ... why should we worry and stop it? If the management aren't ready to play and the workers are ready to go on strike, let's go on strike.' They said, 'No you don't understand, this thing has been negotiated, we have already spoken to other organisations, they are saying we must stop this strike, we have spoken to COSATU; COSATU says no, they think if the workers go out on strike there is going to be war, because there's this war between IFP and ANC, and the workers are going to be caught in the middle, so let's stop this.' Then Martin said to me, they've already consulted people in the ANC, they are saying we must stop this strike, so we need to start negotiating again.[16]

Overruling Makhavhu's objections, the General Secretary agreed to a meeting with Transnet at 9 a.m. the following day. At the meeting Transnet increased its offer slightly, to a staggered increase of 12% and a minimum wage of R925. The meeting adjourned at about 8 o'clock on Saturday night for SARHWU to consider the offer. The problem was that only three of the fourteen-member negotiating team were present. Some attempt was made to get the regional members of the team up to Johannesburg but it was impossible to contact most of them in time and only the 2nd Vice-President, Thobile Majalisa, was able to join the discussions. By Sunday midday it was obvious that the rest of the negotiating team were not coming. SARHWU's democratic procedures required that there should be a full report back to members before any agreement was reached. Members of head office staff who were present argued against taking a decision without the rest of the negotiating team. Simon Mulumone felt strongly that it was wrong to sign without a mandate and Vanguard Mkosana warned ~ainst going against the decision of the NEC.

the 29 September 1991, on a Sunday, I was busy with other comrades
'ng for the strike when I was invited by Martin to join them at our
ᶜfices. There was something urgent to handle. In the offices
~omson and Haysom at Braamfontein was a group of
elected office bearers and some were Head Office
ᵗhat it appears Transnet is prepared to make a
' to hear them. What actually took place is a
ᴜe and one of the mediator panellists were a

form of mediation. Cheadle and one of the mediator panellists were a go-between between these two sides. That session of the negotiations took place without the involvement of the national negotiating team, which included regional representatives. Secondly the decision to open negotiations was in opposition to the resolution of the Special NEC meeting which took place five days ago calling a strike.[17]

Johan Beaurain, a Head Office organiser, was also fiercely opposed to the signing:

At the time when it happened I couldn't understand why he had to sign the agreement. In fact I was present at the time and at one stage I walked out of that meeting when I realised I won't be able to prevent him signing anything. Actually the whole thing was a very emotional thing. People's emotions were high up. They were having expectations about wages but it wasn't only about wages; it was because of the whole political circumstances in South Africa. It was the violence – it made it a very volatile situation. People were angry because people were killed every day and that stress, living under those conditions, made people believe that there is only one way that we can overthrow the system. We must fight them and even if we have to stop everything in the country and overthrow the whole system and create a hell of a chaos here then that is what we must do. There were actually people amongst the SARHWU people thinking about creating that situation where a SARHWU strike will develop and it will be expanded into something where it will be a huge strike, where people will bring the system into chaos and force the government to agree to whatever the ANC wanted to negotiate with them at that stage.

I don't know what forces were there on the side of the management preventing them from coming to an agreement. I don't know if there was also political forces because the right wing at that stage was just sitting waiting for some chaos, creating some chaos so that they can take the whole process back again to nothing where there will be no negotiations … On that day of the negotiations we started on Saturday and we continued on Sunday. On that Saturday Martin took me out a few times, out of the negotiations, trying to speak to me, trying to persuade me, going to buy cigarettes and then we walk and talk in the street and we come back again. And he said to me, '60 000 railway workers are not going to bring about liberation in South Africa. It's going to be a much bigger effort.' I wasn't really impressed with his

17. Interview: Vanguard Mkosana, King Williams Town, October 1997.

191

way of thinking. I didn't want him to continue with signing this agreement. I was very emotional when I realised they were going to sign.

Martin said to me, 'I cannot allow this organisation to be destroyed. These people are waiting for us. They are going to retrench half of this union; they want us to go on strike and I'm not going to allow this union to be destroyed. If I must be kicked out of my position because our people couldn't understand why I had to sign this agreement I still have to sign the agreement. It doesn't matter what happens.' I still tried to persuade him, 'Please, please, the people will never understand; they will never accept you signing this agreement. Please don't do that.' He said, 'I'm going to do it; I've got no other option, it must be done.' So when I left there I was very angry with him – very, very angry – but he just pushed through it. He signed the agreement. [18]

The NMC members present decided to take a calculated risk and to sign what they knew was a controversial agreement. The decision may well have been the right one in the long run, but the timing and what was seen as Sebakwane's deception of his comrades were disastrous for the union in the short run. Although he had called the rest of the negotiating team back to Johannesburg, Sebakwane had signed without waiting for their approval, thus breaking a vital constitutional tradition. What made things worse was that immediately the document was signed, the Transnet team faxed the agreement directly to their managers who released it to SARHWU membership, informing them that they should not go on strike because an agreement had been reached. In doing this Transnet was deliberately attempting to undermine the union. Sebakwane realised immediately that he had been put in a tight spot.

The worst thing you want is somebody else to report to your constituency before you come and report. That undermines everything com-
ꞁletely and that was what happened. When they came with these
ꞁcopies of the agreement, showing everyone, then the perspective
ꞁing haywire. When the negotiators came and we were giving
ꞁlanation of what happened there was, of course, a very
ꞁment telling them. Firstly, they were demanding that
ꞁe gone to talk to management. Secondly, that there
ꞁing to sell this thing when they were not part
ꞁ endless discussions there, very difficult

ꞁn, October 1997.

ones. Finally, there was some kind of agreement, understanding. People flew back to their regions to go and explain what has happened.[19]

The following day, on which the strike had been planned to start, there was much confusion and much anger, especially in the Southern Transvaal. The Southern Transvaal representatives refused to sell the settlement to their members, and on Monday 30 September the President, Justice Langa, and the Assistant General Secretary, Johnny Potgieter, were forced to go to a mass meeting at Delmore in Johannesburg to explain the situation regarding the agreement. The meeting became threatening and only narrowly did they escape assault.

> We were supposed to be going to Delmore for the first day of the strike but we were told that an agreement was signed over the weekend – this was by management! When we went there the leadership accepted that they signed with no mandate and asked for forgiveness for that but people didn't like it. The President, Justice Langa, was driving a Volkswagen Golf and the workers lifted it up with him inside it! They wanted to break him with the car but Nelson Ndinisa and the leadership of the region pleaded with them not to do that and then they left him.[20]

The office bearers and some of the head office staff were dispatched throughout the country to calm the workers but they met with similar treatment. In Cape Town Martin Sebakwane was joined by the Honorary President.

> We went to all these places, split ourselves to go and explain what was happening. I was in Cape Town and ZZ was there as well. We were part of a very tense meeting in a community centre there. The workers locked us up in their office afterwards to say, 'You must really tell us what is happening.' By then, the stories were out that we have been sold. The company has bought farms for us. We have got all kinds of things. We have been bribed with all kinds of things. In Cape Town, I think if ZZ were not there, on our own we wouldn't have handled that situation; it was very volatile.[21]

Occupation

It seemed to Sebakwane that it was still possible to sell the agreement to the membership but he was reckoning without the Southern Transvaal leadership, which was not prepared to let the issue drop. On 5 October a meeting of the

19. Interview: Martin Sebakwane, Johannesburg, November 1997.
20. Interview: Stephen Matlou, Cape Town, October 1997.
21. Interview: Martin Sebakwane, Johannesburg, November 1997.

region's 250-plus shop stewards was called at Wits University by the chairperson of Southern Transvaal, Nelson Ndinisa. Johnny Potgieter, the Assistant General Secretary, was invited to attend but failed to do so, claiming that he was afraid of violence.

> It was a regional shop stewards meeting. A majority of shop stewards were there. We decided that in the NEC when someone from Southern Transvaal stands up and talks, even if you can have a good idea, a constructive one, because it is from you the idea won't be taken up. The national office tell all the other regions not to take whatever Southern Transvaal comes up with, if it's good or bad. They don't want to listen. So we had to make them listen. Chuck them out of the office. [22]
>
> We resolved that we are going to take the leadership by force; we are going to depose the leadership … It was then agreed that people who will take an active part in this will be the shop stewards themselves. We went to their office and we mobilised funds from membership and also some funds from the region to go and hire cars to go and literally look for these guys – the General Secretary, the head office staff, who has got the keys for the safe and so on. The resolution was that we will go to head office and take out the important things first such as cheque-books, and cancel or suspend SARHWU accounts so that they couldn't use the money in the meantime. Then we would confiscate the keys to offices and all property like cars from them.[23]

As it was a Saturday, 20-30 shop stewards accompanied by a traditional sangoma (witchdoctor) from the Transkei and led by Stephen Matlou, who was at that time chair of the City Deep Central Shop Stewards Co-ordinating Committee, went immediately to the house of Simon Mulumone in Soweto and demanded the office keys. Using these they gained entry to the office and on Monday morning when head office staff arrived for work they found it occupied.

> I sat down and gave orders to these comrades – Go to this hotel; Go to this place, that place; the General Secretary is there, Johan Beaurain is there, Johnny Potgieter is there. Part of my work was to scrutinise the documentation in the office between the company and the union, what deals were made. We found that certain things were under way. Discussions took place with the company management without our involvement and without our knowledge, for example about the retrenchment of workers. There was a redundancy and retrenchment agreement which

---

22. Interview: Mandla Nzama, Johannesburg, October 1997.
23. Interview: Stephen Matlou, Cape Town, October 1997.

was supposed to have been signed on the Monday that we didn't know about. The workers were very angry about that.[24]

Staff were told to report to the Southern Transvaal Regional Office. Johan Beaurain, who was responsible for the processing of stop orders, was ordered to hand over accounts and cheque books, but although Beaurain was sympathetic to the views of the Southern Transvaal he opposed their methods. In order to avoid co-operating he absented himself and went underground. Vanguard Mkosana was called to the Head Office by staff to mediate.

> I went in and I found shop stewards had taken over and were answering incoming telephones. They took office keys and ordered all staff to go to the Southern Transvaal Regional Office. Together with Bafana Sithole I met Southern Transvaal Chairman, Nelson Ndinisa and Regional Secretary, Elliot Sogoni. They were fully aware of the situation and were not prepared to intervene and remove these workers from the office. After some discussion they allowed me and Maggie Maunye to handle 'urgent matters'. This relaxed later to allow staff in. On Tuesday 8 October they told me that no one will be able to remove them. The only person they would listen to was Comrade Chris Hani or Joe Slovo [Popular leaders of the SACP and MK].[25]

From the time the offices were occupied, the President, General Secretary, Assistant General Secretary and National Treasurer disappeared without trace. It fell to Mkosana to handle the situation until the Honorary President, Zola Zembe, arrived on 9 October from his Western Cape office where he was the Deputy Chairman of the ANC in that province. Little did he know then that that visit would extend to a period of more than four months of strenuous work. The first Vice-President, Innocent Moshoeshoe, also arrived on the 9 October. ZZ took command of the situation and a special NEC meeting was held in Bloemfontein on 11/13 October.

The meeting was divided and acrimonious, with accusations and counter-accusations of spying flying back and forth. There was reference to previous disputes and the role of SACTU, and Martin Sebakwane and Johnny Potgieter (who had been living in a Johannesburg hotel since his election as Assistant General Secretary) were accused of corruption and misuse of union funds. Eventually it was agreed to call for the suspension of both the national office-bearers for signing the agreement without mandate, and the Southern Transvaal office-bearers for their occupation of the head office. Members of the National

---

24. As above.
25. Interview: Vanguard Mkosana, King William's Town, October 1997.

Management Committee, including the national office-bearers, were requested to go to head office at 8.30 a.m. on Monday 14 October 1991 to conduct the business of the union.

Initially, however, neither side to the dispute would abide by the decision of the meeting. The Southern Transvaal staged a walk-out at the NEC; the shop stewards refused to vacate the union's offices, and the NMC members, who were still in hiding, failed to respond to the summons to head office and instead set about opening up a temporary office in Pretoria. Feelings were running high and Martin Sebakwane was in fear for his life.

> I think we were very paranoid because our relations with certain people in the Southern Transvaal over a long period of time were not really very comradely – to a point that you could not trust something that some of those comrades told to you without having corroborated it elsewhere. I think equally they did not trust us because when the occupation of the office happened and the list of accusations came up, the issues were still the same. They were the same issues that surfaced in the first disagreements – about CIA and impimpi [spies] and all that. So it was a re-hash of the same thing coming back in a different form so many years later – more ferocious, of course this time round.
>
> When I got informed that the offices were occupied I decided, 'No, I am not going to the office. I am not going to be locked up in there.' I wasn't even certain what was going to happen, how much and how deep the anger was, whether this was genuine anger about wages or this was about other things. At that time, it was starting to emerge that there is a whole sector of people who are angry because we have sold out. There was banking on this strike to create the right platform for other things to be built on to the activities. I said, 'Well let the revolution judge us then. We have done our best.' I was in Pretoria, I was in Jo'burg; I was meeting people finding out what is really happening.
>
> The signals that I was getting were really bad signals because I knew SARHWU comrades. I mean there are guns involved, there are all kinds of things, and I thought, 'I am not walking into it blind. I have to know exactly what is happening, exactly what the temperatures are and so on.' You could see that there were people staking out the places where we might be. I thought at that time, 'Why am I continuing in this? I have had it; I have had enough of having to justify my presence in this organisation. Soon we will all be citizens and you don't have to justify anything to anyone. I don't want to be a politician. I don't want to go to Parliament. I just want to be an ordinary citizen.' Until, of course,

finally we met with these chaps because we started to understand that
we can't continue living like rabbits.

There were plans that some sort of assault team would come to
Pretoria to get me because of stories about how much money we had
eaten. Also, we had the chequebooks. Then our side said, 'Well we will
barricade ourselves. Let them come.' It wasn't just idle talk. I mean,
people were wearing their long coats and we know exactly what is at
the back of those long coats! When workers wanted to start storming
each other with guns, I thought, 'No, no. This is really getting out of
hand. It is time to just get it done with and whatever happens, well let
it happen.' [26]

Kidnapped

On 22 October workers staked out a meeting at the Park Lane Hotel in Johannesburg and cornered Sebakwane. He was then taken to the head office where
he was held hostage for three days. Sebakwane bore his captivity bravely. He
was allowed to speak to people on the telephone and made every effort to prevent
his supporters from escalating the situation by storming the office.

Of course, my jailers are comrades that I have done a lot of things with;
I know them. There is the honest worker who believes this is the cause
and this is right as well as those with a personal agenda of some kind.
We used to sit there and play cards and they would buy food for me and
we would sleep at night there and joke about the past. Of course, when
the generals came, they stood at attention and they looked very angry
and busy holding me there! [27]

But Vanguard Mkosana had sleepless nights worrying about his safety and
together with Bafana Sithole set about trying to broker a deal.

We tried to intervene. I think we had a very good relationship with
workers by then; I think myself and Vanguard they respected very much.
But they were listening to no one and when we sat down with them we
realised that there was no way we were going to change their minds.
You could see it in their eye and when they suddenly turn and speak
Venda you must know that they are very angry. Vanguard tried to
persuade them not to do what they were intending to do but they said,
'Look, we love you Comrade Vanguard and Comrade Bafana but what

---

26. Interview: Martin Sebakwane, Johannesburg, November 1997.
27. As above.

197

we have decided is beyond your control.' The railway workers are very harsh and hard workers and resolute when they have taken a decision. Their intention was to kill the general secretary then, we heard it on the grapevine.[28]

The role of COSATU

Following the NEC on 11-13 October, a meeting was arranged for 19 October between those occupying the head office, the regional office bearers and the Southern Transvaal Central Shop Stewards Co-ordinating Committee. COSATU head office received an invitation to attend, but Martin Sebakwane then wrote to ask that they should allow more time for the union to solve its own problems – a move taken by the Southern Transvaal as an attempt to stop any COSATU involvement. The capture of Sebakwane on 22 October made the situation more urgent. COSATU leadership was impatient with SARHWU's problems but recognised that to some extent their failure to give clear guidance to Sebakwane may have been a contributory factor. In any case, the kidnapping of the General Secretary of an affiliate was not good publicity for the federation.

A COSATU delegation of top office-holders Jay Naidoo, Chris Dlamini, and Sam Shilowa went to the SARHWU office and met the stewards, who asked them to produce the President, Treasurer and Assistant General Secretary of SARHWU who were still at large. The stewards were hostile to the COSATU intervention and the meeting was very tense.

> Sam Shilowa advised Jay and said, 'Guys, let's leave. These workers will pounce on us as well. They are angry, let's go.' Then they developed a strategy for rescuing Martin. They called a meeting to COSATU and at last the workers did agree. They came to COSATU with Martin. The strategy was that when they got there we would agree to their requests for a conference to sort out the question of leadership. COSATU agreed, 'You can have your conference, guys. Go back and we'll organise a venue and transport and everything. You go back to your offices.' So they left and Martin remained at COSATU and that's how we rescued him.[29]

At this meeting on 25 October it was agreed that the occupation of the offices would end; the NMC would return hired vehicles to their agents and SARHWU chequebooks would be temporarily kept by COSATU. During his captivity

---

28. Interview: Bafana Sithole, Johannesburg, October 1997.
29. As above.

Martin Sebakwane had been forced to write a letter of resignation which had been faxed to Transnet, COSATU and SARHWU regional offices. This was now withdrawn and it was agreed that his resignation would be a matter for consideration by the NEC, a special meeting of which was to be called on 31 October in Kimberley.

Jay Naidoo and other COSATU office bearers join Zola Zembe on the platform at the special Kimberley Conference, 1991.

At the Kimberley meeting, which was chaired by COSATU, Southern Transvaal proposed that the NMC should be asked to resign and that there should be an investigation of the individual accounts of the NMC members. In his response Martin Sebakwane said that he would accept the decisions of the meeting but that the NEC should investigate the circumstances in which he had been forced to sign a letter of resignation. All regions were given time to present views from their members as to how best to handle the crisis.

The meeting lasted late into the night but eventually there was consensus on the idea that a commission of enquiry should be established, to be composed of representatives of the Triple Alliance (ANC, SACP and COSATU). This would investigate the circumstances surrounding the signing of the wage agreement with Transnet, the letter of resignation by the General Secretary, the closure of Head Office and the alleged mismanagement of funds. The shop stewards who were occupying the Head Office were ordered to withdraw immediately; the NMC was suspended for two months and the Honorary President, Zola Zembe, was put in charge of all SARHWU's affairs until the report of the commission of enquiry. It was agreed that SARHWU would reimburse COSATU R45 000, the cost of the special meeting when finances had been normalised.

ZZ in charge

The partners in the Triple Alliance, who were still preoccupied with the national peace process, were understandably reluctant to embroil themselves in SARHWU's affairs. Eventually, however, as a result of relentless pressure from ZZ, the ANC were persuaded, and Jabu Moleketi for the SACP and Siphiwe Nyanda for the ANC joined Jeremy Baskin from COSATU in producing a report on the problems within SARHWU.[30] In the meantime ZZ set about overhauling the head office administration and teaching the office staff the lessons in how to run a union that he had first learned from Ray Simons and Oscar Mpetha in the 1950s and had used so effectively in London in the West European office of SACTU.

ZZ was angry with Martin Sebakwane for the way in which he had dealt with the crisis and appalled at the low morale and disorganisation that he found at the head office.

> ZZ took control of the organisation. He introduced 15-minute meetings for key management at head office every morning. In addition staff meetings were to be held every Monday. Tasks were given to all members and reports back were made. At this stage SARHWU had R63 000 only in its account and some of our creditors were taking us to court. Maggie and Johan Beaurain were tasked to deal with finances with emphasis on dealing with all our creditors. Simon Mulumone was tasked to keep contact with regions. We moved to the new offices at Market Street on 7 November 1991. The building had four floors of which we needed two. We secured NEHAWU to rent one floor at R2 000 a month.

> The conditions under which we worked were very strenuous, especially for ZZ who was already more than 60 years old. He introduced emergency measures to accommodate financial constraints. Head office was run without petty cash and car hire for head office was stopped, hence he conducted his SARHWU business on foot; regional cash allocations were stopped; staff salaries payments were delayed and media work like publishing *SARHWU Voice* was temporarily stopped.

> All regions were fully briefed on these measures. During this period regions did a lot of work to improve SARHWU. The redundancy agreement between Transnet and the other 12 unions was distributed and discussed by our regions in order for us to formulate SARHWU's

---

30. COSATU, 1992.

position. We participated in the Industrial Council. The problem then was to increase our representation from 3 to 4 in accordance with the Constitution of the Council. Transnet resisted this. We were part of the decision to create a Provident Fund to invest workers moneys from accumulated leaves. Documents for the proposed Transnet Medical Scheme were discussed by the regions.

Comrade ZZ managed to raise funds to help SARHWU. The ITF [International Transport Federation] affiliate in Sweden donated R75 000 for the meeting we held to resolve our crisis. AALC [African-American Labour Center] donated R27 000 for transport to the extended NEC meeting. Comrade ZZ secured Commonwealth TUC offers to support SARHWU education projects. Similarly he got the commitment of the RMT (the railway workers union in UK) to help SARHWU with education and training. They even offered to send their experts to South Africa for this purpose.[31]

In a report on his time in charge from 1 November 1991 to 15 February 1992, ZZ was critical of a number of aspects of SARHWU organisation:

Abuse of the telephone is rife … Some regions sent [telephone] bills exceeding R2 000 during this period of crisis, which puts their consciousness and commitment to question … The exact number of SARHWU members is not known. This reflects poor functioning of our structures … By COSATU standards we are overstaffed. SARHWU wages are very low … There is a need for retraining and upgrading of staff … At the moment there is poor financial accounting and funds are handled by people who have no training in this field.[32]

These findings were reflected in the report of the COSATU Commission of Enquiry that was completed on 20 January 1992.

Report of the Commission of Enquiry

The Commission of Enquiry examined all the accusations made against the leadership of SARHWU. On the substantive issues it concluded that:

• The NMC members were wrong to have met and finalised the negotiations with Transnet. Any further negotiations should have taken place with the full

---

31. V. Mkosana, 1998, p. 26-27.
32. SARHWU, 1992.

negotiating team. Any final agreement should have been presented to the membership for ratification before signing.

- There was no evidence that NMC members received any payments from Transnet to reach the agreement.
- The decision to occupy the head office, given the circumstances surrounding the wage agreement, was understandable. Nevertheless, it could not be condoned. It was clearly unconstitutional and if repeated would lead to anarchy. Comrade Sebakwane was held against his wishes. This behaviour was totally unacceptable.
- The finances and administration at head office and regional offices were extremely poor amounting to 'corruption in the sense of misuse and abuse of union resources'.
- There was *no* evidence of corruption in the sense of major theft in the period examined (January to October 1991) but a more thorough examination of outside donations was needed.
- While it was probable that there were spies within SARHWU (as with any mass organisation) allegations of spying directed against Martin Sebakwane and others were unsubstantiated and divisive.

The chief recommendations of the commission were that the members of the NMC should resign with immediate effect; that the suspension of the Southern Transvaal leadership should be lifted – with a warning that further steps would be taken if there was any repetition of similar events – and that the union should take urgent steps to institute a number of detailed improvements in its financial and administrative systems. In addition, it recommended that the union should oppose as divisive attempts to accuse individuals of being informers and allow NMC members to play a unifying role within the union.

Once the commission had reported, another congress was called and new national officers were elected. Derrick Simoko, formerly Regional Secretary in the Eastern Cape, who had been in the Soviet Union during the leadership crisis, became General Secretary. Nelson Ndinisa, chairperson of the Southern Transvaal, was elected President and Innocent Moshoeshoe, who was not present when the agreement with Transnet was signed, was re-elected as first Vice-President. Other officers were Ezrom Mabyana (Southern Transvaal) Treasurer and Tshediso Moshao (Orange Free State) Assistant General Secretary. Martin Sebakwane stepped down from active participation in the union and took up a position as a trainee manager with Transnet.

Summary

1991 was a traumatic year in the history of SARHWU. Just at the point that the union achieved recognition, when it was finally in a position to negotiate improved wages and working conditions and Transnet was freed from government political control, it was thrown into a crisis which threatened its very existence. The crisis can be attributed to a number of causes.

- *Ideological differences:* SARHWU had always been on the revolutionary wing of the labour movement. As government employees, its members suffered directly from the policy of apartheid, and union policy had always been not to compromise by participating in official industrial relations institutions but to confront them head-on. COSATU policy was to move towards a 'normalisation' of industrial relations and not to jeopardise the national peace talks by undisciplined strikes. The COSATU position was accepted by Martin Sebakwane but not by the majority of SARHWU activists who had been in the frontline of the struggle against apartheid in the workplace and were profoundly suspicious of Transnet management and the National Party. They did not believe in a change of heart and believed that only a show of strength would force concessions.

- *Organisational structures*: The union had a strong democratic tradition enshrined both in its constitution (which could be traced back to the 1930s) and in its grassroots organisation and action. Shop stewards committees had been a key feature of the 1987 strike, when the majority of the national leadership was imprisoned, and of the 1989/90 strike that had resulted in recognition. National and even regional structures were weak in comparison.

- *Inexperienced leadership:* Shop stewards and officials were inadequately trained in necessary negotiating skills and provoked a deadlock. Worker members of the NMC exercised too little control over the General Secretary and did not respond to legitimate complaints. Successive general secretaries, whose responsibility this was, failed to ensure proper financial and administrative procedures.

- *Third Force activity:* The Commission of Enquiry played down the importance of Third Force activity but it is probable that this was responsible for manipulating existing rivalries and factionalism to disrupt the smooth running of the union – both in 1991 and during the preceding disputes in 1988/89. It is also possible that political forces were at work in encouraging the intransigence of the Transnet management and their action to undermine the SARHWU leadership by releasing the wage agreement prematurely.

In many ways the crisis was the product of the particular political juncture at which SARHWU, along with COSATU and the rest of the trade union movement, had arrived. History had speeded up, pitching SARHWU, a revolutionary union founded in the nineteen thirties, into the middle of a sophisticated transition process for which it was ill prepared. The disagreements within SARHWU reflected those inside the liberation movement, between those who were prepared to negotiate a peace with the South African government and those who believed that victory could be won through all-out war:

> People had learned to struggle; people were doing wonderful things that we never thought our people can do; there were engagements with the enemy in all kinds of ways so we wanted to know what the movement meant with this negotiated settlement thing. There were discussions, debates, explanations, differences. In some of the meetings the MK people, the commanders, were walking out and saying, 'This is all selling out.' We had a situation where our own members were also part of the deaths, the dying, the engagements and so on. When we came back home with agreements around a negotiated settlement, working out the different roles that we have to play as different organisations and sectors in the movement was difficult and SARHWU was no exception. How do you de-escalate that heightened level of political consciousness and political action and talk about people coming together? Workers were asking, 'Does it mean now we have to abandon fighting these chaps in Transnet? Does it mean peace with management?' [33]

This confusion led to a renewal of claims and counter-claims about spying and treachery, which were manipulated by those factions inside SARHWU which were opposed to the leadership.

---

33. Interview: Martin Sebakwane, Johannesburg, November 1997.

7

Race and Gender:
Rhetoric or Reality?

I think that you need to apply affirmative action in your own union. Because you haven't got a career path for changed whites in your union and you haven't got a career path for women. I would much rather have gone into the management cadre of the union than do what I have done which is to change my role to a management position – because it was something I enjoyed. But one position after another was filled by blacks. Men! Not women. And there I stood. I was wanting to join the cadre of management in the union, and I would have done a bloody good job let me tell you that.[1]

Introduction

We do not subscribe to the racial classifications imposed by various colonial and apartheid regimes. Indeed, we do not see 'race' as something determined by biology, but rather as something determined by society. As such, definitions and classifications change according to the political and social circumstances. Ultimately, there is only one 'race' – the human race, with different cultures, languages and traditions, which are constantly changing.

The new, 'non-racial' South Africa, however, cannot ignore the legacy of past discrimination based on 'race'. Hence we cannot avoid discussing 'race', and using unscientific colonial categories in that discussion (albeit reluctantly). We

---

1. Interview: Lynette Hugo, Johannesburg, November 1997.

205

look forward to the time when we can only talk about South Africans (as one nation or people), and human beings (as one race).

As an affiliate of COSATU and supporter of the ANC, SARHWU's policy was always one of non-sexism and non-racism. In reality, however, the union had difficulty living up to those promises, like many other South African organisations. During the apartheid era the racist management was all too successful in separating workers of different races from one another. Although there were a few coloured leaders, most of the members and their leadership were always African. In the post-apartheid era legal and ideological barriers were removed, but recruitment of other races was patchy and SARHWU seemed unable to find the right formula for building up a truly non-racial union. At the same time there was a failure to move away from the 'macho' culture which characterised the often violent struggle of the 1980s and thereby to develop structures sympathetic towards women and supportive of their advancement in the union. As a result of these failures SARHWU was in danger of curtailing its own growth and of starving itself of necessary leadership talent.

Race and the trade union movement

As noted in the Introduction, long before the formal implementation of the apartheid system in 1948 the South African government had set about dividing the working class by cutting white workers off from those of other races. White workers were recognised and given privileges at the expense of blacks, mixed-race trade unions were made illegal, and independent African unions were excluded from the industrial relations system. A number of progressive trade unions attempted to maintain working-class solidarity by forming parallel 'sister' unions to accommodate different races and by helping to form independent African unions. Nevertheless, the trade union movement became increasingly divided on racial lines.

A few, mainly communist-led, white unions resisted this trend and joined the unregistered affiliates of the Council of Non-European Trade Unions (CNETU) in founding the non-racial South African Congress of Trade Unions (SACTU) in 1955, but the alliance of SACTU with the ANC and the imprisonment or exile of most of its activists drove SACTU underground. The remaining unions, organised in the Trade Union Council of South Africa (TUCSA), became closely identified with government policy and it was not until the 1970s and 1980s that open and independent trade union activity was revived. The new organisations were, however, still split over the question of race, with one federation allied to the Black Consciousness Movement, one closely linked to white progressive intellectuals, and one bringing together the remnants of the old SACTU affiliates with a strong anti-apartheid platform.

Race and the railways

The South African Railways played a major part in the implementation of the 'civilised labour' policy in the 1920s and 1930s. The Railway and Harbours Administration became a major employer of Afrikaner labour, initially in un-skilled occupations and subsequently in artisan and supervisory positions. Jobs were reserved for whites, and other races were confined to the low-paid position of general worker, with no security of employment or pension rights.

Management operated a policy of 'divide and rule'. White workers were represented by unions, but these were divided by trade and grade (for example Footplate, Technical Workers, Salstaff) and even the Afrikaner Spoorbond failed to win recognition to negotiate for all white workers. All general workers had to belong to the employer-controlled, racially divided Staff Associations for which subscriptions were automatically deducted from pay – either the Coloured, Indian or Black Staff Association.

Race relations in the industry were directly affected by the political context. As the government was the employer, opposition to management and opposition to apartheid were the same thing. White workers were identified by blacks not as fellow employees but as tools of management and the apartheid system. The unfairness and brutality of some white supervisors inspired deep racial hatred in many blacks who were already subjected to the oppression of apartheid in their daily lives. Unfair treatment was applied to Indians and coloureds as well as to Africans but the institutionalised racial divisions in South African society and the finely graded distinctions made between different groups were a barrier to solidarity in the workplace and retarded the development of a unified response.

Johnny's story

Johnny Potgieter was the son of an African father and a coloured mother. The story of Johnny Potgieter illustrates the effect of apartheid on one man. He began work on the railway in 1982 and became a Shop Steward for the Coloured Staff Association. In 1986 he was elected the first Chairperson of SARHWU in the Northern Cape and in 1991 became the national Assistant General Secretary.

> I was born 1965, 15 January, in Upington, a township called Sunset, now known as Progress. My father was Tswana. My parents were not married and my mother had to rent a house in her name because my father being African he was not allowed to rent a house in a coloured

township. They separated about 1968 and she got married to a coloured guy who became my stepfather. My stepfather used to work on these little farms and later on he joined the railway also. But because of me being the child of a Tswana that caused some friction in the house. My younger brother was fairer in complexion than me and his hair was softer than mine and to my stepfather those were really big issues. Before I even became aware of something like apartheid I knew it was a mistake to be black – from my early childhood. In order to maintain a good family atmosphere, in 1971 my mother decided to send me, at the age of seven, to her parents' family – to her late mother's aunt. I lived there in Louisberg, in another coloured township – today it is completely demolished.

I stayed there for two years. In 1973 my mother came to fetch me but in 1974 I went back to my mother's aunt and continued my schooling. Then they moved to the Orange River Scheme where the Boers were given farms to irrigate. I stayed there for a few years but this thing of me being black was always an issue in the family. I bear my great grandfather's surname and people always had remarks about that so I became used to that, always having to do all the dirty work and so it became part of my life. They moved from there back to Upington and I was left in the care of one of her in-laws. Then my late grandmother's eldest sister found out about it and she said she didn't like it and came to fetch me.

That was the happiest part of my life – to be accepted just for being a child and not for who you are. I stayed there until 1978 when I went to Cape Town to live with my mother and my stepfather. But it was just history repeating itself. I couldn't even eat at the table on Sundays when my stepfather was at home; I had to sit outside just to keep the peace. He said he would not work for the child of a kaffir who wouldn't work for him when he was grown up so my mother made the decision. I implored her to let me go and work so she wouldn't have all this hassle. I started working there at the age of 14 in 1979 for the municipality. I lied about my age and said I was 16 … One week later I came to understand what apartheid means in the workplace. I knew it was wrong to be black but when I started working now I understood what this whole thing of apartheid was all about.

Certain people were anti-black and always had racist remarks. Then there was the issue of the Boers. Whether he had Standard 1 or what, he was white and in charge. I came to understand it there. There was this white guy and he used to say in Afrikaans, 'This one isn't really a kaffir, I don't know what he is.' In terms of jobs there were guys from Transkei who worked as a separate team and only coloureds and whites were in charge. The manner in which you were dismissed was there wasn't a hearing or any kind of enquiry. He would just say, 'OK, send him back home,' and that was it.

In 1982 I came to Kimberley to live with my father's mother. I joined the railway on 29 February as a labourer at the electrical locomotive depot. When I started in the railway, being classified a coloured I started sweeping. You had to jump to attention every time you saw the boss. I was lucky, I started with the luxury salary of R200 a month. There were production bonuses – a person who worked with an artisan would get a bigger bonus than the one who was sweeping floors. They used it in a punitive way because every cent made a difference. They would move you and put you somewhere else to punish you, to feel the pinch. They robbed me of my first year's bonus but it's a government department. You can write as many letters as you want. They say, 'This is the situation. You accept it. That's it!'

My difficulty with this situation of Coloured Staff Association and Black Staff Association was that you had the whites over there with their own ablution facilities – they were different. We [Africans and coloureds] were all grouped together and yet there was this division – very deliberately. We saw that these unions were 'Yes Men' unions. A few months after I started working there, because I was quite outspoken, I became a shop steward for the Coloured Staff Association. The Black Staff Association was BLATU by then. Because of the close relationship we all had there I didn't distinguish between a BLATU case and a Coloured Staff Association case. If somebody approached me with a problem I would take it up. There at the office they would make an issue out of that. They knew if it was me who had written something and then they would say, 'Go to whoever was the BLATU representative'. We were fighting that system but they would bring the national representatives of those two unions there and parade them to try to keep us apart.[2]

---

2.   Interview: Johnny Potgieter, Kimberley, October 1997.

Race and SARHWU

On paper SARHWU had impeccably non-racist credentials. Its formation in 1936 was the result of collaboration between white communist organisers (in particular Ray Alexander), coloureds (who took the first leadership positions) and Africans. SARHWU adopted a non-racial constitution and in 1955 became a supporter of the Freedom Charter which looked forward to a South Africa free from any racial inequalities. At the re-launch in 1986 the original constitution was revived and support for the aims of the Freedom Charter was restated. Nevertheless, the union did not remain free of the racial tensions which characterised the rest of South African society, and the role of both whites and coloureds was at times a bone of contention.

The apartheid era

Even within the progressive trade union and anti-apartheid movement inside South Africa there was an imbalance of power between whites, who had the advantages of money, education and access to external support, and blacks, who were in a much more vulnerable position. Blacks accepted whites ideologically and needed them on a practical level because of the resources at their command, but whites were frequently resented personally by blacks in a hurry to take control of their own future even if it meant making their own mistakes. Understandably they were also treated with deep suspicion as possible spies or entryists with an axe to grind. Whites also found it difficult to adapt to working in a virtually all-African environment. These points can be illustrated by the role played within SARHWU by two very different whites: Mike Roussos and Johan Beaurain.

As noted in the previous chapter, SARHWU owed a lot to Mike Roussos. The overseas funds which were raised for the re-launch of SARHWU were largely the result of the efforts of SACTU's external offices and overseas visits by white progressives like Mike Roussos who were able to travel abroad. Roussos played a major role in setting up administrative structures and as a public spokesperson for the union during the 1987 strike. He was undoubtedly committed to building up SARHWU as a stable and efficient trade union but his abrasive personality and his race combined to make him the focal point for the fierce faction fighting which broke out in 1988, overshadowing the living wage campaign. It was argued, with some justification, that as a white, he could not communicate effectively with the membership of the union and could have little understanding of the problems of illiterate railway workers. He was accused of ambition (by those who probably had ambitions of their own), and he had to go because he could not accept electoral defeat and continue to work alongside those with whom he disagreed.

Roussos was of Greek extraction, an educated outsider who had become involved in left-wing politics and the trade union movement when at Wits University. In contrast, Johan Beaurain was an Afrikaner born in the Free State and a genuine railway worker, an electrician working for SATS in Durban. Astonishingly, he became a member of SARHWU in 1987.

Johan's story

I had previously belonged to the White Staff Association but in 1987 I decided to join SARHWU. I had some little problems as a worker but it was mostly political frustration in that I didn't feel like I had a home. I was very isolated in my political thinking and I didn't have an organisation to belong to. Once I heard about SARHWU then I realised that I was at home there because what they are fighting for is also what I would like to see come about. I was working in Durban but in 1988 the railway transferred me to Johannesburg.

When I got there I started to suffer a lot of intimidation from the white workers. They frightened me that they would kill me; in fact they said to me that they will get a worker to kill me; they said it in so many words. They said – in fact I still remember one of them telling me, 'Man we are going to get the kaffirs to kill you, to burn you.' And they said that in front of our black people who could hear him, and he wasn't scared to say it. And then I realised that this is no joke, they are serious, you know? And they have killed people in that same depot.

I was working with one man, who is now a SARHWU official, though then he was just an ordinary worker. During the short time I was working there they also intimidated him just because they want to see how I am going to react. Sometimes they hit him on the head like that, or play very rough with him to see if I am going to intervene to try and stop them. Trying to provoke me, that type of thing. I realised that I was sent there so that they could get rid of me in a way that was much easier for them to intimidate me. But that realisation of course came very much later. I only realised that many years later, when I fought back. At that time I didn't know what was happening. It was just a situation that was totally new to me because I wasn't very political. In fact I knew very little about politics before I joined SARHWU; I was just a naive worker who grew up in the Free State and had very little political experience.

When I brought the intimidation to the attention of the authorities they just ignored me and then later on they charged me with absenteeism and dismissed me, although they were responsible for the absenteeism. After I was dismissed I continued to fight to try and get back and I took them to court but of course the case never reached the courts. In fact I lodged two applications in the Supreme Court and both of those applications were thrown out. I started to get ill. I was on medication for depression but luckily at that time I became more involved in the organisation and through my organisational involvement I rid myself of that depression completely. I was just lucky also that a political changeover [Mandela's release in February 1990] came at the same time, otherwise I'm sure I would have landed up in some hospital where they treat psychiatric patients. I wouldn't have survived these times if it wasn't so lucky that things are changing at the same time as when I started fighting.

After I was dismissed I continued to fight them in the Supreme Court and when I lost those cases, in 1990, I started working in SARHWU's office as an organiser. At that time Martin Sebakwane was the general secretary and I started working very closely with him and questioning about a lot of things that I didn't understand. I wanted to know – I had many questions. And then we started organising white workers; we had a special focus on trying to organise the white workers.

At that time our purpose was to motivate our own members, to go out of our way to go and approach the white workers so that it won't be an effort of one organiser organising everyone. We were not very successful even though a lot of white workers joined SARHWU. We learnt a lot through the difficulty of bringing white workers and black workers together in one union and all the difficulties around that, because white workers were staying in their own communities and black workers staying in different communities. After those white workers joined the union they are striving to communicate with us and the more conservative elements in their own community.

They were having difficulty to explain why they are now in a union which has got a majority of black workers in it. And that was not an easy task for people who had just joined the union so many workers drifted away from the organisation again for reasons unknown to us. We

> didn't really understand what problems they experienced when they go
> home at night after they have been with us through the day.[3]

Beaurain became embroiled in the internal politics surrounding the resignation of Martin Sebakwane. Although he disapproved of Sebakwane's action in signing the 1991 wage agreement, he refused to throw in his lot with the leaders of the coup, and when they took over the leadership of the union he inevitably shared the same accusations of being an informer that were levelled against the former General Secretary. Nevertheless he continued to work for SARHWU – as an organiser in the Western Cape – until he resigned on health grounds in 1997.

In the 1980s it was unusual for any white person to work in a black organisation. It meant abandoning their own community and suffering the hostility of the government and their fellow whites. This was especially so for Johan Beaurain who, unlike Mike Roussos, did not have the support of educated white middle-class colleagues of like mind. Both Roussos and Beaurain appear to have been to some extent misfits, exceptionally determined, 'bloody-minded' and unwilling to compromise. SARHWU accepted both, but at a time of transition their race made them vulnerable to personal suspicion and for neither did SARHWU become a permanent home.

It is not surprising that early attempts to recruit white workers were not very successful. SARHWU had a reputation as a revolutionary organisation, and even after whites began to accept the end of apartheid they were still not comfortable with its militant culture and open political stance. The situation of coloureds was somewhat different, although also shaped by the racial divisions created by the apartheid system. In the railway hierarchy they were classified as a separate group and accorded some privileges over Africans, but their material living conditions were little better. They were despised by the whites but felt themselves superior to Africans, and to a large extent held themselves aloof from their co-workers for fear of suffering the same penalties for opposition to the government. Nevertheless, towards the end of the 1980s they began to respond to SARHWU's efforts at recruitment in the Northern and Western Cape and to abandon their separatist organisations.

As noted earlier, Johnny Potgieter left the Coloured Staff Association to become a founder member of SARHWU in the Northern Cape. He later became Assistant General Secretary of the union nationally. On joining SARHWU in 1986 he immediately set about recruiting both African and coloured members. The process was a difficult one and progress was slow because the railway management

---

3. Interview: Johan Beaurain, Cape Town, October 1997.

continually harassed the organisers and victimised those known to have joined. Nevertheless, with the impetus of the 1987 strike in the Southern Transvaal, Potgieter ran a resignation campaign that successfully undermined the employer-controlled Staff Associations.

> I was recruited by Charles Ntlangula ... On 17 December, on a Wednesday, I received my joining slip and I was elected chairman the next day. On joining the union we were full-hearted, only to be confronted in January when the Boers have awakened. They tried to block us on all kinds of things but while they were recovering from the shock we would go to field camps and start organising the workers. Once they found that out, once we were returning from where we had gone to organise we would be intercepted by the security police. They would confiscate joining forms. The railway was in cahoots with the Special Branch because they pointed us out and had our records. The railway police was just freshly integrated with the SAP [South African Police] at that time. Our organising was severely hampered.
>
> At the time of the eruption of that [1987] strike there was an NEC to discuss the response of the railways to the comrades in the Southern Transvaal. The decision then was if there is no positive change we will all try to come out. At that time we were the youngest region. On returning to the Northern Cape we had three depots which were more or less effectively organised but these were on the outskirts of town and we could see that the impact of Special Branch and the army would have neutralised us and blocked us. Our strategic position was weak from all angles. Also the support we had from the UDF and the youth organisations was under tremendous attack from the state security apparatus ... and we were very much infiltrated by the enemy forces. The decision was never not to strike. The decision was, 'Can we strike and sustain a strike?' I remember the night we had the meeting here with comrades from Bloemfontein, we were 120 or less and it was mostly from those three depots. And they were also divided on racial lines. Only at one of them did the majority of the coloureds support SARHWU.
>
> Our high point was in '87 [after the strike]. We had these resignation books for people to resign from the staff associations. In '87 we decided to take it a step further and use the G27 [form] and inform management directly, 'I'm resigning'– because they ignored SARHWU. People had dual membership. Even though they despised these apartheid associations they were forced to belong to them. When they were now confronted with individual letters of resignation signed by an employee

they had no other option than to implement them. But with that came a lot of other problems because they saw the who and who. They tried to be difficult, victimise people. If you got a bonus of R78 a month you were shifted to a place where it's only going to be R12, that kind of thing. Comrades had people at home to support so it's another kind of struggle going back there and saying, 'Since I belong to SARHWU I'm earning less.' People individualised things. But gradually the conscious-ness raised.[4]

In the Western Cape SARHWU was mainly African at first, despite the high proportion of coloured labour in that area. After the 1989 strike, however, a conscious effort was made to separate coloured workers from the Coloured Staff Association and recruit them to join SARHWU. Branches were formed in the predominantly coloured, more rural areas such as Worcester and Friedenburg.

In '91, '92 they started to flock in, especially from the rural areas. We were sharing the same pay. Because of apartheid we were divided but we were treated the same so there was no real conflict of interest.[5]

By and large it can be said that, despite some residual racial tensions, coloureds were well integrated into the union. A number were elected to leadership positions and even the disgrace of Johnny Potgieter, who was forced to resign following the COSATU enquiry into corruption in 1992, did not generally take on a racial complexion.

The post-apartheid era

We realised it's a much more complex issue than just to organise white workers into a union and think that they will stay in the union. It's a whole social transformation that has to take place really before we can unite white and black workers of Africa. That will not come over one year; it will take us many years.[6]

The 1994 elections signalled the end of legalised apartheid but not of the racialisation of South African society. Wealth, education and skills remained in the hands of whites, and the segregated labour market continued to put the interests of black and white workers in opposition to one another.

---

4. Interview: Johnny Potgieter, Kimberley, October 1997.
5. Interview: Thobile Bangiso, Cape Town, October 1997.
6. Interview: Johan Beaurain, Kimberley, October 1997.

White workers in the public service were pulled in two directions. On the one hand their instinct was to cling to their segregated right-wing unions and to fight to protect their jobs against black competition and affirmative action. On the other hand they recognised that the threat of restructuring, privatisation and overall job losses in the sector could only be faced successfully if black and white workers presented a united front.

For its part, SARHWU recognised that both the introduction of non-racial industrial relations in accordance with its constitution and the continuation of its bargaining strength in a shrinking industry pointed to the recruitment of white members. But the history of racial hatred in the workplace was almost overwhelming.

From time to time black and white workers made common cause in opposition to oppressive management actions. A number of whites did join the union. In 1991 SARHWU claimed around 1 500 white members and in the same year there was a prolonged strike in the Northern Transvaal against the dismissal of white members. Nevertheless white members rarely stayed long. According to officials many were over demanding, wanted special treatment and refused to use the branch structures. There were problems of language and communication and

Joint action by black and white workers brought SAA to a halt, December 1995.

216

there was also the matter of SARHWU's political culture: it was hardly surprising that ordinary whites felt uncomfortable in branch meetings which still began and ended with the singing of revolutionary songs and chanting of ANC slogans. There were, however, some whites who were prepared to be open and to adopt a non-racial perspective. When white cabin crew in dispute with South African Airways (SAA) decided to join SARHWU, Lynette Hugo became chairperson of the branch.

Lynette's story

I come from a very conservative Afrikaans family. I was schooled in Afrikaans after which I left for Stellenbosch University. After completing my three years at Stellenbosch I joined the airline and I started to fly as a cabin attendant. I was quite a happy cabin attendant for all those years, and I would say that I was quite oblivious to any problems. I was fully aware of the apartheid system that was in the country, but I think that every white can say that they chose to do nothing, and so did I choose to do nothing.

It wasn't until 1993 that I started to think, well I must look a little bit further than just my own pleasure. At that time the cabin staff were in big trouble. We had only white unions. We had different white unions, and none of those unions I've ever belonged to. I've never been a unionised kind of person. I've been very individualistic which has been a trait of white people. They're not really very collective thinkers. I went to the union [SARHWU] and said, 'I'm prepared to help, please help me.'

I was chosen to be the chairperson of the branch but when I had my very first meeting it was as if it was a white union in a black union. That was the most amazing thing, we had almost no black members, we had only white members. Our steering committee and our shop stewards were white except for one black. It was run, basically, by a bunch of racists trying to ride on the back of SARHWU, and that was also how they sold the membership of SARHWU to the cabin crew.

I cannot actually elaborate on my career as unionist without saying exactly what made me believe so much in the cause as a white person. Because I think that is what reconciliation is. Reconciliation is not to say, let's forget the past and get it over and done with. For me as a white person it is to realise exactly what I've done all those years by choosing to forget it, because you're actually choosing to forget the suffering of

217

millions. It is to say, 'Listen, what do I do now to make it better? What can I do to contribute, to actually make this a better place?'

So at my very first meeting I refused to participate as a chairperson or as a silent member unless I could have affirmative action applied in my own union – because I felt that the blacks boycotted the election process due to the fact that they did not want to serve with the same whites who they perceived to have been racists, and I did not blame them. At that meeting we introduced seven ad-hoc shop stewards and it was with those guys that we started to work.

That year was very frustrating for me because I didn't know anything; I didn't even know what the term 'negotiation' meant. Those guys were very instrumental in leading me. I did not know much about power. I did not know much about how things happened, and we started to embark on an entire programme. I said to them, 'Teach me about you; teach me about your life and show me the places where you've grown up.' And I made all the shop stewards go to Soweto. We had wonderful times. I think that it was also because of that that eventually we were left with a group of people who accepted the change, and it was actually wonderful to start working with people like that instead of people who were seeing colour.

The conservative whites broke away, but that did not deter us. Whatever we said we'd do, we did. We said, 'Right, we were going to bring in closing of the wage gap, we were going to give full attention to the Turn Strategy [affirmative action programme].' At that time on-board services did not have one black manager but in two years time we transformed, single-handedly, literally, this place. We overthrew the management of the time and currently we have almost 50% black. We did that by the very first strike and that was in November 1995.

We took management by surprise. I drove from Pretoria, it was a wildcat strike and they didn't know what was happening. They tried to ignore us. They didn't believe that we could actually gather power. It was actually quite amazing. We had two strikes after that, of which one was the privatisation strike. That was quite a successful strike and then after that it was the de-recognition strike. Management tried very hard to break us, but I don't think they will ever be able to break the spirit that was born here. Even though we now have a backlash of very conservative white unions, it's not something which is going to last.

Now I have moved to a management position. I wanted to join the union management but when I asked there was no reply. You know, I struggled with it for a long time. When I applied for management I got a mandate. I said to my shop stewards, 'If there is one that objects, I will not apply.' And it took a whole day, the deliberations. At the end of the day, about 5 o'clock that afternoon, they stuck up all their hands, and they said, 'We give you consensus to go; we want you to go.' But I am still a member. I would like to see someone stop me! SARHWU is something that will always stay part of me.

It was just after that that the whites and the blacks completely split up again. It's a lack of changed leadership. The whites have been led by a person that was very confident; I inspired them. At the time it was easy for them to accept change because I was there, I was an example of somebody who accepted change. Now that person is gone, and the white conservatives came in and said, yes, well you see she just wanted to give everything to blacks. If you still had a mixed leadership committee, changed whites who were actively and visibly playing a very hard role, you would not have seen so many whites leaving. But now it looks as if it's a white and a black union.

Even today still I experience a hell of a lot of discrimination because I have chosen to show visibly exactly where I stand. Whites in the beginning saw me as something dirty. They didn't really want to associate with me, but they liked the power and they liked the things I was winning. They all hoped to get something personal out of it so they were quite happy to follow us at first. And I would say that the whites that have broken away now just find it totally unacceptable to be associated with blacks as such. I think it has got a race connotation to it. I believe it's part of the everyday problems that we experience in this country.

From my own family, my own friends and from my background? Yes, now that was quite a hard time, because the more I tried to explain why I have made certain decisions in my life, the more I was shot down by the normal kind of things that people were saying. By now they've accepted it. People at first react violently, then they accept it, you know. When my family speak to me, they say to me, 'In any case you're ANC.' They don't include me, they don't expect me to react favourably to their comments. So they know, and they respect that as well at this stage.[7]

The failure to retain white members at SAA must be seen as a failure not only by whites, who did not want to change and compromise, but also by a union

---

7.   Interview: Lynette Hugo, Johannesburg, 1997.

hierarchy that was not prepared to provide the necessary leadership. To a certain extent things were left to chance and when whites drifted back to their own unions there were certainly some on the SARHWU side who were not sorry to see them go.

SARHWU and gender

Throughout its history SARHWU was fortunate in attracting strong and committed women, including Ray Simons who was instrumental in helping to found the union in 1936, Rita Ndzanga who was imprisoned for her work in the 1950s and 1960s, and Catherine Mavi the acting secretary of the revived union in the Transvaal before the official re-launch in 1986. Nevertheless, women's role in the railways and ports and in the day-to-day affairs of the union was always a subordinate one.

One of the reasons for this was that women suffered from gender stereotyping. The unskilled work that blacks were confined to by the railway administration during the apartheid era was seen as being traditionally 'masculine', so the number of women employed was small and their interests tended to be over-looked. At the same time women were discouraged from seeking promotion and from joining and becoming active in their union by the traditional domestic role assigned to them by men – within the family, in the workplace and in meetings and negotiations. By 1997 the percentage of women employed by Transnet was still only 10%, of which one fifth were SARHWU members. Women were concentrated in telecommunications and administrative jobs at one end of the spectrum and in low-paid unskilled cleaning jobs at the other end.

The apartheid era

The histories are given briefly below of five women who worked for SARHWU during the apartheid era. They illustrate the importance of their role, their courage in difficult circumstances and the ways in which gender relations and race relations have interacted in their lives inside and outside the union. Three worked as Regional Administrators, employed to perform clerical jobs in different regional offices, one is a railway employee (now SARHWU Regional Treasurer of the Northern Transvaal), and one is a former organiser in Northern Natal who became SARHWU National Gender Co-ordinator.

Nomanese Signoria Maxhakana and Bukie Motloung began working as Regional Administrators at the time of SARHWU's re-launch in 1986.

Nomanese's Story

Nomanese Signoria Maxhakana was born in a rural area in 1959 in what was to be designated the independent 'homeland' of the Transkei by the apartheid regime.

> When I was a girl I was in the rural area so I had to go and fetch water and wood and to plough with oxen. When I was at primary school my father used to wake me at half past 3 or 4 so before I go to school I should go and plough. At 6 o'clock I was released so that I can go to school! I looked after my father's cattle. We were five, me and my two brothers and two daughters from my father's brother, so we would know, 'My day is Monday so I will be absent from school on Monday.' I finished primary school in 1975 and passed my standard 9 in 1980. My mother died in 1976 so I went to my father's sister to get a job but unfortunately I became pregnant and I had my first daughter in 1982.
>
> I didn't get married. I met a guy from Port St Johns. He was working at the municipality offices and I fell in love with him. My father's sister quarrelled with me when she found I'd got an affair. She told me I would get pregnant but you know how it is with young girls. First love sometimes makes little girls crazy! I was at that stage of craziness. Then, as my aunt said, I became pregnant. And when I was pregnant everything happened as my aunt told me. The guy went away and she told me so. Everything was exactly as she told me but it was too late! I raised money so that I could come to Durban to do some commercial subjects and those commercial subjects are what led me to work here in the SARHWU offices. I was employed by SARHWU in September 1986 as Regional Administrator. The person who was at the office at that time was David Moeti who was Regional Secretary. The person who was General Secretary was Ntai Sello. Sello was at the Head Office but he came from here in Durban. At that time there was a lot of harassment of the organisers and it was hard to work for the organisa-tion. The police were not allowing the organisers to work freely. They visited the offices again and again raiding the filing.
>
> When I came to SARHWU I knew nothing about politics. I wasn't involved in any politics so I learned everything when I was here in SARHWU. When I first came there were pamphlets on the history of SARHWU and how it was oppressed by the Boers and that made me know that it's not easy to get freedom. First of all I learned how to take the cases of the workers. If David wasn't at the office I took the details

and then I would tell him that workers at such and such a depot have got a problem of this nature. Then Mr Moeti tried to develop me so that I could deal with cases so that if he was not available at the office I could help the workers. There was one time when he was detained for three months and I was alone at the office. That was a tough time for me because I wasn't good at helping the workers but I tried my best because when workers come to the office they expect you to assist them. I told myself I was going to do it and I did it. [8]

Bukie's story

Nombukiso (Bukie) Motloung was born in Gauteng in 1957. She began working for SARHWU at the time of its relaunch and, with Catherine Mavi, ran the Southern Transvaal regional office throughout the 1987 strike.

When I joined SARHWU, Comrade Marvi was regional organiser. Our union was not launched by then. She was Acting Secretary and at the same time doing the organising. Then after SARHWU was launched we had a new leadership in our head office and she came back to Southern Transvaal region. I was working with her hand-in-hand. She was a person who liked to show people who didn't understand their job like I was when I was originally appointed as administrator.

She was the person who used to show me how to do my job; each and every thing I am doing now is from the experience I gained from Catherine Marvi and Comrade Mike Roussos. She was always in the depots recruiting members. Whilst I'm in the office doing my administration she was in the depots organising the workers. She was visiting the depots during lunchtimes and coming back to report to the office.

Soon after I began working for SARHWU I experienced the strike of 1987. We were in COSATU House, 8th floor. The head office and the regional office for Southern Transvaal were both there. On one of those days I was on my way to work after I was busy washing at home. I heard on the news that COSATU House is bombed. But I came to work; I didn't decide I'm not going there because COSATU House has been bombed. I found that people were standing outside the building and there were these red and white tapes showing that we mustn't go to the offices; we must stand outside there. Then we moved to Khotso House to service the members who have lost members of their families.

---

8.   Interview: Nomanese Maxhakana, Durban, November 1997.

After the strike of 1987 we had a strike in 1989 where our members were shot and some were killed. Again Comrade Marvi was the only strong woman who was taking those people from the railway line. Some of them were taken to hospital, some to the office and some to a doctor based in Mayfair. We had the files of the deceased members and we had a list of those who were arrested. We kept the information because every month the family members were coming to the office to get the allowance of R200 to feed the families.

We had women members as well as men but not so many because they thought that women cannot do the jobs being done by the men, like driving the train or selling tickets. The women were just cleaning the toilets or making tea.

Some of them now are busy applying for the jobs like administration but we are still fighting as a union to negotiate with the company that they should allow those who have got long service in the company to apply for better positions. SARHWU is doing workshops to teach and train women that they should apply for the jobs that are done by men. Like now, we're having workshops that are done by COSATU.[9]

Under the apartheid government the conditions experienced by black women railway employees were as harsh as those experienced by men. In fact they fared worse because they were discriminated against as women in addition to discrimination as workers and as blacks.

Elizabeth's Story

Elizabeth Kekana began to work for the railway in 1983. Although she had attained Standard 8 she was unable to find other employment and so became a toilet cleaner at a railway station.

One day I was sitting in Pretoria Station looking for a job in the newspaper and a lady said to me, 'There are vacancies in the railway. I don't like that kind of work but maybe you can go for a job.' Because I was worried, not employed and suffering I applied for a job cleaning the toilets and cleaning the floor at the station. When I got there I found two white guys and they employed me.

I have got five children. When I first began it was very difficult in the workplace working with white men who don't want to understand if you have got a person sick at home and you have to go home. They say you can't just go. They just gave instructions. We had to work from

9. Interview: Bukie Motloung, Johannesburg, October 1997.

8.30 to 4.30, standing. Working with male workers is also difficult because when a woman is working with them they undermine her. They don't say anything that can help them. They have that way of saying, 'We can't hear anything from a woman. A woman is a woman and has to sit back.'

I worked for the railway for 10 years as a toilet cleaner, not promoted. I tried to apply for other things but there was no chance in that position. It was very difficult. It was horrible. Sometimes you would come in the morning and there was blood or somebody had blocked the toilet and there was water everywhere but people wanted to come in and it was too difficult to do your job. The management was not sympathetic. It wasn't a nice job and there wasn't enough money to support the family. I earned R140 per month.

I started to become a member of SARHWU when I arrived at the company. At that time there was that thing of BLATU where they told you that you had to sign a stop order. It went on up to 1989 and then we changed from BLATU to SARHWU. Shop stewards were elected but at that time it was only men because women were supposed to be in the kitchen and we are not supposed to sit with them in their meetings and the like.

We just accepted that. Management didn't understand clearly. They were still hard. They didn't understand what a shop steward is. We had to fight to get some of the things right. Unless you strike or fight against that you don't get anything. In a depot when the management doesn't want to co-operate with a shop steward you have to sit down and say, 'If you don't want to talk with that man we are not working.' Our hands were our weapons because we blacks, when we work, we use our hands, and if we don't work that work stands still.

My husband is a policeman working for SAP. I was on strike in 1989. It was very difficult because my husband didn't like to see me in that strike because he didn't understand. And you know how difficult it is when your husband is a policeman. He is forced to get instructions from his seniors. When we were on strike and it come to the push of marching and all that he was involved from the police side and I was here. He had to fight with me at home and say, 'Go to work.' And I cannot go to work alone! The whole station is closed and everybody is on a march so how am I going to work? We quarrelled. My parents had to interfere, my brothers had to interfere – to talk to him so that he can understand that whatever the workers are doing I have to do.[10]

Despite the additional disadvantages that they suffered, many women were highly politicised and became involved in the trade union movement and in the underground struggle. Among these were Nomvuyo Mtyekisane, who later became Regional Administrator and then organiser in the Western Cape, and Veronica Mesatywa, organiser in Northern Natal and then the union's first Gender Co-ordinator.

Nomvuyo's Story

Nomvuyo Mtyekisane became involved in SARHWU through the ANC.

It was really early when my father met with ANC people and joined – I think it was during the '40s. So he was actively involved in the ANC and my mother got involved in the '50s. The time I started to notice anything at all was about 1960 when I was a toddler. We almost grew up alone. Our parents were actively involved in politics, going out night and day, being detained and we were left alone with neighbours and that kind of experience. But at the time we never noticed anything bad about it because we enjoyed the moments when we were with our parents and with their comrades because it was like a meeting place. I remember selling papers like *New Age* and other papers of the movement, before the ANC was banned.

Since my parents were in and out of jail it didn't occur to us when we got older not to join them, we had that thing in our mind – that there is an oppression that needs to be challenged. I attended secondary school in the Transkei and I got involved there. My father passed away after being released from detention in 1977. After the '76 riots they were detained for underground activities and he died immediately after he was released. After then we did not have a chance of going back to school and I became involved in the struggle. I met some people who were involved in the struggle in the community, so I started getting involved slowly but surely. I joined the youth movement and I got involved there and I filled the position of regional women's co-ordinator, because we were having problems in the organisation of not having women involved.

We were doing that job but it was not easy because they saw the area of struggle as being a man's world. Girls were not that much interested

---

10. Interview: Elizabeth Kekana, Pretoria, November 1997.

in going for it, so they needed a bit of a push. I couldn't say I achieved a lot, but at least I made a small impact. There was something wrong within the organisation. The exploitation of women sexually by the comrades of the opposite sex. That's what I fought left, right and centre. You know its very flattering for a girl; a leader, a male comrade, approaches you. And they fell for it because they were not well matured. And then, men will be men. They take this one this week, the other one that week. That was one problem. And the fact that our meetings were held late, so others were not allowed from their homes. Those are the small things that I was looking into, because I wanted to know why these people are so reluctant to come to our organisation or are being driven away. Then I tackled the leaders and threatened to call a meeting and tell people how they were retarding the progress of the organisation. That's how I was dealing with that problem. And you know, I was winning. Because they were afraid of being embarrassed and I promised them the biggest embarrass ever!

The first campaign that I can highlight was in 1986 when we set about reintroducing the ANC. We launched a campaign where we declared it above instead of under ground. We were working through nights and having meetings where you talk from 6 o'clock in the evening and see the windows becoming dark and after that you see the light of sun coming through the curtain. And then in the morning we'd go and hide in some places and again in the evening we'd go and hang the flags of the ANC in stations and terminals, wherever people are grouped, when people are going to work and so on. I remember that day when we saw the soldiers seeing these flags for the first time in many years. The way they tore them apart was as if they thought they had the person who had put them there! We were hounded like dogs after then. We were sleeping wherever, going with rucksacks because wherever we are once the time to sleep comes we just sleep there.

After those struggles I happened to join with a group of MK who were coming from outside. They happened to be placed in my home so I could look after them because the person who was going to be their reception was detained under Section 29. They were in trouble because some people were believing they are informers, other people are not. It was something that was being sown by the system to divide us, to retard the struggle because all the time we were fighting each other they were advancing. I was afraid because I no longer knew who was right and who was not but I felt I must try so I helped them. Luckily then everything was cleared up and I started working secretly with them and other groups coming inside. I was the person who goes out and seeks money and seeks help for them and hides them. It was very difficult. I used to walk past the Hippos [armoured vehicles] and all the time the people I was working with were being looked for and it was announced on the television that anybody who was sheltering them would be treated the same as them. I had to get money and yet comrades were suspicious and were refusing me.

I worked like that for some time until I broke. I was so angry. We were being frustrated by the system and by our own comrades at that time. And unfortunately for me I couldn't handle the pressure that we were undergoing. I developed a skin problem because of the pressure and I was told in hospital to play a very inactive role if I want to be alright. After being hospitalised I was called to Botswana for a crash course in the military. It was a very short one because they saw that I wasn't okay. I think they thought that it would be too much for me. But I'm telling you that I was so furious because I wanted to do it, because at that time I didn't fully realise what the pressure did to me.

After that the ANC was unbanned and things simmered down. I involved myself instead in some community projects and then in 1992 I was recruited by Comrade ZZ to work with SARHWU. He knew I was involved with my parents in the ANC and he encouraged me to apply for the job of Administrator for the union in the Western Cape. I was reluctant because at that time I had never worked with the unions but he told me that the working-class struggle was just another part of the same thing. Fortunately I followed it up and I got the job and I worked as an administrator from then until I became an organiser in 1997.[11]

Veronica's Story

Veronica Mesatywa gained her trade union experience as one of the leaders of a famous strike at OK Bazaars before joining SARHWU as an organiser in 1990.

In 1978 I got my first employment. I was employed by a shoe factory as a machinist but I did not survive very long there because there was a lot of exploitation and the management was not even prepared to listen to our complaints. I was expelled because I was starting to organise the other women and we were starting to put our act together. Next I was

---

11. Interview: Nomvuyo Mtyekisane, Cape Town, October 1997.

employed by a home for the aged but I survived only nineteen days. I could not take the oppression which was there so I left.

I went out again to look for another job and I got a part-time job with the OK Bazaars. We were all employed as casuals and we found that we were not treated the same. There were coloureds, Indians and white people who were employed after us, who were getting full-time jobs before we did. I decided to take up the matter. At that time, the people were not unionised; they were using these liaison committees. I took up the matter with them and we fought until they gave us full-time jobs. Even then it was very difficult because, again, we were so much oppressed. We found that the liaison committee was not doing anything for us so we tried to look for a trade union.

There was a union which was established which is CCAWUSA, Commercial Catering and Allied Workers Union of South Africa, and in 1980 those organisers came to visit at the OK Bazaars to come and tell us about it. On that day I was the only person who joined the union – because I was just liking what the union does for the workers. But I asked those organisers, 'Can you please leave the joining forms so that I would be able to talk to the others?' They left the joining forms with me.

OK Bazaars is a national company but within that shop I was working in I said, 'I want to make sure that we get fifty plus one per cent of the workers.' In order to get that I had to utilise my own time because I couldn't use the company time. So I used my tea break; I used my lunch. By the time the organisers came back maybe only ten of the people in the shop were not members. From there, we took up the struggle but there was a problem because we were not recognised yet. We tried to negotiate issues with the management but they were telling us, 'You CCAWUSA people are not recognised so we can't discuss anything.' Because I was the one who always took the initiative the management persuaded the people to elect me as a representative on the liaison committee. They hoped that I would give up the trade union. They said I must call a meeting. I had to know how do they feel; do they still have confidence in the liaison committee or not?

Then they said, 'No, no. We feel that we would rather do away with the thing, with the liaison committee. We have to go for a union.' Then I said, 'OK, I am going to draw a petition.'

During my lunch break I ran down to the offices of FOSATU which were very far from the OK where I was working. They helped me to draw up the petition and then it was typed. The following day they brought it for me and then I made everybody sign it. When I counted the numbers I found that most of the people had signed the petition, even the white employees! I submitted the petition and they said they are going to send it to the OK Bazaars [head office]. From there a letter came back saying, 'You people at Chapel Street must know that you no longer have a liaison committee. You don't have any representation any more because you have chosen that you want to be in a union when you know that the union is not recognised.' But we said that although we were not recognised we were still going to operate.

Near where I was working there was another OK. I went there and from there we went outside organising all the other shops. Then there was a national strike in OK from 1985 -1986. I was also involved there. We were detained during that strike. What I liked about that strike was that we were militant! We were all together and we were all saying that we will never go back until we achieve what we went out for. Myself, when we were on strike, I used to say that if people feel that they want to turn back they will all come back but I will never come back. I will remain alone and stay until the problem which we went out for is solved. Unfortunately I really was the last one to go back because of the detention!

Then in 1989, when a new management came in in the OK Bazaars where I was working, I started to have problems where they were trying to say my till was always short, this and that so I said, 'No – I must look for another job. Let me leave OK now.' At that time I thought about the trade unions but unfortunately I could not get a job with the trade unions so I got job with an insurance company called African Life. There were many women, more women than males but even within the insurance company I found that wherever there are women working conditions are very poor and the wages are very poor. It is even worse when you find most of the people are African people. African women are being oppressed as women and then by their colour again. When I joined that insurance company I found that women are victimised like anything.

While I was dealing with that insurance company I was delegated to work specially with Transnet workers [SATS at that time]. When I went to different depots to sell the insurance to the workers I found that the working conditions were poor and I tended to spend most of my time discussing work-related issues instead of selling my product. At that time there was still that spirit of the 1987 strike. I tried to ask them about

SARHWU but they said, 'No no – don't ever ever mention that name! SARHWU is not good at all. The people who are members of SARHWU are murderers.' I said, 'Why are you saying that? Is there anybody you know here who has been killed by members of SARHWU?' They said, 'No.' Then I asked them, 'What union do you belong to?' and they said, 'We belong to BLATU.' I saw they were lost because I asked them, 'What has BLATU done for you so far?' and they couldn't say.

A month later I went again to the PX. When I was just passing by, going to another depot I heard them shouting at me, 'Veronica, Veronica, please come here.' I went and they said, 'Look here. There's this one guy who is coming from Durban. He is a SARHWU member. Can you speak to him? Maybe he can tell you, because we can't be caught speaking to him because we are not SARHWU members.' I spoke to the guy. We discussed and discussed and discussed and we started to organise them one by one – at that time I was not working for SARHWU, I was still working for this insurance company!

Then immediately after that they said, 'Look here. We are going to open an office here in Pietermaritzburg. Could you please apply for the post of organiser?' The office was opened and there was no organiser, no one. They tried to encourage me to apply for the job. They said, 'Look here. We have got two posts – the post of an administrator and the post of an organiser.' I said to myself that at the moment I don't want to work as an organiser because the railway is purely male. Maybe I won't succeed if I go there. Because I've seen from previous companies I've worked for that even where there were more females than males women were suppressed. No matter that they were there in numbers, they were suppressed.

I said, to myself, I'm a black lady; I don't think I would succeed; I'd rather apply for this post of an administrator. So I applied for the post of administrator. I was called for interviews. We were so many that at the end of the day I was shocked when I received a letter from them stating that, 'Looking at the interview, we feel that, although you are female, we would like to employ you as an organiser.' I said, 'What am I going to do? Should I deny or shouldn't I deny this?' I went home. I spoke to my mother about this. My mother said, 'No no no no no. You must not deny it. Take it! Take it!' So I responded that, OK, I would be able to assume my duties on 1 October. When I assumed my duties I said, OK, to be able to succeed within this purely male sector I must make sure that I am assertive. I'm going to be assertive, knowing what goal I am going to achieve. I said I must not take myself any more as a female, especially as a black female. I must take myself as an organiser who is like all the other organisers. From there I set my course.[12]

The post-apartheid era

There are very few women who are being advanced in SARHWU itself. And again I've got to come back, what's good for the goose is good for the gander. If the country has embarked on an affirmative action policy, I don't think the unions can exclude themselves from it. Because definitely we've got to give attention to the place of women. I think that if we actually make an audit of women in SARHWU, in higher positions, in influential positions and so forth, we will find there are very very few women. Those are the kind of things that I think SARHWU needs to work on in the future. Because SARHWU will die if they don't give attention to those things.[13]

Unfortunately (although not surprisingly) gender stereotyping and sexist attitudes did not end with apartheid. Women clearly had the capacity to work on equal terms with men but they were constrained by the gender roles assigned to them. When Nomvuyo first began to work for SARHWU in 1992 she found a lot of difference between that and the ANC organisation that she was used to. Although there was continuing prejudice against them by those who saw the area of struggle as being a man's world, women within the ANC were actively encouraged to play a leading role, and sexual harassment and gender stereotyping by males were condemned. As gender co-ordinator in the Western Cape she had struggled with some success to change male attitudes so it was a shock to her to find that these still went unchallenged within SARHWU.

If you were an administrator you were expected to be prepared to perm your hair to look smart and so on. And I wasn't like that because I was coming from the struggle in the community. That's the way I grew up because we never had those kinds of things because we're always busy. The first question I was asked by a shop steward when I came here was, 'Administrator, why do you not go to the salon and perm your hair so that you look smart so that we can be proud of you?' I said to them, 'People, you have hired me here to come and work, not to come and look beautiful.' Two of our shop stewards which are in leadership are

---

12. Interview: Veronica Mesatywa, Johannesburg, October 1997.
13. Interview: Lynette Hugo, Johannesburg, November 1997.

still talking about that today! They said, 'You are very tough to give an answer like that in a house full of shop stewards, men only and you are the only woman. Everybody was looking at you and thinking that you will run away and cry.' And our shop stewards were impressed.

Anyway, that is how the women are being treated in each and every area; you are treated like an ornament, a tool. People need you to look the way they like. People need you to listen. People need you to talk when you are allowed to talk. And then it was even worse within the trade unions because the working-class men are the majority and they believe that men are the ones who are supposed to go out to work, women are supposed to stay at home. Those are the hardships that we had to endure. And it's up to you to say, 'Do I challenge this or not?'[14]

As the only woman organiser in SARHWU, at the time Veronica felt that she should make a special effort to encourage Transnet to employ more women workers, to recruit more women members for SARHWU, and to improve the lot of women within the union.

I found that within the area of Pietermaritzburg there was only one black female. Those who were there were only white females. That female was just doing mere sweeping and making tea and then when I asked her about her qualifications, the woman was having a certificate of Standard 10 but because she is a black woman she was denied the right to be one of those within the offices where you find that some of them did not even have education up to Standard 7.

Within these offices, because most of our members are illiterate people, there is a breakdown of communication. They can't communicate with these people. So within the depots we started to recommend that they should start employing African women. We went to each and every depot to fight for an African person to be employed there. The first place we were successful was a depot in Pietermaritzburg, in Victoria Street, where they employed an African lady, to deal with all the office work and to communicate with the workers.

Being a person who is active in COSATU, I was also very much active within the Women's Forum which was established at COSATU in 1987. So I asked myself – I am participating in this COSATU Women's Forum but in SARHWU where is this Women's Forum or gender or whatever? I felt that we should do something within SARHWU itself. We started to encourage one another – could you please participate

14. Interview: Nomvuyo Mtyekisane, Cape Town, October 1997.

within COSATU on women's issues and so forth? At that time it was even difficult within SARHWU because we found that when they negotiated they were not negotiating anything about women's issues within the Transnet bargaining council. We started discussing and phoning one another and talking about women's issues at our staff meetings. Finally everybody is aware that women are also important within the workplace.[15]

Once it became clear that an ANC government would be in power, the attitude towards SARHWU by the management of Transnet changed and there was some success in negotiating improvements in conditions and increased opportunities for women workers.

It was felt that, looking at the changes within the country, when we were talking about affirmative action we had to consider the employment of women. Now SARHWU started pushing issues such as, why shouldn't women be employed as train drivers? Why shouldn't women be employed on welding? Why can't women be employed to do those things? That's when we started discussing that doors should be open for women within Transnet to apply for whatever job they feel they can do. Because as women we knew that if women want to achieve something they don't fail. As it is now, within the main bargaining council we've got one woman who is sitting there.

Now SARHWU is taking up women's issues. Within Transnet, when a woman was pregnant there was no maternity leave. If a woman was pregnant they had to tie up their stomach and if they give birth today, tomorrow they have to go back to work. Now I can say that we have achieved on that one; although our maternity is still only three months we are going to negotiate to try to achieve the standard which is being achieved within the government – four months' paid maternity.[16]

Together with Maggie Maunye, the then national administrator for SARHWU, Veronica campaigned for an increased awareness of gender issues within SARHWU.

Within the office itself you find that women are there and males are there. We found that we were still suppressed as women by these male comrades who we were working together with. When we are working outside we are saying that our workers within the workplace who are

15. Interview: Veronica Mesatywa, Johannesburg, October 1997.
16. As above.

233

females are suppressed but when we come back to where we are working ourselves we find that we are being suppressed by the same comrades.

We felt we had to do something; we had to try and establish a structure within SARHWU which would be looking at women's issues. Maggie was dealing with the structure until she left for the Parliament. Then we decided that although there are issues which touch women alone these issues do link with our male counterparts. That is when we felt that we should not have just a women's forum, isolated, with we women sitting dealing with women's issues alone. We felt if there is somebody who is full time dealing with these matters at least somebody is responsible for gender matters. [17]

In 1994 the COSATU Congress recommended that in order for all affiliates to take up gender issues, each one should employ a full time Gender Co-ordinator. Women within SARHWU were sceptical that the union would be prepared to take such a step but in 1995 the proposal was put to a full staff meeting and recommendations were made to the National Office Bearers who agreed to the employment of a full time Co-ordinator. The post was advertised and Veronica Mesatywa was appointed by the NEC in 1996.

The President, Nelson Ndinisa, made an attempt to bring the union into line with COSATU and ANC policy on gender. Steps were taken to recruit more women members, to involve women more in the mainstream activity of the union as shop stewards and office holders and to educate the male membership about the importance of gender relations in the workplace and in union structures. Regional delegations to the NEC were mandated to include at least one woman and a structure of regional gender committees was set up.

Nevertheless, progress was slow. Many regions brought their office administrator rather than a woman shop steward and women delegates rarely spoke, feeling overpowered by the male approach. The NEC refused to support a woman candidate in the COSATU elections and there was also opposition to a proposal for guaranteed seats for women.

It's better than then now. You get a shop steward woman, whereas at that time it was hard to get one woman who is active, let alone being a shop steward. But within the trade unions is not easy. People are going to the meetings, you are left to answer the phones but at the end of the day we are expected to know everything that they want from you; even if you were not in their meetings you need to know whatever their needs

---

17. As above.

are, whatever information they need; you are doing many jobs under the name administrator. You are even an organiser, an effective organiser too. But you are not seen as that. People give you tasks and you do them; you don't get credit for them. But I think that's how it is in many places.[18]

Elizabeth Kekana was elected as a shop steward for her depot in 1995 but when she attended the regional congress she found that she was one of only two women workers who were present.

There was a congress in September 1995. When we arrived at the congress we were the only two women workers there. They elected me as the treasurer of the [Northern Transvaal] region and they accepted that women should be there. But even now there are some issues where they say that it's not necessary for women to be a leader. I accept that because a change is very difficult. Maybe it will take a long time for them to accept. Last year, 1996, we decided that we must have a structure, a gender structure, and SARHWU has employed a Gender Co-ordinator. We had a workshop and called all the women from SARHWU to show women are there within SARHWU and women have

A woman member shows her enthusiasm at the SARHWU congress.

to be developed within SARHWU. Comrade Ndinisa said that all the male shop stewards must develop women so that they can be empowered as leaders and show that SARHWU goes with what government is saying. I was elected for being a chairperson but we are still practising. We are around 30 but maybe next year we will have more shop stewards. We have resolved that if women are active we must bring them in.[19]

In the Western Cape Region there was a genuine effort to increase the participation of women.

18. Interview: Nomvuyo Mtyekisane, Cape Town, October 1997.
19. Interview: Elizabeth Kekana, Pretoria, November 1997.

We need women becoming leaders. We need shop stewards and the branches need to make space for women to become leaders and we need to find ways and means of electing people. It's not a difficult thing; we need to go and talk to the structures and where there are active women and say, 'Well, elect women' and make sure that the women are then also developed, as all new shop stewards have difficulty, especially when starting as a shop steward. It's not an easy task; it takes a lot of time and women have a problem in the home also if their partners wouldn't like them to be having meetings and they expect them to go and cook. There are those kinds of barriers and COSATU resolution does try to address that. It's not going to be an overnight task. We went to a branch where they were saying, 'Look, we've tried to bring women but cannot'. They must see it as a task and know that we've moved SARHWU from being just African workers who are now united with coloured workers; now we must bring women or else we are not really uniting workers. That's just part of ongoing tasks.[20]

Nadeema Syms joined SARHWU in the Western Cape in 1994 and was elected as a shop steward shortly afterwards but she found that attitudes to gender issues still had a long way to go.

There are very few women within our organisation. The majority are men and it can be quite intimidating, especially when you are still learning about the organisation. Coming to the gender issue you will find that in SARHWU we are struggling at this stage in building our structures. To take the port of Cape Town, for instance, you will find that most of the women that we do have are casual and the others are in certain grades and they don't want to become active in the organisation because they are scared of being victimised.

One of the issues we are raising is how we can be active in organising the women. The problem we are experiencing with women is that the organisation is so dominated by men that women don't feel that they can go to the men asking for advice. We are in the process in getting women leadership in. So if a woman is active we want to make her a shop steward and get her more involved and recognised. At the end of the day we need to make people realise that women in organisations can also be leaders.

Women need to help one another, and with the women of SARHWU the one thing I've found is that when we get together it doesn't matter

---

20. Interview: Evan Abrahamse, Cape Town, October 1997.

who you are, we just click. It doesn't matter if you are a manager or a general worker, when you come together and you talk about the issues you realise that the issues are the same. As women we need to realise that we need to stick together. That doesn't mean that we need to overpower the men. One of the issues is how can we create a platform so that the voice of the women can more easily be heard?

We also need to ask ourselves what we can do to get more women, especially black women, into the company. The company would say that they are looking after the interests of women but when they appoint from outside it's mostly males so we need to ask how do we get women on the operational side. For the first time now we have got a woman crane driver and she is a SARHWU member. After so many years! And this is a woman with four children. That shows that if the doors are open a woman can achieve that. Our focus should be: how can we empower these women?

If people feel threatened they will oppose. People will always be resistant to change and this is a change for this organisation. We never had women before and suddenly they are coming to the forefront. To be able to say this woman is capable of doing 1, 2, 3 for some men cannot be easy. You must also remember the different culture. Most of the women are mothers and the men are saying, 'No it is not your place to be here.' How do you cope with that? It is a challenge for everybody and you have to ask yourself how would I have coped if I was in that person's shoes? You can't take that person and hit him over the head and say, 'Come right over now.'

It is a process basically sensitising all the men in the leadership, all the men on the ground floor, everybody in the workforce, all the members of SARHWU – sensitising them to what are gender issues. Why do we need to bring women in? In the past what has the role been for women? It's always been subservient. How do you change that? It won't happen overnight. What we need to look at is telling people what are the issues, informing them what the obstacles are … You will find that some males will only listen to males but if you convince some then they will show the others. It's a process but it is difficult! As a shop steward I've learned that if you are sensible, if you have a value system and if you know facts you will be amazed what people will support you – if they know what you stand for and that you are not trying to manipulate the situation. That's a lesson nobody else could have taught me except SARHWU and that I'm very glad of.

Women do have these problems in our culture. I am Muslim, I am not married and I come from a background where when the man comes home the food must be ready and the wife doesn't go to any meetings when he is at home. Her responsibility is to sit at home and look after the children. That is what my mother did. Suddenly for those women to change is very difficult and they may meet with physical abuse or mental abuse as well. Within our leadership we also experience that problem that the men don't give us support. The minute a woman gets a position higher than a man they feel inferior because the woman has a new status and according to society that isn't right – he should be the breadwinner of the house. He sees that as a threat to himself and unfortunately some men are then very brutal. They don't accept that there is a change. That is the way that they were brought up. [21]

The root of the problem is that both men and women are still insufficiently educated about the difference between 'women's issues' and gender – the power relations between men and women, the roles that they play, how this is supported by ideology, and how it obstructs the achievement of equality in the workplace and in society at large.

People don't understand. Most of them think it's the same as Women's Forum. If you go to the depots some of them ask what else you want. We have to recognise gender issues but they seem not interested. The women themselves don't recognise the importance of gender. They don't want to be shop stewards because there are men and if you say that we women should have a role in the organisation they don't buy it! [22]

Such confusion leads to hostility towards gender issues even at leadership levels.

They feel, 'Oh, women! Do you think that you can do this 1, 2, 3?' There's still that thing of not trusting us as women, thinking that we can't achieve anything. Even when you come up with a good suggestion, because it is coming from a woman it is not taken into consideration. There are programmes which we should run but you find that when it comes to the gender budget you are not getting money to run those programmes. If the issues are other issues which are not women's issues you find that that particular meeting is being funded. You go and participate in COSATU meetings but you find our women sitting

21. Interview: Nadeema Syms, Cape Town, October 1997.
22. Interview: Elizabeth Kekana, Pretoria, November 1997.

thumb-sucking because we didn't discuss the matter at home. Some of them now are starting to participate although the pace is still slow.

Where the problem lies is in the education of the trade union. There is a resolution from the President that SARHWU is prepared to educate and develop women in different categories within the trade union but when we are discussing issues you find that they will say that women don't have the capability. I don't agree with that. Women are capable of all things. The problem is training and developing skills. If a person is semi-skilled, in order to empower her you have to train her.

There are obstacles which prevent them participating in every meeting of the trade union – the time the meeting is called, the venue. Another thing is the home responsibilities. For many they can't leave their child unattended because they don't have the money to take the child to the childcare facility or to pay the neighbour to look after the child. The trade unions themselves don't provide childcare facilities within the meeting venues. At our congress in 1995 I wrote a letter proposing that SARHWU should provide childcare facilities for the women participating in the congress and they treated it like a joke! 'You women! You want more things. It will never happen.' But I don't think it will never happen because other unions have started to provide childcare facilities so even SARHWU, if they really mean that they are prepared to develop women, should provide childcare facilities.

Women are also denied the chance to take up shop steward positions because they feel that if I am taking a shop steward position I'm taking an extra job which will also require most of my time. This is why you find when it comes to elections women keep on nominating males. Another thing is the way they are brainwashed by some of our male comrades so they don't have confidence in other women. We tend not to have confidence in other women. Another thing is that the environment where the elections take place is intimidatory to women. I would be very happy one day to see at least one or two women within these National Office Bearers. Before we point the finger at management for not appointing women we should practise it at home and have women within our leadership.

Women should be given an opportunity to grow. In this head office they laugh at me when I say I'm like a blind person just seeing with poor, poor vision. When they ask me, 'Why are you saying that?' I say that the way this office operates isn't the way I'm used to. As women we aren't developed. You are confined wherever you are. If you come with this skill you end up having just that skill. As a woman you aren't asked to represent SARHWU in a meeting but I don't only want to attend meetings about women's issues. I want to be in other meetings to see if women's problems are being taken care of. [23]

As noted at the outset of the chapter, commitment on paper to non-racism and non-sexism is easier than transformation of a long-standing culture. South Africa as a whole is still grappling with how to do it while also trying to tackle innumerable other basic and pressing problems.

The new trade union leadership will no doubt be judged, among other things, on whether it can develop the policies and educational programmes that will be needed to weld black and white, women and men, into an effective and united union that develops and respects and uses the strengths of all its members.

---

23. Interview: Veronica Mesatywa, Johannesburg, October 1997.

8

SARHWU in a New Era

Introduction

The Government of National Unity (GNU), elected in 1994, inherited an ailing economy. The main objective of the National Party's economic policy had been to maintain high wages and a prosperous life-style for the white minority, together with high profits to encourage capitalist enterprises. There was a heavy reliance on gold to provide export earnings while local industry was protected against external competition, and the public service and parastatal organisations were used to provide sheltered employment for government supporters. Investment and productivity were low, and in order to ensure profitability it was necessary to keep the wages of the black workforce down and to suppress trade union opposition. Black unemployment was high, health and education services poor and other social services for the majority of the population virtually non-existent.

The role of the trade unions during the 1980s had been to fight the combination of state repression and employer hostility responsible for the continuing oppression of their members. Trade unions became politically engaged and played a major part in bringing the apartheid regime to the conference table to negotiate the transfer of power. This was recognised by the Triple Alliance between the African National Congress (ANC), the South African Communist Party (SACP) and the Congress of South African Trade Unions (COSATU). The Alliance fought the 1994 election on a single platform and with a single party list, and the new government gave the trade unions a role in economic decision-making

241

through their inclusion in the tripartite National Economic Development and Labour Council (NEDLAC).

In theory the trade unions were now in a position to influence government policy in the interests of their members. In reality, COSATU soon found that by committing itself to an alliance in which it played a junior role it had undermined its ability to act independently and to challenge those aspects of government policy with which it disagreed. This was illustrated by the unions' failure to win key points in the debate on the 1995 Labour Relations Bill and to prevent changes in the policy on privatisation which took place almost immediately after the election of the GNU. On both issues COSATU resorted to extra-parliamentary pressure by strikes and demonstrations but failed to push them home and accepted compromise solutions.

Privatisation

The clash over privatisation placed particular strain on the relationship between COSATU and the ANC. The Reconstruction and Development Programme (RDP), which had been adopted by the Triple Alliance as its economic platform for the April 1994 election, emphasised state-led investment and development as the primary means of redistributing wealth and overcoming the inequalities entrenched by the apartheid system. As early as October 1994, however, the reality of the economic situation, coupled with the need to ensure a peaceful transition and the pressure brought to bear by the international community, encouraged the 'moderates' within the new cabinet to propose a different role for the public sector. A six-point plan was put forward based on the privatisation of government assets to raise funds for the economic empowerment of the black population, and at the end of 1995 the ANC adopted a policy document *The State and Social Transformation,* reversing previous policy on public ownership. This was swiftly followed by an announcement by the then Deputy President, Thabo Mbeki, that the government was proposing to privatise key public enterprises.

This change in policy by the ANC without reference to its Alliance partners created tension within the Triple Alliance and threw into question the relation-ship between the trade unions and government in the post-apartheid era. The SACP and trade unions in the public service and parastatals were strongly opposed to what they saw as the effective abandonment of the RDP and the adoption instead of neo-liberal policies, which they believed would lead to major job losses. A protest campaign was launched and COSATU unions took to the streets as they had done in the 1980s – but this time against their 'own' government.

The union protest brought about some modifications but no fundamental change in government policy. In February 1996 government and labour (COSATU, the Federation of South African Labour Unions and the National Council of Trade Unions) signed a National Framework Agreement (NFA) on the privatisation and restructuring of state assets. Unions agreed to the restructuring of state assets in order to increase economic growth and employment, meet basic needs, develop infrastructure, reduce state debt, enhance competitiveness and efficiency, and develop human resources. In return government recognised the legitimacy of the state playing a role in productive sectors of the economy and accepted that 'restructuring is not necessarily geared towards reducing state involvement in any economic activity'.[1] Organised labour in general and the employees of the relevant enterprises in particular were to participate in the formation of policy, and restructuring should not occur at the expense of the workers. Every effort should be made to retain employment and a social plan should be implemented to assist workers affected by retrenchments.

The agreement temporarily papered over the cracks but the differences between the government and the unions remained. COSATU supported the restructuring of state assets for 'the upliftment of South Africa's people'. It was prepared to accept the sale of a portion of the equity of parastatals provided that the state remained the major shareholder and that sales excluded institutions central to the RDP. It was, however, opposed to privatisation being the central tool of government policy. The government paid lip service to these concerns but it insisted that privatisation was a fundamental policy of the ANC and would be implemented.[2]

In June 1996 the Minister of Finance, Trevor Manuel, presented the government's new macro-economic framework policy document *Growth, Employment and Redistribution* (GEAR). The policy contained ambitious targets for growth and job creation and looked to privatisation and de-regulation to drive the economy. In the same month the Minister for Public Enterprises, Stella Sigcau, announced the setting up of committees to formulate proposals on which restructuring options should be pursued for each parastatal. By June 1997 strategic stakes in eleven public enterprises had either been put out to tender or sold off, and plans were well advanced for eight more to follow by the end of the year.[3] Employee representatives were involved in these decisions as laid down by the NFA, but in reality 'ill informed and under-resourced trade unionists [were] more often than not confronted with privatisation which [was] already

1.   *South African Labour Bulletin*, 20(2), April 1996; pp. 18-22.
2.   *South Africa Survey*, 1997, pp. 399-401.
3.   M. Ray, 1997, pp. 11-15.

underway' and they were powerless to stop it. The situation was further clouded by the involvement of trade union investment companies 'jostling for a piece of the privatisation pie'.[4]

The future role of trade unions

In July 1996 COSATU set up a commission to enquire into the future role of trade unions in the changing political and economic circumstances in South Africa (the September Commission). NEDLAC and the new Labour Relations Act (LRA) encouraged a shift in labour relations

> away from the old adversarial model characterised by high levels of conflict, union repression, discrimination, cheap labour and authoritarian management styles to a more co-operative model based on collective bargaining, greater participation, organisational rights, effective resolution of conflict, and higher levels of co-operation resulting in greater flexibility and improving productivity outcomes.[5]

The Commission report, published in May 1997, came up with an ambitious vision of expanded union participation in decision making, the transformation of the public sector and the development of 'social unionism.'[6] In reality, however, the unions were constrained by a capacity crisis following the mass exodus of experienced leaders to take up posts in government and business. They suffered from a high level of staff turnover and a shortage of qualified personnel and found it difficult to maintain the level of service to members and the democratic structures of their organisations, let alone to research and develop policies and make meaningful contributions to the boards of companies.

At the same time many unionists – particularly at the activist/shop steward level – felt ambiguous about the form of change which had taken place and the kind of ideology which supported it.[7] NEDLAC seemed to them to be less an opportunity to influence policy, more a way of tying the unions into supporting and implementing ideas which, in the short term at least, were against the interests of their members. The framework of the LRA, while giving more recognition to unions, was in fact remarkably similar to that established by the Industrial Relations Act in the 1920s and signalled a continuity of approach rather than a radical departure.

---

4. As above.
5. A. Smith, 1997, p. 71.
6. See *South African Labour Bulletin*, 21(5), October 1997, for details and discussion of the Commission's proposals.
7. See A. Smith, 1997, and J. Baskin, 1996, for discussion of the capacity crisis in trade unions.

COSATU took part in high-profile discussions such as the NEDLAC Jobs Summit held in 1998, but it was clear that the rhetoric of participation far outstripped the reality. GEAR's over-optimistic targets for growth and job creation predictably failed to be met, and by the end of 1998 employment had actually fallen to 1980 levels. An Alliance Summit was held at which agreement was reached to realign macro-economic policy with reconstruction and development objectives to address the social deficit, but the government continued with its programme of privatisation and GEAR remained official policy.

Conflict or Co-operation?

The history of wages with SARHWU was always linked to a struggle. The struggle for the R1 500 was at a time SARHWU was not recognised. It was not even allowed to put its demand formally on the table. So it became a culture that wages were linked to a broader struggle or insurrection because that is how SARHWU was always prepared. When it went into a strike it was war. [8]

The recognition of SARHWU in November 1990 and the negotiated agreement between the National Party and the ANC brought a fundamental change in SARHWU's situation. As an affiliate of COSATU and a long-term ally of the ANC it was now committed to support for the political settlement and the avoidance of civil disorder. At the same time, as a member of the Transnet Industrial Council, it was no longer excluded from the industrial relations machinery but an integral part of it, and committed to play by the rules. This change in circumstances meant that both leadership and membership had to learn an entirely new language and style of behaviour, with the emphasis less on strikes and violent action and more on negotiation and compromise. The transition was not an easy one.

There was very little experience of negotiation within SARHWU because it was previously unrecognised. Traditionally no negotiations took place without prior consultation with the membership. The rank and file wanted to control the leadership. It was common practice for shop stewards to accompany negotiators to any meetings, and any alteration to the mandated position had to be endorsed by the membership. Failure to abide by this procedure would lead to the removal of leaders and in the climate of the times the organisers sometimes went in fear for their lives.

---

8. Interview: Bonnie Thekisho, Kimberley, October 1997.

> Sometimes if there was a big strike the workers would call you an
> impimpi if they didn't find you at the office. They would see the reports
> in the media and then you as an official don't have them. Then people
> come to the office and say, 'Where are the reports? Yesterday on the TV
> we read that SARHWU is going to be recognised. Why don't you have
> that information?' In 1989/90 I had to go into hiding for a period of two
> months because I feared for my life, thinking that they will come and
> chase me away! [9]

This attitude and the faction fighting which accompanied it led to a rejection of
offers of training by Transnet, and held the union back from effective participation in negotiations about restructuring in 1990. Bongani Nogaga, then Acting
Secretary of the Southern Natal Region, was threatened and accused of selling
out.

> That cost us a lot. It was when the company was starting to reshape
> itself. We were bogged down with infighting while they were deciding
> how the company should operate and who is needed and not needed.
> There was going to be retrenchment. There was something we should
> concentrate on. Then when we started to have marches and so on
> management said, 'You had your chance. There were meetings and you
> decided not to attend! Therefore we can't wait for you; decisions have
> been made.' We lost quite a number of workers and it was bitter for me
> because it was my first experience of negotiations. [10]

Mistrust of the leadership and faction fighting were responsible for the overthrow
of Martin Sebakwane when he went against his mandate in negotiating the wage
agreement in 1992. It also led to the replacement of Elliot Sogoni as Regional
Secretary of the Southern Transvaal in the same year.

> It was a question of unfounded beliefs. Some of them were saying he
> was attending meetings without being accompanied by shop stewards
> and that he had entered into agreements with management – agreements
> that were not for the benefit of the workers. I think mainly it was a
> question of the militancy that we had created in the workers. They would
> go to the extent of analysing even the way in which you talk. If you are
> soft, they believed, 'No, he cannot be a leader.' If you talk slowly, they
> believed, 'No, no, no there is something wrong here.' You had to be
> vigilant. You had to stand out there and shout and then they realised that
> this is the man who is the leader! That type of thing was happening.

---

9.   Interview: Sello Tshwaribe, Kimberley, October 1997.
10. Interview: Bongani Nogaga, Durban, October 1997.

> People complained of minor issues, and they made them into serious
> things. If a manager does a thing they sit down and discuss in their
> meeting and say, 'He is doing this because he still has that belief of those
> old times when black people were being oppressed.' Then they go out
> on strike. Sometimes you find that it is such a small issue that had they
> decided to send a delegation to go and meet their managers it would
> have been solved there. It was that type of militancy that these workers
> in fact believed in.[11]

The new leadership that succeeded Martin Sebakwane and his team was well
aware of the need for a new approach. The imminent end of apartheid meant also
the end of feather-bedding for Transnet, and the process of splitting up the
company into different business units with a view to privatisation had already
begun. The process involved a large number of potential redundancies and it was
important that SARHWU should secure the best deal for its members that it
could. To support this drive the union requested and received the facility of
release of key members as full-time shop stewards on full pay. The first of these
was Stephen Matlou who had succeeded Nelson Ndinisa as Chairman of the
Southern Transvaal.

> I used the opportunity of the ANC's unbanning effectively. Because of
> being a full-time shop steward I was able to attend all kinds of political
> education and training in the ANC, SACP and COSATU. Then I started
> to operate nationally. I was a national SARHWU negotiator between
> SARHWU and the company and I was a peace maker *vis à vis*
> SARHWU and the white unions created by management. I used to be
> a go-between – to soften them. SARHWU could put its positions
> without diluting them and I would then make them acceptable to these
> guys. I'd also take the leadership in negotiations. First I'd caucus them
> and make them swallow what SARHWU is going to say then I'd take
> the lead in the negotiations with Transnet.[12]

As General Secretary Derrick Simoko worked to build up a relationship with
Transnet managers and to develop a less adversarial bargaining strategy. This
became easier following the election of 1994.

> We have changed the approach to not putting up a demand on the table
> but demanding that management declare their budget to the union. We
> have managed to settle with management without any pressure from
> labour demanding that management should bring more. We think that

---

11. Interview: Johnson Gamede, Johannesburg, November 1997.
12. Interview: Stephen Matlou, Cape Town, October 1997.

> transparency as introduced by the new management in Transnet is saving a lot and workers are becoming very confident in their leadership and their management which is predominantly black at present.[13]

Nevertheless members were still extremely militant and reluctant to compromise.

> It is the culture of railwaymen. When they have demanded something they expect to get 100% what they have demanded. That has been a problem in this union and is still a problem. At NEC meetings people would come with mandates from different regions. We'd agree, for example, on 8%, and the NEC mandates the negotiators. When the negotiators get to the table things are different. They find that we cannot get 8%. In fact the company cannot offer 8%. But when they come back after months of intense negotiations the membership says, 'We didn't agree on six. We said eight.' That's the problem![14]

These differences between leadership and rank and file were made worse by the changing industrial situation. Union leaders felt that their hands were tied by militants who did not understand the mechanics of negotiation.

> Although the workers have not yet achieved what they fought for, they *are* liberated in terms of the national liberation struggle. We need to go out to our members and say, 'Let's ask ourselves whether the strategy that we used before 1994 is still the right one to use after 27 April 1994.' Because if we leave those workers as they are, instead of them being an asset to the country and their unions, they might become a liability. Their struggle is still based on the old same concept and they still believe that the only way in which you can make somebody listen to you and respond in a manner which will make you happy is when you go out on strike. We still have members in the region [Southern Transvaal] who, when they talk to a manager and he is not prepared to listen to them, they take him out and throw him out of the premises of the company!
>
> I think our union is standing on only one place. We are still being guided by the old militancy that we used to have before 1994 and times have changed. We need to make this company productive; that is the role that we must be seen to be playing as SARHWU. We cannot say we are fighting for liberation. We have attained that. We are free. We need to make a contribution so that at the end of the day if I demand a

---

13. Interview: Derrick Simoko, Johannesburg, October 1997.
14. Interview: Arthur Mosikare, Kimberley, October 1997.

fourteen percent increase I am able to say, 'I have made a contribution. Give me that. I deserve it.'

But there is no movement towards that and we need to focus as a union more on that to change the beliefs, the minds of the people. If we are not going to do that, we are not going to have SARHWU within the next four or five years because management will take decisions that this particular business unit is not making money, let's give it to a private person. The more we play our role as workers making the company productive, the more we will see jobs created. The company will be able to compete with any other company out there. We would be able to take them head on and say, 'Now you are playing with fire.' [15]

Many of the rank and file, on the other hand, saw union leaders as neglecting democratic structures and failing to protect the interests of the workers.

Our main purpose was not to fight with the comrades. It was to bring to their attention that they must understand that in this organisation we won't let anybody kill worker control and democracy. Because if we do that we will be agreeing to autocracy; that is, any individual can do what he likes or she likes. We have got these people who have gone to university who are telling us, 'Now the struggle is over. You have got democracy; you must stop struggling.' But how have we got this democracy? Economically where are we? In our belief the struggle will never end. Our belief is that it isn't a question of if you are black or white. We are talking about problems. To me it seems we are compromising everything. We are lacking political direction. We don't have politics and we are stagnant. [16]

The impatience of the members was a major problem in allowing a stable leadership to develop.

People on the ground start feeling that the leadership don't do enough. And because of the apartheid that was there they feel that leadership is pro management – that you drink tea with them, you interact with them and therefore you forget to deliver for people. That's one of the reasons why leadership has to change from time to time. If a person is outspoken on the floor they want to send him up with the aim that they will dilute the established leadership. It's fair that the membership should be able to change leadership if they want to but some people are slow starters, some people learn by mistakes. If you are not given a chance they will

15. Interviews: Arthur Mosikare as above; Johnson Gamede, Johannesburg, November 1997.
16. Interview: Mzaman Silus Mabunde, Johannesburg, November 1997.

take you out and put someone else in and they don't know what they are losing. They should give leadership at least three terms of office so that it can be properly built up and give them a fair chance. People want more money than the leadership can deliver. That's why I say we need people from the shop floor to mix with experts to build up a team. Because we can never negotiate what they want.[17]

Running the Union

Some of these differences must be put down to problems with the internal running of the union. Historically, SARHWU was not good at developing sound financial and administrative systems and 'capacity' problems have continued into the post-apartheid era.

In the red

When SARHWU was relaunched in 1986 efforts, led by Mike Roussos as Education Officer, were made to set it up on sound financial and administrative lines. Some funds were obtained from international supporters; two offices (National and Southern Transvaal) were set up in COSATU House, and education and training of office staff were undertaken. Unfortunately, however, much of this was undermined during the course of the 1987 strike. SARHWU offices were destroyed by bombing, documents were seized and officials were arrested. The union was left in the hands of the rank and file leadership who were harassed by the police and who had no administrative or financial experience.

When the strike ended the membership had grown but the ability to communicate with, and service, that membership had actually shrunk. Lack of money was a fundamental problem. Subscriptions were fixed at a flat rate of R1 per member and were collected at the workplace. Income fluctuated and a certain amount was always siphoned off for branch expenses with only a fraction ever reaching Head Office. It was not possible to pay organisers regularly so these were recruited on an ad-hoc basis from the ranks of political activists and dismissed workers willing to work for a share of what they could collect.

We got a salary after six months. The subs were hand collected. You go to work but at the end of the month when you need to bring something in there is nothing there. Some of us were naughty. We used to hide the

---

17.   Interview: Ezrom Mabyana, Johannesburg, November 1997.

subscription books and say we didn't receive that money for that month in order to feed ourselves! [18]

The leadership of SARHWU admitted that the financial affairs of the union were out of control.

We never owned anything from our parents. We never had money so we never learned how to manage it. You learn to manage it because you have it, you know. Now also, at an organisational level, we didn't have money and we never learned to manage organisational funds. By the time any funds came we were so deep in debt that we had to go and feed the monster [pay off debts] so that we increased the debt even more.

We had to cultivate friendly travel agents, bank managers, cultivate all key resources that we will need. We always were in the red but we had hotels which knew that if they accommodate us one day, when we catch a jackpot, we will pay them. At the same time we would prepare and cultivate another one so that if it got really bad with one who said they will never have us again we had somewhere to go. You must always have the next one ready, cultivated, and you pay on the day when friends overseas have sort of remembered you! If you have a big contribution from overseas, you get them to keep it on access because you know you will be back again in so short a time and you will be in the red for so much again.

During periods of a strike, once management has sealed off its facilities and transport from us we don't have mobility. Out of the '89-90 strike, our total motor vehicle bill was 100 000 Rand. We didn't have money for petrol. We would hire cars then change them for another one with a full tank so that we could continue to do the work. There was a lot of malpractice but to a large extent the work was also getting done. You couldn't be all over the country at the same time. It wasn't even an expectation, because there are local leaders who must also exercise a certain accountability and sort of command in the area. And the nature of the expenses and the difficulties about finances meant that we couldn't keep tabs on everything.

Our financial systems were in a mess. It is an oxymoron to say they were in a mess. In fact they were never even there because to have a financial system you have to have the money to manage! Thinking back, we had a million courses on handling finance by all these NGOs that had money to teach people and when they offered you couldn't say no.

---

18. Interview: Sello Tshwaribe, Kimberley, October 1997.

> We kept sending people to these courses but it is no surprise that the
> first time we really had money these courses didn't help. Because you
> go, and it is nice to have the nice conference food and you are away
> from the stresses and strains of the office but you never get to practise
> the skills because there is no money to practise it on. We never really
> had administrative systems, which later on became one of the big
> criticisms and accusations about finance. [19]

This situation continued even after the recognition agreement when the setting
up of stop orders meant that there was a regular flow of income coming into the
union. The auditors' report in October 1990 noted that there were 'a number of
weaknesses and breakdowns in the control and administration of the union funds'
and made a series of detailed recommendations to improve matters.[20] These
recommendations were followed up by a National Finance Workshop in March
1991, where it was stated that the organisation's funds belonged to the membership and that as a matter of urgency SARHWU needed to adopt a financial policy
which would clearly show how the union's funds should be accounted for. [21]

There was, however, slow progress in implementing the decisions made at the
workshop, and in September 1991 a special Regional Executive Committee
meeting was convened by the Southern Transvaal. As the region with the largest
membership the Southern Transvaal members considered that union funds were
'their' money. A motion to withhold funds from head office was defeated, but
the Regional Secretary wrote to the General Secretary demanding that a special
NEC should be called and making veiled threats of further action if satisfaction
was not forthcoming. [22] The showdown came with the revolt over the signing of
the wage agreement by the NMC on 30 September and the occupation of the
head office.

Militants from the Southern Transvaal linked the acknowledged financial
confusion to the signing of the wage agreement without a mandate and accused
members of the NMC of corruption and of having been bought by the Transnet
management. The Commission of Enquiry set up to investigate the crisis in the
union noted that it had received allegations of corruption and maladministration
too numerous to mention.

As noted in Chapter Six, the Commission investigated the accounts of the
head office and the personal bank accounts of the NMC as far as it was able. It
concluded that there was no evidence of corruption in the sense of major theft

---

19. Interview: Martin Sebakwane, Johannesburg, November 1997.
20. Auditors' Report, Douglas and Velcich, 31 October 1990.
21. SARHWU, 1991, p. 22.
22. E.M. Sogoni to General Secretary, 9 September 1991.

but that maladministration existed on a massive scale and that 'corruption in the sense of misuse and abuse of union resources' was widespread. It also noted that, although it had not been possible to investigate the financial affairs of the regions, there was every reason to believe that similar problems existed there.

The language of the report is criticised by Johan Beaurain, who felt that SARHWU was being unjustly criticised for failings that were common in the trade union movement in general.

> They said things in that report which are just simply nonsense. They talked about corruption. They say there is no corruption in the sense of big sums of money disappearing but there was corruption in the sense of the necessary control systems to prevent corruption that did not exist. But it can only be described as corruption if those systems were deliberately not put into place in order to be corrupt. The system wasn't put into place because it wasn't a priority at the time. There were other issues, more political issues, that were more important than to concentrate on setting these systems into place. I don't see that you can call it corruption. How many unions even today have got those systems in place to prevent corruption? [23]

These comments highlight the fact that many of SARHWU's leaders still thought of themselves as political activists rather than as administrators. They were more used to hiding funds, cutting corners, living from hand to mouth and lying to creditors than drawing up financial accounts. Few were trained for their new role and even Martin Sebakwane, who was university educated, had no head for finance. Others, like Johnny Potgieter, were carried away by the change in their circumstances from poverty to riding around in cars and living in hotels and, in the opinion of many, became corrupted in a moral sense if not a financial one.

The financial and administrative reforms put in place by Zola Zembe during his brief time at head office (described in Chapter Six) provided a sound basis on which SARHWU could build for the future. In 1992 Ezrom Mabyana, then Treasurer of the Southern Transvaal region, was elected as National Treasurer. Financial controls were improved along the lines recommended by the Auditors' Report and the Commission of Enquiry. Nevertheless, old habits died hard. In 1992 the First Vice-President, Innocent Moshoeshoe, was accused of irregularities over an overseas donation and forced to resign, and in both the Southern Natal and Northern Transvaal regions branch officials were accused of the theft of union money. Payment of staff salaries, car hire and telephone bills, all of

23. Interview: Johan Beaurain, Cape Town, October 1997.

which should have become systematised, continued to cause problems, and the rank and file remained mistrustful of the leadership's control of their money.

Organising and organisers

At the time that SARHWU received recognition the exact number of SARHWU members was not known. (The union estimated it as 50 000 but Transnet only agreed to process stop orders for 34 000.) There were few full-time organisers, and those that there were tended to be dismissed workers taken on by the union as the only way of helping them. In order to operate in the new era it was necessary to know the location, number and condition of the membership and for that reason the union needed to employ and train additional full-time organisers and office staff. [24] Additionally, a number of former SACTU operatives were brought into the union from exile to act as education officers. Education and Publicity Departments were set up by Vanguard Mkosana, who started a SARHWU newspaper to communicate with the membership and a training programme for shop stewards (see Chapter Six). But all this was disrupted by the October 1991 coup and the subsequent change of leadership.

SARHWU administrative staff at a COSATU computer training session.

24. Interview: Derrick Simoko, Johannesburg, October 1997.

The Honorary President's Report for this period emphasised the need to educate workers from the ranks and to undertake a survey of training needs for full time staff. It also noted that the number of staff employed by SARHWU was more than the size of membership demanded, and that by COSATU standards SARHWU was overstaffed. Unfortunately, however, little was done to act on these recommendations. The Education Officers were recalled from their regional deployment to work from head office making the union appear increasingly centralised to the membership. According to Derrick Simoko,

> When we started in 1992 the administration in the union was in tatters and even the filing was bad. When we looked at it we found that the staff we had was not trained in administration. We made attempts to improve the training but though they had experience of working for the union only a few were trainable as far as administration is concerned. This was not due to the fact that they don't want to but because of the past. The level of education is very low so we seem to be milking a fat bull. [25]

In November 1992 Vanguard Mkosana left SARHWU to work as a public servant and much of the work which he had done to improve communication with the rank and file collapsed. Over the next five years other trained and experienced leaders also left – some like Nelson Ndinisa (National President) and Stephen Matlou (Southern Transvaal Chairman) were recruited to work as managers for Transnet. Others like Bafana Sithole and Maggie Maunye (National Administrator) were elected as ANC members of Parliament in 1994.

Even as late as 1997/98 the problems of organisation had still not been solved. Regional officials complained of late arrival of salaries and poor communication between the centre and the regions.

> The morale of the staff nationally is down. Maybe that is due to the leadership. Currently we haven't received our salary advice. You receive it three weeks after it is due. You don't know who to consult – You ask X and X refers you to Z and Z refers you to Y. That is frustrating. The workers come to the office and harass you with their problems. Sometimes you wake up at four in the morning, drive 400 km to attend to some problems. It is very pathetic and you really want to help them because you have those political convictions. But when you come back you've got nobody to complain to when *you've* got problems. We must realise now that the days of the struggle are over. We are employees

---

25. As above.

now but nobody cares. The latest thing was, 'The railway workers got 7,5% so we'll give you 7,5%, non-negotiable.' You get pushed by your employers and by the workers. That's why I said because the morale of the staff is low, the future of the union is poor. [26]

At the same time, it was said that the workers, in whose interests the union should be run, were getting a raw deal, and poor communications added to the gap between rank and file and leadership.

I think we have a serious problem when it comes to servicing our members. Right now, with the seven branches that we have in the region [Southern Transvaal] not a single branch has got an organiser. It is a truth that at one stage we had too many organisers but when you looked at what they could offer to the members of the union, they had nothing, absolutely nothing. What was happening was that members went on a strike and in any strike there would be casualties. Some of them were dismissed, and the union felt bound that it must give employment to those people. I don't think that was a very good decision. I think the union must give employment to people who are going to be able to service the members.

We have a membership out there that is longing for trade union education, people that need to be guided at each and every occurrence that takes place. We need organisers to give them direction, to give that education because education cannot be found in a workshop room. It also goes on out there in the field, when we are helping with problems. This is not happening in this region. We are now three organisers short. We felt that the best way of using those officials who are still left in the organisation was to bring them from the branch offices to the regional office. But still we have people in the region who don't know what a trade union is because of that business of taking people into the office simply because they had been dismissed for being involved in a strike. The workers themselves are not getting enough service and they are complaining because when they want us we are not there for them. [27]

Communication is not very good. If there is something at the top we have a three-monthly NEC. Then we debate it in the regions and the regions are supposed to tell all the branches and local shop stewards. It's between the regions and the people on the ground that information doesn't flow properly. If one morning I go to my depot I find that there

---

26. Interview: Anonymous regional official, Kimberley, October 1997.
27. Interview: Johnson Gamede, Johannesburg, November 1997.

are questions and that the depots have not been properly informed even though it has been debated.[28]

The Future of SARHWU

> Our objective as SACTU was to unite the working class of South Africa. Our aim should be to transform society, to get rid of poverty, get rid of illiteracy, make sure there are jobs and bread for the workers. The principles of what we do as a union will not change but the tactics may have to change. Transnet ceases to exist so SARHWU loses its identity. There is also emerging joblessness as a result of the changing economy. These problems need to be looked at. How in the next 10-15 years are we to maintain the railway as a key transport industry and fight job losses? We have to find new ways of addressing these problems. [29]

In 1994 the future of the union seemed uncertain. The changes in the South African transport industry which began in the 1980s had a damaging affect on SARHWU. Between 1980 and 1987 jobs in the industry declined from around 266 000 to just under 199 000, with jobs in predominantly black grades falling by nearly 41 000.[30] Over the next five years Transnet was prepared for privatisation. It was restructured into business units, regional offices were closed down and yet more jobs were lost by means of dismissals, natural wastage, early retirements and redundancies. The new government had made promises on education, health and housing and was not willing to continue the heavy subsidy which Transnet had received from the previous regime to protect staffing levels and keep loss-making services open. Despite increased consultation and participation at higher levels, grassroots industrial relations were still very bad and were characterised by low trust and poor line management. In 1994 at Kaserne alone there was an average of one serious industrial relations incident a month.

In 1995 the union was involved in a number of industrial disputes, beginning in January with a protest against the dismissal of a worker in the PX (Parcels) division of Transnet. This grew into a wider confrontation over the use of private contract labour at a time when in PX 4 000 jobs had been lost in the previous year and the number of drivers at the City Deep depot had fallen by two-thirds. In many ways this was a typical SARHWU strike with action initiated at the grassroots which was then capitalised on at national level. Workers threatened

---

28. Interview: Ezrom Mabyana, Johannesburg, November 1997.
29. Interview: Tshidiso Moshao, Johannesburg, October 1997.
30. R. Roux, 1989, pp. 90, 92.

to eject contractors from Kaserne depot and blockaded the City Deep container depot to prevent the private road contractors who had replaced Transnet drivers from collecting containers. In retaliation Transnet applied for an interdict and locked out its employees, on the grounds that the 1993 agreement with SARHWU recognised the right to strike but not the right for the union to 'interfere' with company business. [31]

In July of the same year wildcat action by Transnet workers in Cape Town, Durban and Kimberley closed the two harbours and effectively paralysed rail services in the Northern Cape. This time the dispute was about wages. Members of SARHWU and other unions took joint action in protest against the slow progress of negotiations and less than a week later agreement was finally reached giving workers the long-awaited minimum of R1 500 a month. This was followed by stoppages and demonstrations linked to the COSATU anti-privatisation campaign and in December by a major national strike at SAA against the proposed privatisation of the airline.

Despite the good relations at senior level and SARHWU's participation on Transnet boards and councils it seemed that there was very little influence that the union could exercise effectively. The contraction of the railways continued, making it increasingly difficult for SARHWU to protect the jobs of its members, and in 1998 membership had fallen to around 35 000 from over 40 000 only three years before. Clearly it was essential for SARHWU to review its position. It needed to develop strategies which would enable it to meet the challenges presented by the changing economic and industrial relations situation without abandoning its democratic tradition and without losing sight of the main objective of improving the lives of its members. As an affiliate of COSATU, the union already had a voice in government policy-making circles but it was a muted one. It was clear that the private sector was going to be a major player in determining the direction of economic development, and as a public sector union SARHWU's influence was relatively small. SARHWU's leaders therefore decided to fight the contraction in the industry and in their membership by a bold policy of strategic financial investment, restructuring for more effective collective bargaining and merger with other unions.

SARHWU Investment Holdings

SARHWU's philosophy was a socialist one. It supported the ownership of the means of production by working people and had expected this to be the policy

---

31.   I. Macun, 1995, pp. 14-15.

of the ANC in power. However, the collapse of socialism in the Soviet Union had changed the balance of international forces in favour of capital. The new government's policy was consequently more social democratic than socialist. The National Framework Agreement reached between the government and unions in 1996 recognised a number of restructuring options for parastatals including outright privatisation, out-sourcing of services, granting concessions to the private sector and setting up Strategic Equity Partnerships (SEPs) between government, labour and private business. The union allocation of Transnet shares was to be no more than 9% although more could be bought if they went into a consortium with black business.

Following the election of the ANC-led government and the adoption of positive action programmes, South African businesses were suddenly keen to attract black directors and managers and to make strategic alliances with individuals and organisations perceived to be close to the ruling party. Approaches were made to SARHWU by a number of companies (some of which offered shares as an incentive to form a relationship), and by this means SARHWU had acquired direct investments in insurance, scrap metal and advertising businesses. But sections of the union were opposed to the idea that SARHWU itself should be directly involved in the ownership of capitalist enterprises. For this reason it was decided to set up a separate investment arm.

In November 1996 SARHWU Investment Holdings was set up in response to a decision of the NEC for SARHWU 'to facilitate the meaningful participation of its membership in the mainstream of the economy'. [32] The company was 70% owned by a special SARHWU Enablement Trust appointed by the membership, which was set up at the same time, the remaining shares being divided between SARHWU Executive Trust, representing the managers of the company (15%), and two private partners (15%). It was set up with four directors and two alternate directors, four of whom were national office holders of SARHWU (Ezrom Mabyana, Treasurer, James Phera, Deputy President, Tshediso Moshao, Deputy General Secretary and Bonakele Jonas, President).

The aim of the investment company was not to make a profit for SARHWU. The stated vision was, 'A South Africa in which labour plays a pivotal role in the restructuring and development of the economy', and among its objectives was 'To pursue privatisation and other joint venture opportunities in transportation and related businesses'.[33] SARHWU as an organisation was not to be a beneficiary. According to Derrick Simoko who was General Secretary at the time,

---

32. SARHWU Investment Holdings, 1997, p. 4.
33. As above pp. 5-6.

Once the company makes profits the board of trustees will decide how workers are going to benefit individually. The Board of Trustees is accountable to SARHWU and they don't have the right to act without a mandate. The tendency of other union investment arms has been to benefit leaders and union officials but we are setting up a policy to benefit workers. We do have some ideas. For example, bursaries for disadvantaged children of workers, projects which will create employment, and a provident fund which is a direct benefit to workers. [34]

But some rank and file members were afraid that SARHWU's leadership would become distracted from the union's main role and become too closely identified with employers' interests at a time of crisis for individual workers who were facing redundancy.

When we elected them they were OK, but since last year in our view in SARHWU there is no more democracy, no accountability. We start asking ourselves the question, 'Are we still a union or are we now managers?' There is a conflict of interest between the two. Although we are not opposed to the new developments, the issue here is, 'Are you going to be a referee, or a player at the other end?' Since we started this thing, this investment company, people are no more interested with the members; they are more interested with this investment. [35]

The focus of the leadership is going on business. When an important meeting is taking place, they are nowhere to be found, because when you attend the meeting of a business you are entitled to something – when you attend the meeting they pay you. But when you attend a meeting for the workers you won't get paid, only at the end of the month, not for the meeting. That's why now members of SARHWU are resigning but some are remaining and want to see where the money is going. [36]

At the national congress in 1998 the operation of SARHWU Investment Holdings was criticised and delegates insisted on the distribution of individual share certificates to all members. It was agreed that current office holders of the union would not also act as directors of SARHWU Investment Holdings or accept fees or benefits from the company or from other boards on which they acted as union representatives. At the time of writing, it is unclear how this decision might affect the policy and operation of the Trust.

---

34.   Interview: Derrick Simoko, Johannesburg, October 1997.
35.   Interview: Mzaman Silus Mabunde, Johannesburg, November 1997.
36.   Interview: Mandla Nzama, Johannesburg, October 1997.

Restructuring and Reform

We need to try to implement something that will encourage people to join SARHWU. You can see in other unions that they are improving benefits because there is a social need and they are making the membership grow. But we are still stagnant. We need to research what other unions are doing for their growth. I believe if SARHWU is still there in the future, that will be the only idea to make the membership grow. [37]

As well as seeking to influence the direction of policy through its investment arm, SARHWU leaders needed to tackle the decline in membership more directly. Serious attempts were made to improve financial accountability, to offer better conditions of employment for union employees and to provide a more efficient administrative back-up to organisers and therefore ensure a good level of service to members.

We established a SARHWU Provident Fund for staff. We had a staff of about 63 at that time. We established a SARHWU Medical Aid Scheme which is administered externally for the staff and we went computerised. We got salary packages that we put in place and another thing we have done is to lease some of the office equipment and cars. We put in place a membership administration system where we can pick up how many members we have in a particular area, and we established a car scheme where members of staff who need to travel are provided with them. And not forgetting the funeral scheme for staff. [38]

At the same time a decision was made to restructure the organisation of the union, nationally and regionally, so that it mapped more closely on to the structure of the Transnet Bargaining Council. This was divided into a main bargaining chamber covering issues affecting workers across the board, and separate chambers for business divisions such as Spoornet (the main rail network), Metro-Rail, Portnet, SAA, Autonet and Support Services. National officers were allocated responsibility for each business division supported by regional officers and shop stewards from the division concerned. In this way expertise was developed and regional rivalry and factionalism diminished through members recognising their shared interests and working together to overcome common problems.

Although the unofficial industrial action in 1995 had finally won the elusive R1 500 minimum wage together with improvements in other benefits, the

---

37. Interview: Ezrom Mabyana, Johannesburg, November 1997.
38. As above.

financial instability of the company and the threat of privatisation created new challenges. Under new management (including a number of former SARHWU leaders), Transnet attempted to improve industrial relations. Information-sharing sessions, an affirmative action council, a training board and a Transnet Strategy Council were set up with 50% union membership. At the same time SARHWU and the other main Transnet unions (the Footplate Staff Association, the Transnet Allied Trade Union, the Black Labour Trade Union, the Technical Workers Union and the Salaried Staff Association) began to work together to form a united front against further redundancies. The logic of the situation dictated that unions should merge to form more efficient units.

This process was begun by the 1998 merger between three mainly white FEDUSA-affiliated unions which operated in Transnet and its business units, the Salaried Staff Association (Salstaff), the Employees Union of South Africa (EUSA) and the Technical Workers Union (TWU). The merger gave the new union a combined membership of 27 000, giving it added weight in the bargaining council and enabling it to offer improved services to members. This gave an impetus to talks about mergers between SARHWU and other transport unions which had been taking place on and off since the launching of COSATU in 1985.

Merger

> I was part of the union immediately after its rebirth in the Kimberley area. A very important part of my life was spent in SARHWU. It was my school and what I know today is because of SARHWU so it's a very special relationship. It was my home and I think it will remain like that until the day I die. I love this union and I feel that I've contributed much to SARHWU – to such an extent that I cannot afford to see SARHWU disintegrating because it will mean something about my efforts – that I've built this and now people are coming and tearing it apart and it pains me. Whenever I hear that there are problems it pains me. [39]

Since its re-launch in 1986 it has been the policy of SARHWU to merge with other unions in the transport industry in order to comply with COSATU's 'One industry one union' resolution. In reality, however, there was considerable reluctance to bring this about. This did not only come from officials afraid of losing their positions and constituencies. There has also been a fierce loyalty to SARHWU on the part of those rank and file who were persecuted for belonging

---

39. Interview: Johnny Potgieter, Kimberley, October 1997.

SARHWU becomes SATAWU: Leaders celebrate the end of the rivalry between SARHWU, BLATU and TATU, October 1998. (Left to right: Ephraim Mothlako, Bonakele Jonas, Tony Naidoo, Dan Phiri, Johnson Gamede, Moses Matsemela).

to the union in the eighties. There was marked opposition to the idea of abandoning the name of the union and the political tradition that it denoted, and fears that the identity of the union would be diluted by merging with non-Transnet unions. As a result, although talks with the Transport and General Workers Union (T and G) took place on and off over a period of almost fifteen years little progress was made.

> The problem is that since 1985 SARHWU and T and G have been agreeing that they will merge but there hasn't been any visible concrete action. What were the reasons for that? The problem was that SARHWU wouldn't have been SARHWU as it is now. It would have been something else – a transport union which is a merger between SARHWU and T and G. The problem was:

> 1. Our membership was not willing to move over to this new union; the leadership was not willing to move. Actually Sam Shilowa in one meeting in Durban actually summed it up precisely the way it was. He said, 'You make as if you are running but you are not running.' SARHWU national leadership was not taking the lead, motivating the membership and making the membership accept it. The leadership had that responsibility to sell it to the members but they didn't. Why was that? The problem was that SARHWU was afraid that it was going to lose its influence if we merge in this new union.

> 2. It was also a problem of strategic approach – SARHWU was militant and believed in the masses, marching against the bosses and all that sort of thing. T and G was perceived by SARHWU as nice gentlemen who cannot go out and fight. They are boardroom sort of people not activist cadres. That then became a stumbling block.

263

3. There were certain views to the effect that, 'How can we as SARHWU merge with T and G because ideologically there are people the T and G is embracing that we cannot embrace.' They could go to all different donors in the world without looking at the strings that go with the aid that is being offered. SARHWU was selective in choosing as to where to get aid, with whom to have friendship and solidarity in terms of exchange programmes and things like that. SARHWU believed that T and G was not socialist enough. They could take anything and no worry.

It was frustrating because SARHWU leadership and the NEC would say these things but when you go to COSATU meetings people failed to say, 'We are not going to merge because of these things.' What we'd do was to hide behind peripheral reasons such as, 'What about the general workers members of T and G? What about the security workers?' That was not the issue. The issue was the ideology; the issue was leadership and influence in the union. Nelson [Ndinisa] was prepared to go for it but the majority of the leadership in SARHWU was reluctant.[40]

More pressing for SARHWU was the need to establish its supremacy over other unions in the public service transport sector. The management's tactic of using BLATU members to strike-break against SARHWU had led to violent clashes and deaths on both sides, leaving a legacy of mistrust and hatred which probably held back many BLATU people from coming to SARHWU. Following the strike management continued to recognise BLATU and to collect subscriptions even though it had been demonstrated that workers wanted to join SARHWU. The 1989/90 strike saw further violence, and management continued to support BLATU up until the signing of the recognition agreement in 1991 and in some regions even later.

BLATU used its historical advantage to negotiate the wage increase for its members in 1991 which precipitated the crisis in SARHWU and the replacement of Martin Sebakwane as General Secretary. It also continued to challenge SARHWU in terms of benefits for members. The more far-sighted of the BLATU leadership, however, could see the writing on the wall. BLATU membership was already falling and SARHWU's relationship with the ANC meant that it was likely to replace BLATU as the union most favoured by government and management. With the encouragement of the SARHWU Honorary President, Archie Sibeko, BLATU President, DP Phiri and SARHWU Deputy Secretary

---

40. Interview: Stephen Matlou, Cape Town, October 1997.

Tshidiso Moshao met in Kenya in 1992 and agreed to work together to improve the relationship between the two unions and between SARHWU and the smaller Transnet Allied Trade Union (TATU).

This was a start but progress was slow. There were many practical problems to be solved and historical enmities to be overcome. Disappointed by the slow progress being made along the road to 'One industry, one union', Archie Sibeko decided to intervene again. He located the BLATU office on Cape Town Station, and went in and introduced himself. Fortunately the President happened to be there and the two men hit it off from the start. Trust was established and lines of communication were opened. There was still a long way to go but the chances of success seem to have been significantly improved by this encounter.

Even so, it was not until the end of 1998 that the merger was completed. The imperative came from changes in the Transnet Bargaining Council and the merger between Salstaff, the ESUSA and TWU. This made it essential that the old enemies should put aside their differences and come together. New agreements laid down that unions would only be eligible to participate in the bargaining council if they represented a minimum of 15% of Transnet employees, including 'critical grades' (i.e. skilled and semi-skilled grades). Of the three unions SARHWU was the largest with 35 000 plus members compared to 6 000-7 000 in BLATU and just under 2 000 in TATU. The unions were, however, strong in different grades and geographical areas, with SARHWU representing mostly unskilled African workers while BLATU organised mainly in Gauteng, Northern Province and KwaZulu-Natal, and TATU was based mainly amongst Indian and coloured workers in the Western Cape. A merged union would be able to hold its own with the newly merged former white unions, would be able to provide better service and attract more members, and would carry more weight with management and government.

There were, however, a number of difficulties to be addressed. The ideological difference between the three unions was illustrated by their affiliations. BLATU was affiliated to the National Council of Trade Unions (NACTU), TATU was non-aligned and SARHWU was affiliated to COSATU. There were differences in dues and benefits, organisational structures, location of offices, staffing, assets and liabilities which needed to be brought into line, and the idea needed to be sold to the members, who were reluctant to lose their separate identity. Talks between SARHWU and BLATU began in earnest in March 1996. In August 1996 TATU joined the process but withdrew again due to internal problems. In March 1997 the name South African Transport and Allied Workers Union (SATAWU) was adopted and in June 1998 TATU rejoined the discussions. A programme of action was adopted by the NECs of the three unions involving a period of co-ordinated parallel operations culminating in the launching of the new union at a special congress which met on 16 December 1998.[41]

Once the merger with BLATU and TATU was successfully achieved, the agenda moved on to the final realisation of the 'One industry, one union' mandate through merger with the Transport and General Workers Union. Here the difficulties proved to be even greater and the process was, once again, slower than hoped for. Ideological differences were no longer such a major issue, but the vested interests involved in the two unions made it difficult to solve the organisational problems inherent in such a merger.

SARHWU proposed that rather than work in a top-down way the new union should respect the democratic tradition of SARHWU and build a new relationship with the T and G from the bottom up. The two unions were already working closely with one another in a number of regions and it was agreed that this should be used as a model on which to develop more formal structures that would be the building blocks for eventual merger. This was accepted by some parts of the T and G but not others. It was agreed, however, to aim for a joint conference in October 1999 at which the merger of SATAWU and the Transport and General Workers Union would finally be launched.

The Fight Ahead

The role of the union has changed. The government today who is in power is our own government. I have participated in putting those people in power. People who are in government today are the people who have actually struggled. People have access to the government today via trade unions so in that context things have changed. But in terms of the worker on the ground, to be honest there's very little which has transformed and changed. So the perception is that everything has changed but in the practical and real world things have not changed on the ground. We have already lost a lot of experienced people. The danger is if all experienced people leave there will be a weak organisation. There is still a need for a strong trade union movement. We need to fully realise social transformation, fight the effects of globalisation. Government will move away from the left to become a referee not a player. Only through a strong organisation can we realise our objectives. [42]

---

41. M. Musi, 1998, pp. 14-15.
42. Interview: Nelson Ndinisa, Johannesburg, October 1997.

In early July 1999 Transnet announced massive losses in two of its business units, Fast Forward (formerly PX) and Spoornet. Losses in Fast Forward amounted to some R1,5 billion over the previous three years, and the cash flow in Spoornet during 1998 had fallen R244 million short. Plans were in hand to sell off Fast Forward and to introduce 'radical and immediate transformation' so as to restructure Spoornet in line with customer demand and to make operating savings of R3,8 billion by March 2000. This would entail 'a significant reduction of employees' – rumoured to be around 18 000 in Fast Forward and 27 000 in Spoornet.[43]

The announcements came on top of retrenchments already announced at SAA in preparation for the sale of a 20% stake to Swiss Air and produced a dilemma for SATAWU. As a member of a variety of Transnet bodies it was already aware of the problems of the company, and under the National Framework Agreement it had already participated in discussions on restructuring, but it had been largely powerless to influence the outcome. Workers affected by the proposals were mostly uneducated, unskilled and unlikely to benefit from any of the limited redeployment or retraining initiatives that had been proposed. They were becoming angry at the union's seeming inability to protect their jobs. Reductions on the scale planned would lead to a dramatic fall in SATAWU's membership and further weaken its ability to influence decisions. The merger with the Transport and General Workers Union that might have increased their muscle was not yet completed.

At the beginning of August 1999 the then Public Enterprises Minister, Jeff Radebe, announced that he was preparing a legal framework to advance the government's restructuring and privatisation programme and that the restructuring of Spoornet was an urgent necessity. Along with the communications parastatal, Telkom, Transnet was high on the list for privatisation, but unlike Telkom, 30% of which was privatised in 1997, Transnet was still relatively untouched (apart from SAA). A major problem was the pension and medical fund liabilities which were a legacy of the policy of over-manning and inflated benefits for white Transnet employees adopted by the apartheid government as a means of rewarding its supporters.

Conclusion

For much of its life SARHWU was forced to fight for workers' rights by allying itself with the political struggle against apartheid. The direct links between

---

43. *Citizen*, 9 July 1999; *South Africa Times* UK, 14 July 1999.

SATS/Transnet and the governing regime and the harassment of activists by the railway management made it impossible to build a stable trade union organisation. Nevertheless, the union survived because of its militancy and because of the commitment of its members. The problems faced by SARHWU's successor, SATAWU, have changed but they are still great. Workers are no longer faced with systematic racial harassment or denied opportunities purely because of the colour of their skins, but they *are* still faced by unemployment and economic hardship – partly the legacy of the apartheid system and partly the result of global changes which have affected the South African economy.

The government has recognised that restructuring of state assets must not create more poverty pockets.[44] As noted by Karl von Holdt, co-ordinator of the September Commission on the future role of trade unions, 'There is an alliance with the government. A much wider range of agreements and concrete concessions can be won. On the other hand … the old repertoire of demands, mass actions and victories does not match the complexities of relations and outcomes.'[45] SATAWU must fight to overcome these problems. To do so it needs an efficient, modern administration, but it is all too easy for union leaders to become alienated from their membership. Policy and action must be built on a firm foundation of grassroots democracy and organisation.

SARHWU led the way for SATAWU and the positive aspects of the tradition of commitment, militancy and democracy inherited from SARHWU must be retained. The objective is not only to win short-term economic gains for those who are employed and are members of the union but to bring about social transformation. As a union organising workers in the largest parastatal in South Africa (currently the country's fourth largest employer), SATAWU is in a pivotal position. Political action to influence the direction of government policy is therefore as essential a weapon today as it was during the apartheid years.

---

44. Jeff Radebe, quoted in *South Africa Times*, UK, 11 August 1999.
45. K. von Holdt, 1995, p. 16.

Glossary

Autonet	Road Transport division of Transnet (formerly *RTS*)
Braai	Barbecue, celebration
Broederbond	Order of senior Afrikaners (now Afrikanerbond)
Caspir	Armoured vehicle used by SADF
Check-off	See *stop order*
Hippo	Armoured vehicle used by SADF
Impimpi	Spy
Induna	Supervisor
John Vorster Square	The central police station in Johannesburg
Muti	'medicine' given by *sangoma*
Panga	Heavy cutlass
Sangoma	'Witch doctor'
Spoorbond	Afrikaner-based railway union
Spoornet	The railway division of *SATS*
Stoep	Verandah
Stop order	Method of collecting union subscriptions by deduction from wages at source.
Third Force	Under-cover network of *agents provocateurs* sponsored by senior elements within the military and state security force
Transnet	Reorganised and renamed South African Transport Services after the dissolution of *SATS*

Currency values are given in old values where appropriate: the Pound (£), which was generally at a par with the Pound Sterling, comprised twenty shillings (s) each of twelve pence (d). It was replaced by the Rand in 1961, at the rate of two Rand to the Pound. The exchange rate has fluctuated since and in mid-1999 stood at more than R9 to the Pound. The 1961 rate of R2 has been used in all conversions.

Abbreviations

AALC	African-American Labour Centre
AEU	Amalgamated Engineering Union
AMWU	African Mine Workers Union
ANC	African National Congress
ARAHWU	African Railway and Harbour Workers Union
AZACTU	Azanian Confederation of Trade Unions
BAWU	Black Allied Workers Union
BLATU	Black (Transnet Allied) Trade Union (at first Black Staff Association)
BMWU	Black Municipality Workers Union (later MGWUSA - Municipal and General Workers Union of South Africa)
CCAWUSA	Commercial Catering and Allied Workers Union of South Africa
CCSATU	Co-ordinating Council of South African Trade Unions
CFLU	Cape Federation of Labour Unions
CGT-Railway	Railway sector of French CGT union confederation
CIA	Central Intelligence Agency (USA)
CNETU	Council of Non-European Trade Unions
COSATU	Congress of South African Trade Unions
CP	Communist Party
CPSA	Communist Party of South Africa (to 1953)
CTSWU	Cape Town Stevedoring Workers Union
CUSA	Council of Unions of South Africa
EUSA	Employees Union of South Africa
ESCOM	Electricity Supply Commission
FNETU	Federation of Non-European Trade Unions
FNV	Netherlands Railway Union
FOSATU	Federation of South African Trade Unions
FWU	Furniture Workers Union
GAWU	General and Allied Workers Union (dissolved 1987)
GAWU	Garment and Allied Workers Union (launched 1988)
GEAR	Growth, Employment and Redistribution
GLAA	General Law Amendment Act (various dates)
GNU	Government of National Unity
GWU	Garment Workers Union
GWU	General Workers Union
ICA	Industrial Conciliation Act, 1924
ICFTU	International Confederation of Free Trade Unions (western-leaning)

ICU	Industrial and Commercial Workers Union
IFP	Inkatha Freedom Party
ILO	International Labour Organisation
ISCOR	Iron and Steel Corporation
ISTA	Iron and Steel Trades Association
ITF	International Transport Federation
JBSWU	Johannesburg Boot and Shoe Workers Union
JCATU	Joint Committee of African Trade Unions
LACOM	Labour Committee
LC	Local Committee (of SACTU)
LRA	Labour Relations Act
MA	Master of Arts degree
MACWUSA	Motor Assemblers and Component Workers Union
MAWU	Metal and Allied Workers Union
MGWUSA	Municipal and General Workers Union of South Africa
MK	Umkhonto we Sizwe (Spear of the Nation)
MWU	Municipal Workers Union
MWU	Mine Workers Union (white)
NACTU	National Council of Trade Unions
NATAU	Namibian Transport and Allied Union
NBU	Native Bakers Union
NCWU	Native Clothing Workers Union
NEC	National Executive Committee
NEDLAC	National Economic Development and Labour Council
NEHAWU	National Education, Health and Allied Workers Union
NFA	National Framework Agreement
NFW	National Federation of Workers (at first NFBW: National Federation of Black Workers)
NLWU	Native Laundry Workers Union
NMC	National Management Committee
NOC	National Organising Committee (of SACTU)
NUM	National Union of Mineworkers
NUPE	National Union of Public Employees (Britain), now absorbed into UNISON.
NUR	National Union of Railway Workers
NUR	National Union of Railwaymen (Britain) (now *RMT*)
NURAHS	National Union of Railways and Harbours Servants
UTW	National Union of Textile Workers
OFS	Orange Free State (now *Free State*)
PAC	Pan Africanist Congress

PE	Port Elizabeth
PWI	Public Works Installations
PX	Parcel Services
RDP	Reconstruction and Development Programme
RTS	Road Transport Services
SAA	South African Airways
SAAWU	South African Allied Workers Union
SACP	South African Communist Party (from 1953)
SACTU	South African Congress of Trade Unions
SADF	South African Defence Force
SAFTU	South African Federation of Trade Unions
SAIF	South African Industrial Federation
SAP	South African Police
SARH	South African Railways and Harbours
SARHWU	South African Railway and Harbour Workers Union
SATAWU	South African Transport and Allied Workers Union (launched 1998)
SATLC	South African Trades and Labour Council
SATS	South African Transport Services
SATU	South African Typographical Union
SATUC	South African Trade Union Council
T&GWU	Transport and General Workers Union (sometimes *T&G*)
TATU	Transnet Allied Trade Union
TLC	Trades and Labour Council
TMA	Transvaal Miners Association
TUACC	Trade Union Advisory Co-ordinating Council
TUC	Trades Union Congress (Britain)
TUCSA	Trade Union Council of South Africa
TWU	Technical Workers Union
UDF	United Democratic Front
WPWAB	Western Province Workers Advice Bureau
YMCA	Young Men's Christian Association
ZZ	Zola Zembe, a k a Archie Sibeko

Sources quoted

Books

Baskin, Jeremy (1991), *Striking back: a history of COSATU*, Ravan Press, Johannesburg.

Brown, G Gordon (ed.) for Union Castle Mail Steamship Co Ltd (1937), *The South and East African Yearbook and Guide*, Low, Marston and Co, London

Bunting, B. (1964), *The Rise of the South African Reich*, Penguin, Harmondsworth

Callinicos, Luli (1987), *Working life: factories, townships and popular culture in the Rand 1886-1940, A People's History of South Africa Volume 2*, Ravan Press, Johannesburg
(1993), *A Place in the City*, Ravan Press, Johannesburg

Davies, R.H. (1979), *Capital, State and White Labour in South Africa 1900-1960*, Humanities Press, New Jersey

Durban-LACOM (for SACHED), (1986) *Freedom from below: the struggle for trade unions in South Africa*, Durban

Fine, R. with Davis, D. (1991), *Beyond Apartheid: Labour and Liberty in South Africa*, Ravan Press, Johannesburg

Hindson, D. (1983), *The pass system and the formation of an urban African proletariat in South Africa*, D.Phil thesis, University of Sussex

Hirson, B. (1990), *Yours for the union: class and community struggles in South Africa*, second edition, Witwatersrand University Press, London.

Houghton, D H (1969), *The South African Economy*, Oxford University Press, Oxford

IDAF, *Women under Apartheid*, London

Kraak, Gerald (1993), *Breaking the chains: Labour in South Africa in the 1970s and 1980s*, Pluto Press, London.

Lewis, J (1984), *Industrialisation and trade union organisation in South Africa 1924-1955; The Rise and Fall of the South African Trades and Labour Council*, Cambridge University Press, Cambridge

Luckhardt, K. and Wall, B. (1980), *Organize or Starve! The History of the South African Congress of Trade Unions*, Lawrence and Wishart, London

Marks, S and Rathbone, R (1982), *Industrialisation and social change in South Africa: African class, culture and consciousness 1870-1930*, Longman, London.

O'Meara, D. (1983), *Volkskapitalisme: Class, Capital and Ideology in the Development of Afrikaner Nationalism, 1924-1948*, Ravan Press, Johannesburg

Ringrose, H.G. (1951) *Trade Unions in Natal: Natal Regional Survey, Volume Four*, University of Natal/Oxford University Press, Cape Town

Seidman, Gay W (1994), *Manufacturing militance: Workers' movements in Brazil and South Africa 1970-1985*, University of California Press, Berkeley.

Sibeko, A. (1996), *Freedom in our Lifetime*, Indicator Press, University of Natal, Durban

Simons, H.J. and R.E. (1969), *Class and colour in South Africa 1850-1950*, Penguin, Harmondsworth

Articles

Bonner, P. (1982) The Transvaal Native Congress, 1917-1920 in Marks, S. and Rathbone, R. *Industrialisation and Social Change in Africa*

Doyle, A. (1961) Striking out under the Republic, *Fighting Talk*, July 1961

Edwards, I. (1986) Recollections: the Communist Party and worker militancy in Durban, early 1940s, *South African Labour Bulletin* Volume 11 No. 4, February-March pp 65-84

Green, P. (1986), SATS Workers on Track, *South African Labour Bulletin*, Volume 12, No. 1 November/December pp 27-39

Lambert, R. (1985), Political Unionism and Working Class Hegemony: Perspectives on the South African Congress of Trade Unions, 1955-1965, *Labour, Capital and Society,* Volume 18, No. 2, November pp 244-277

Matiko, J. (1987a), SARHWU: Organising railway workers, *South African Labour Bulletin*, Volume 12 No 3, March/April pp 1-9
(1987b) SATS 'No' to SARHWU, *South African Labour Bulletin*, Volume 12, No. 4, May/June pp 1-7

Roux, R. (1989a) SARHWU – Problems and advances since the 1987 strike, *South African Labour Bulletin*, Volume 14, No. 2, June pp 74-93
(1989b) Labour Action, *South African Labour Bulletin*, Volume 14, No 25, October-November, pp 119-122
(1990) SACTU: End of an era, *South African Labour Bulletin*, Volume 14, No 8, May

Newspapers Reports and Pamphlets

Board of Trade and Industries Report No. 282

Cape Argus, Cape Town

Carnegie Commission, (1932) The Poor White Problem of South Africa

COSATU, (1992) Report of the Commission of Enquiry into Problems within SARHWU, Johannesburg

Fighting Talk, The Guardian, Cape Town

Haarlov, J. for Scandinavian Institute of Labour Studies, (1983), *Research Report No. 68: Labour Regulation and Black Worker's Struggles,* Uppsala

IR Data and Union Profiles, IR Data Publications, Rivonia

Mkosana, Vanguard (1998) *My Deployment at SARHWU,* King William's Town

National Union of Railwaymen (NUR) (1987) *Solidarity with South African Railworkers*, London

Native Economic Commission, 1930-32 (1932), UG 22

Negro Worker

Race Relations News

Report of the Native Economic Commission, 1930-1932, UG 22, 1932

SARHWU, (1992) *Honorary President's Report Covering the Period from 1.11.91 to 15.2.92*, Johannesburg

SARHWU, (1937), *We Want to Live,* Cape Town

SARHWU (1991) *Report on the Financial Workshop held on 22nd/23rd March 1991 at the Park Lane Hotel,* Johannesburg

SARHWU, (1997), *the Voice of the Voiceless,* Port Elizabeth

SARHWU Investment Holdings (1997) *Introduction to SARHWU Investments,* Johannesburg

South African Labour Bulletin (SALB), Johannesburg

Auditors' Report, Douglas and Velcich, October 31, 1990

IIR Information Sheet, April 1987, Johannesburg

INDEX